The Promise and Peril of Entrepreneurship

The Promise and Peril of Entrepreneurship

Job Creation and Survival among US Startups

Robert W. Fairlie, Zachary Kroff, Javier Miranda, and Nikolas Zolas

The MIT Press
Cambridge, Massachusetts
London, England

The MIT Press would like to thank the anonymous peer reviewers who provided comments on drafts of this book. The generous work of academic experts is essential for establishing the authority and quality of our publications. We acknowledge with gratitude the contributions of these otherwise uncredited readers.

This book was set in Stone Serif and Stone Sans by Westchester Publishing Services. Printed and bound in the United States of America.

Library of Congress Cataloging-in-Publication Data

Names: Fairlie, Robert W., author. | Kroff, Zachary, author. | Miranda, Javier (Economist), author.
Title: The promise and peril of entrepreneurship : job creation and survival among US startups / Robert W. Fairlie, Zachary Kroff, Javier Miranda, and Nikolas Zolas.
Description: Cambridge, Massachusetts : The MIT Press, [2023] | Includes bibliographical references and index.
Identifiers: LCCN 2022033263 (print) | LCCN 2022033264 (ebook) | ISBN 9780262545358 (paperback) | ISBN 9780262373982 (epub) | ISBN 9780262373975 (pdf)
Subjects: LCSH: New business enterprises—United States. | Small business—United States—Management. | Entrepreneurship—United States.
Classification: LCC HD62.5 .F365 2023 (print) | LCC HD62.5 (ebook) | DDC 658.02/20973—dc23/eng/20220919
LC record available at https://lccn.loc.gov/2022033263
LC ebook record available at https://lccn.loc.gov/2022033264

10 9 8 7 6 5 4 3 2 1

Contents

Contents

Preface

How many jobs are created by the average entrepreneur? Do these created jobs last or do they disappear quickly? How many entrepreneurial firms survive each year after startup? Although the answers to these questions have enormous economic, policy, and societal consequences, surprisingly there are no definitive answers. How we define entrepreneurial firms—often a function of data availability—will determine the answer. The goal of this book is to ask fundamental questions about what an entrepreneurial firm is, and to answer these questions from a broad perspective. In the process we provide new facts about entrepreneurial job creation, firm survival, and the early-stage dynamics of startups.

The idea for the book dates back to an earlier research project by the authors that examined why and when some entrepreneurs take the leap into hiring their first employee. The project involved using an early "beta" version of some of the Census Bureau data used in this project. The findings from that earlier project sparked broader discussions about a much more ambitious project of creating a panel data set capturing the entire universe of startups in the United States—from their earliest possible inception, through the hiring of their first employee and eventually their possible exit, and to analyzing job creation and survival among those startups. The inherent challenge was to link existing data sets so we could expand and broaden existing definitions of "the entrepreneurial firm" and to identify all startups. This required multiple iterations and improvements in data linkages, and ultimately resulted in the creation of the data set introduced here, the Comprehensive Startup Panel (CSP), tracking all startups—both those with and those without employees.

The idea for the chapter focusing on racial inequality in the book originated from previous work of the authors on racial disparities in business outcomes and access to capital published by the MIT Press, *Race and Entrepreneurial Success: Black-, Asian-, and White-Owned Businesses in the United States* (2008). The contributions of disparities in business outcomes to broader racial inequality are becoming well known, but we know much less about inequality in the startup process. We have built on the earlier research by focusing on startups in this book.

We hope that the book will serve as a useful source of information for policymakers and business leaders, as well as a valuable research and instructional tool for professors, researchers, and students. We also hope the book raises questions about the definition of an entrepreneur. We propose some potential definitions of entrepreneurship and offer the tools to broaden the discussion. Anyone interested in learning more about entrepreneurial job creation and survival should find guidance in this book. We hope that numerous academics, researchers, policymakers, and students use the new Comprehensive Startup Panel to conduct their own research and build on the findings presented here. The possibilities seem endless.

The data can be accessed via an approved research proposal through the Census Bureau's Federal Statistical Research Data Center (FSRDC). As of 2022, the FSRDC has partnered with more than 50 research institutions and has 31 centers operating throughout the United States. Interested parties can apply through the following link: https://www.census.gov/about/adrm /ced/apply-for-access.html.

Three of the authors worked at the US Census Bureau during all or part of the several years taken to complete the book. Any opinions and conclusions expressed herein are those of the authors and do not reflect the views of the US Census Bureau. All results have been reviewed to ensure that no confidential information is disclosed. The Census Bureau's Disclosure Review Board and Disclosure Avoidance Officers have reviewed this data product for unauthorized disclosure of confidential information and have approved the disclosure avoidance practices applied to this release. DRB Approval Numbers: CBDRB-FY22-004, CBDRB-FY22-CES007-002.

Given a project of this length, there are many people to thank for providing comments and suggestions. These comments and suggestions were especially useful for creating the data set, exploring job creation and survival, and defining entrepreneurship. We benefited from numerous discussions with colleagues and policymakers. Special thanks go to Ronnie Chatterji, Emin Dinlersoz, Christopher Goetz, Nathan Goldschlag, Brian Headd, Shawn

Klimek, Josh Lerner, Ross Levine, Ben Pugsley, David Robinson, and Bulent Unel. We also benefited from discussions with seminar participants at Duke University, Stanford University, the National Academies of Science, US Census Bureau, Small Business Administration, Louisiana State University, University of Oklahoma, University of Nevada, Reno, the FSRDC Conference at UCLA, the SOLE meetings, and the NBER Entrepreneurship workshop for helpful comments and suggestions.

We also thank family members who have been incredibly supportive during the past several years of writing this book. Robert Fairlie thanks Rebecca London, Zoe Fairlie, Jessica Fairlie, and Barbara Fairlie for their patience and support. Zachary Kroff thanks his family—Julia, Marie, Kate, and David—for their endless encouragement and contagiously cheerful support. Javier Miranda thanks his family and friends (they know who they are). Nikolas Zolas thanks Adelina Zolas and his two children, Elise and Adrian, for their love and support.

1 Introduction: Entrepreneurship

Federal, state, and local governments spend billions of dollars each year on incubators, training programs, loan programs, tax breaks, and investor incentives to encourage business formation, with one of the primary goals being to create jobs. The popularity of public policies to foster entrepreneurs is not limited to the United States but is widespread around the world (OECD 2017b). Government expenditures, however, are often made without careful consideration of how the benefits of these programs are measured in terms of the number of businesses, number of jobs, or total payroll created relative to the costs of running these programs.[1] In response to these concerns, there have been recent calls for more emphasis on program evaluations and other ways to better measure these benefits. The US Government Accountability Office (GAO), for example, recently recommended that the Small Business Administration (SBA) use outcome-based measures, such as job creation, rather than focus on output-based measures, such as the number of loans approved and funded, to evaluate the effectiveness of its programs (Congressional Research Service 2020).[2]

As a starting point for understanding the potential benefits and costs of government programs, however, we first need answers to broader and more basic questions related to entrepreneurship, such as how many jobs the average entrepreneur creates and what percentage of entrepreneurial startups survive one, two, or more years. Surprisingly, definitive answers to these two general questions do not exist. To be sure, the federal government releases two statistics on startup job creation and survival rates—each startup creates six new jobs on average, and 50 percent of startups survive up to five years (US SBA 2017). The numbers on survival are part of the mythos of the riskiness of entrepreneurship and are widely disseminated in the press and even in popular culture. However, in these government statistics on job creation and survival rates, startups are strictly defined as new *employer* businesses and do not include the vast number of businesses that start with no employees or start as potential new employer businesses before any employees are hired. Although the government and statistical agencies have long had the ability to measure these nonemployer businesses, pinpointing their start date and linking them to their potential employer business futures has proven difficult.

In this book, we redefine the start date of a business from when it hires its first employee to when it either hires its first employee or first has revenues. This new, alternative, and expanded definition of a startup includes all businesses that start without employees and moves the start date back in time for those that hire employees after their first year in existence. Taking this approach is not easy and requires linking two disparate sources of Census Bureau data on nonemployer and employer businesses. By linking these data sets, we create a new compilation of administrative data that reflects the new and fuller universe of business startups. The new Comprehensive Startup Panel (CSP) data set tracks job creation and the survival of every business startup in the US economy from the initial startup year to up to seven follow-up years. The Comprehensive Startup Panel tracks the outcomes and movements of the original startup but does not differentiate between exits via permanent closures, ownership changes, acquisitions, or reorganizations.

Using the new data set, we provide the first answers to three fundamental questions about entrepreneurial job creation and survival based on the universe of US startups: (1) How many jobs are created by the average entrepreneur? (2) Do these created jobs last or do they disappear quickly? and (3) How many entrepreneurial firms survive each year after startup? We answer these questions using the broadest definition possible of an entrepreneur and then narrow this definition to accommodate tighter definitions. Government policies promoting entrepreneurship are not limited to high-growth-potential startups; many often target individuals interested in starting smaller-scale businesses for the first time, with the primary goal of simply making a living for the owner and the owner's family. For example, the SBA (2020) notes that assistance and training services provided by Small Business Development Centers (SBDCs) are "available to anyone interested in beginning a small business for the first time or improving or expanding an existing small business, who cannot afford the services of a private consultant."[3] SBDCs also make special efforts to reach out to socially and economically disadvantaged and underrepresented groups.

In addition to providing answers to these fundamental questions about entrepreneurship, we reevaluate documented patterns in entrepreneurial job creation and survival using this new database. We assess whether job creation is being driven by a few extremely successful startups or whether there is a continuous upward shift in the employment size distribution across all startup firms. Relatedly, we examine whether nonemployer startups make notable contributions to employment several years after startup. Finally, we examine which sectors of the economy lead in job creation among startups and which have relatively low turnover rates.

The answers to these questions are not only important for policymaking purposes but also shed light on the fundamental nature of entrepreneurship. Is entrepreneurship about creating innovative products, services, and jobs (i.e., Schumpeterian entrepreneurship), or is it increasingly about job independence (being one's own boss), contract or consulting work, schedule flexibility, or being part of the gig economy (Hamilton 2000; Hurst and Pugsley 2011; Katz and Krueger 2016; Levine and Rubinstein 2016)? In other words, is entrepreneurship about creating *jobs* or creating *a job*? Is it about creating a long-term job or just a temporary job? And finally, is it about taking risks (Kihlstrom and Laffont 1979; Knight 1921) or about diversifying risk (through undertaking multiple job activities)? Obviously, there is no correct or universal answer, and your own perspective may determine how you define entrepreneurship.

The US Bureau of Labor Statistics (BLS) defines entrepreneurs as new employer establishments (US BLS 2020).[4] We use a similar general approach of defining entrepreneurship as business formation, but our starting approach is to include the universe of business startups and not limit the focus to new employer businesses or establishments.[5] The classic studies of entrepreneurship, such as Knight (1921), Schumpeter (1934), and more recently Kihlstrom and Laffont (1979), Jovanovic (1982), and Evans and Jovanovic (1989), which have helped establish entrepreneurship as an independent field in economics, do not limit the definition of entrepreneurship by employer, incorporation, or any other status. This is important because estimates of job creation per *employer* startup may offer only a partial view and will necessarily overestimate job creation per *any* startup if most nonemployer startups do not eventually hire employees. Nonemployer firms account for both the majority of startups and total firms in the United States, yet they are not often mentioned in the entrepreneurship literature. Also, employer firms will be classified as new businesses even if they actually started many years earlier with no employees, and jobs eventually created by nonemployer startups could be allocated to the wrong startup cohort.[6] The inclusion of nonemployer startups is also important for measuring survival rates over time because many nonemployer firms might exit before ever hiring an employee. Knowing how many high-tech startups, for example, that never make it to the point of hiring employees would be useful for calculating levels of job creation and survival per high-tech startup. In general, ignoring the nonemployer history of firms might miss important early entrepreneurial dynamics that are crucial to understanding the relationships between and among entrepreneurship, job creation, and survival.

The standard approach to measuring startup job creation includes counting only the number of employees hired. But entrepreneurs create jobs for themselves, and those jobs are not always counted as employee positions in the data. Thus an alternative approach for calculating startup job creation might be to add the owner's job to counts of jobs created per startup. Although the "entrepreneurs create jobs for themselves" argument is often made in the policy arena, an important question is whether the business ownership jobs last very long. A new job is created for the owner in the startup year, but if the business exits quickly, then this owner job disappears. Additionally, a worker hired by a startup is paid a wage or salary, whereas the owner might be losing or making very little money in the first years. On the other hand, many nonemployer startups have no intention of hiring employees. Their goal might be to make a living or supplement income through a self-employed business activity. Similarly, contract work and consulting count as business activities with the goal of providing income for the owner, but not necessarily with the goal of creating jobs for others. Increasingly, what used to be formal employer-employee relations are shifting to contractual arrangements. Because of these concerns, the creation and potential loss of business owner jobs should also be considered in the economic welfare calculus for at least some entrepreneurship policies.

Understanding the early-stage dynamics of entrepreneurship is important: starting a business is difficult, with many potential barriers and risks. Conducting market research, identifying competitors, writing a business plan, and calculating startup costs are all recommended but represent knowledge and skills that not everyone has. Inadequate access to financial capital also represents a major barrier to starting a business. Obtaining loans or attracting investors is difficult, and not everyone has enough savings to fund their own business ventures. Other startup decisions and activities, such as finding a store location, choosing an organizational structure (e.g., sole proprietorship or incorporation), applying for business licenses and permits, and obtaining business insurance can also be daunting for some would-be entrepreneurs.

Hiring employees is also an important and difficult decision and represents one of the major thresholds that entrepreneurs encounter when starting or operating their businesses. Hiring employees entails additional registration, tax, and legal requirements, as well as health insurance, workers compensation, and unemployment insurance issues, which might be especially daunting to small business owners considering hiring their first employee.[7] But perhaps the most important consideration for the owner is whether current and future revenues are large enough to cover the extra expenses of having employees. Even putting aside the issue of hiring employees, growing a business and surviving is no easy task. Startups often need additional injections of financial capital to make it through the first few years of operation. Decisions regarding expansion, such as adding new locations, finding new clients, and exporting to new markets, are risky and can lead to failure if done prematurely or incorrectly. Adding to all these concerns, but often not considered seriously enough at startup, survival also relies on luck and good fortune as unforeseen events such as recessions, pandemics, natural disasters, new competition, or changes in consumer trends can doom even the best-laid plans of the most talented entrepreneurs.

These difficulties and additional barriers to starting and growing businesses can be even more severe for certain groups of the population. In the book, we build on the analysis of startup job creation and survival to explore who owns these startups. We are particularly interested in identifying disparities in startup ownership. For example, are Blacks over- or underrepresented in the ownership of startups? Do women own a proportionate number of startups relative to their numbers in the labor force? To shed light on inequalities in startup ownership across different groups we make comparisons between the demographic composition of startup owners and the demographic composition of the broader US labor force. We explore differences by race, ethnicity, gender, age, nativity, veteran status, and owner's education level.[8]

Of particular interest are the barriers faced by minority entrepreneurs in creating new businesses because of implications for broader racial inequality. Wealth disparities, differential access to financial capital, discrimination in lending, and differences in human capital, family business background, and business social capital limit business creation and success among minorities (Fairlie and Robb 2007b, 2008). We zero in on disparities in access to startup capital because of the importance of startup capital to the successful launch of a business. We provide new evidence on racial and ethnic differences in levels of financial capital used among startups and the sources of this capital. The analysis is not limited to one minority group but examines the constraints (and possible advantages) faced by Black, Latinx, Native American, and Asian startups.[9] We then examine how initial job creation differs by race or ethnicity and whether these patterns are related to potential barriers such as limited access to financial capital or lower levels of human capital among startups owned by underrepresented minority groups.

It is surprisingly difficult to find nationally representative data on the demographic characteristics of startup owners. The Comprehensive Startup Panel that we create from administrative data, for example, does not currently contain any information on owner characteristics. For this task, we rely on microdata from the US Census Bureau's Survey of Business Owners (SBO), which is unusual in that it captures detailed information on both the owner and the business. To focus on startups, we select new businesses started in the year before the SBO survey was conducted. A major advantage of the SBO for this analysis is that it consists of a large sample based on the same underlying data used to create our startup panel data set and includes both nonemployer and employer startups. It does not, however, capture the universe of startups and is limited to only one year of data.

The findings presented here on race, startup capital, and job creation have implications for broader racial inequality. Business ownership provides an important source of income and wealth accumulation. Roughly one in ten people in the workforce own a business as their main job activity, and these owners hold a disproportionate amount of total wealth in the United States (Fairlie and Robb 2008). Business owners also create jobs for others, and often those jobs are located in local communities and may be held by workers of the same race or ethnicity as the owner. Relevant to the US economy, if minority entrepreneurs face liquidity constraints, discrimination, or other barriers to creating new businesses or expanding current businesses, these barriers could translate into efficiency losses downstream. Barriers to entry and expansion are potentially costly to US productivity and local job creation, especially as minorities represent a growing share of the population.

Outline of the Book

The chapters of the book present the data, methods, and findings from our multiyear project on entrepreneurial job creation, survival, and ownership demographics. We discuss how we create the new data set that follows the universe of startups in the United States, the novel and important findings from analyzing these and related data, and the implications for evaluating policy and the fundamental nature of entrepreneurship.

Chapter 2 poses the question of how to define and measure a startup. The answer is difficult because there is no clear demarcation point at which a business starts. For example, does it start with the idea for the business, or when the owner starts working on the business, or when the business first has revenues, or when the business hires its first employee? Following the US Census Bureau's approach of tracking businesses through tax records either from revenues or from payroll in the Business Register, we present data showing the total number of businesses in the United States. We present numbers using these Census Bureau definitions and separate the statistics by nonemployer versus employer and business versus establishment classifications. We also compare these numbers to the number of self-employed business owners from household surveys conducted by the US Bureau of Labor Statistics.

We then present information on the age distribution of businesses and focus the discussion on defining, measuring, and counting all startups in the US economy. The common focus on new employer businesses to generate statistics on job creation and survival rates provides only a partial view because it does not include the vast number of businesses started with no employees or the possible existence of new employer businesses before employees are subsequently hired. We provide a detailed discussion of how the Comprehensive Startup Panel data set is created and describe how it can be accessed for future research. Using this new data set, we present the total number of startups in the United States and numbers by industry.

Chapter 3 provides new findings from the Comprehensive Startup Panel data set on job creation. We explore several different aspects related to job creation. First, we compare the number of jobs created by startups to the total number created by existing firms, an exercise that demonstrates the massive contribution of startups to job creation in the US economy. Second, we document the number of jobs created by the average startup. Third, we examine how job creation changes over time with age of the startup from the initial year to seven years later. We next examine how average payroll per employee changes over time among startups and compared to nonstartups. Finally, we use regression analysis to examine how startup job creation differs by industry and evolves over time after controlling for other factors, such as business climate and macroeconomic conditions.

The analysis next turns to entrepreneurial survival. Chapter 4 explores survival rates and patterns for the universe of startups. We document the quick drop-off in survival during the first few years after startup and examine how survival rates differ by industry. We again use regression analysis to explore the evolution of startup survival over time after controlling for macroeconomic conditions and industries.

Chapter 5 builds on the two previous chapters by exploring the dynamics of job creation and survival. We first explore why the average number of jobs created per entrepreneur remains relatively constant over the years since startup. Patterns in the average number of jobs created per entrepreneur conceal a substantial amount of heterogeneity in the underlying dynamics of job creation by startups. We explore alternative explanations for the relatively flat pattern. Related to this question, we examine whether the strong upward trend in average number of employees per surviving startup can be attributed to a few very fast-growing survivors or to a larger number of steadily growing survivors.

Another important type of underlying heterogeneity that we examine is the movement between not having employees, having employees, and exits. We focus on a key transition in the employment process for many startups in the US economy, which is from having no employees to hiring the first employee. In this case, the owner of a startup has to make a commitment to payroll and figure out more complicated hiring procedures, regulations, and taxes. We examine this transition carefully by focusing on the timing of when nonemployer startups take the leap to employer status. We build on the analysis of the Comprehensive Startup Panel data set to explore dynamic business conditions such as sales, change in business assets, or intellectual property acquisition, milestones that are associated with hiring the first employee, using data on a sample of startups from the Kauffman Firm Survey.

Two broad questions about the definition of an entrepreneur are explored in chapter 6. The first is related to timing: Do nonemployer startups create jobs one, two, or more years later, and if so, do they make a sizable contribution to job creation in the United States? Previously it was difficult to answer this question because of data limitations. The second and related question is whether the low levels of job creation per entrepreneur and the low survival rates found in our startup panel data set are simply due to an overly inclusive definition of entrepreneur (i.e., one derived from using the entire startup universe): If we restrict the population of startups to be less inclusive and require a stronger signal of commitment by entrepreneurs in the startup year, do we continue to find low levels of job creation and survival?

In chapter 6, we also propose a refinement to including the universe of startups for calculating job creation and survival statistics. We exclude sole proprietor startups without an employer identification number (EIN), resulting in a selective subgroup of startups that includes all employer startups and all nonemployer startups that are incorporated, S corporations, partnerships, or sole proprietorships with EINs. In each of these cases there is a much stronger business registration requirement than for sole proprietorships without an EIN. The restriction should remove many consultants, hobby entrepreneurs, and gig and contract workers, who often do not have an ultimate goal of hiring employees. The inclusion or exclusion of sole-proprietor, nonemployer startups is a difficult decision to make in measuring entrepreneurial job creation and survival, and whether one does so or not depends on the research or policy question addressed. Instead of deciding whether entrepreneurship is best measured by the universe of startups or by our new, non-sole-proprietor definition of startups, we consider the two measures as lower and upper bounds, respectively. We push the analysis further by creating a third measure of job creation that adds the number of owners to standard employee-based calculations of total jobs created per startup.

Chapter 7 pivots from examining job creation and survival among startups to answering the important question of who owns startups. We use SBO microdata that include detailed owner information such as race, ethnicity, gender, age, and education level to explore ownership patterns. Focusing on new businesses in the SBO sample, we explore four general issues. First, we provide a detailed analysis of who starts businesses in the United States, exploring patterns across demographic groups and comparing them to the characteristics of both older surviving businesses and the broader US labor force. The comparison to the broader US labor force in particular sheds light on the representation of different groups of the population in the ownership of startups. Second, we explore levels and sources of startup capital because of their importance in the startup process. Third, we examine whether job creation per startup differs by the race or ethnicity of the owner. Finally, we combine the separate analyses to identify potential barriers to success faced by minority-owned startups. We focus on constraints imposed by limited access to financial capital and lower levels of human capital.

In chapter 8, the concluding chapter, we summarize and interpret the main findings from the book and discuss promising avenues for future research. We take a step back and place our definition of the start of a business (i.e., the first time a business entity has revenues or hires employees other than the owner) in the context of the broader spectrum of the different stages of business creation. There are several possibilities for examining stages along the startup timeline, and we briefly review some example data sets capturing different stages. We then discuss how our Comprehensive Startup Panel data set allows substantial flexibility in how one defines entrepreneurship and in exploring many additional questions around entrepreneurial job creation, survival, and growth. The new data set and the findings presented here provide a jumping-off point for future research on entrepreneurship using these data. We also discuss and provide examples of the ability to link the Comprehensive Startup Panel data set to other Census Bureau data sets. Matching the startup panel data set to other data sets can extend the timeline on which startups are measured, provide more information about the characteristics of startups, and shed more light on early-stage business outcomes among startups. The chapter concludes by reviewing the lower and upper bounds that we provide on the number of jobs created per startup and survival rates, with a discussion of the implications of these new statistics for entrepreneurship research and policy.

Main Findings

The main findings from our analysis of the new Comprehensive Startup Panel data set and SBO data on the demographic characteristics of startup owners are as follows:

1. The average annual cohort of 4.1 million startups in the United States creates a total of 3.0 million jobs in the first year after startup and employs 2.6 million workers five years later. Without these jobs created by startups, net job creation would be negative as older businesses lose jobs on average.

2. Using the broadest definition possible of a business start and excluding the entrepreneur's own job, we find that the average entrepreneur creates 0.74 jobs in the first year after startup and employs 0.63 workers five years later and 0.57 workers seven years later. These statistics account for entrepreneurs exiting over time and thus, by definition, creating no jobs in those years.

3. Using instead a selective definition of entrepreneurship that includes employer, incorporated, partnership, S corporation, and sole-proprietorship-with-EIN startups but excludes sole-proprietorship-without-EIN startups, we find that the average entrepreneur employs 2.56 employees one year after startup and 2.15 employees five years later.

4. Adding the startup owner's job as an additional potential job in the calculation of job creation per startup, we find that total jobs (including the owner's) created per startup are 1.33 in the first year after startup, dropping to 1.19 two years later and 0.97 five years later.[10] In the early stages, startups provide a large number of jobs for owners, but these owner jobs disappear as startups exit, an observation responsible for the sharp decline in total jobs per startup over time.

5. All of our alternative measures indicate job creation levels per startup that are substantially lower than the numbers often cited by federal statistics that focus on new employer businesses, which show six new jobs per startup (US SBA 2017).

6. When the broadest definition of a startup is used, survival rates are extremely low, with a large shakeout occurring in the years immediately after startup. After one year only 59 percent of startups survive, and after two years only 47 percent survive. The rapid decline in the number of surviving startups begins to taper off, and after five years, 33 percent of startups survive.

7. Although job creation is higher among the selective group of startups, survival rates remain low, with 64 percent surviving after two years and 45 percent surviving after five years. We view these levels of survival

rates as upper bounds, but they are still lower than the numbers cited in federal statistics that focus on new employer businesses, which show 50 percent of startups surviving up to five years (US SBA 2017).

8. Exploring the rich heterogeneity in job creation dynamics across the universe of startups, we find that rapid job growth over time among surviving startups mostly offsets the negative influence from extremely high exit rates. When the broadest definition of an entrepreneur is applied, surviving startups employ an average of 1.90 employees five years after startup and 1.96 employees seven years after startup.

9. Examining heterogeneity across industries, we find a few major industry groups or sectors that are job creators. For example, Manufacturing and Accommodation and Food Services have average employment levels that are much higher than average per startup.

10. Survival rates are mostly similar across industries, differing from the large variation found across major industry groups for job creation levels. For example, the five-year survival rates for startups are 32 percent in Construction, 35 percent in Accommodation and Food Services, and 38 percent in Manufacturing, compared with 33 percent for all startups.

11. Exploring whether there exist milestones that nonemployer startups often reach before hiring their first employee, we find that higher levels of business assets are associated with nonemployer businesses making the transition to employer firms. Having intellectual property, which includes patents, copyrights, and trademarks, also has a positive association with making the nonemployer-to-employer transition.

12. Nonemployer startups make substantial contributions to job creation after the initial year. Separating businesses with and without employees at startup, we find that nonemployer startups employ an average of 319,000 workers in the seventh year after startup, representing one-seventh of the total 2.3 million jobs created by all startups seven years after startup. Ignoring previous nonemployer years misses important early-stage entrepreneurial dynamics as one-fifth of businesses hiring their first employee have some prior nonemployer history.

13. Turning to ownership patterns, we find that 7 percent of startups are owned by Blacks, 9 percent are owned by Latinxs, 1.0 percent are owned by Native Americans, and 6 percent are owned by Asians in the United States. Compared to the demographic composition of the US labor

force, Blacks are underrepresented among startups, constituting 12 percent of the labor force; Latinxs are underrepresented (constituting 14 percent of the labor force); and Native Americans are underrepresented (1.5 percent of the labor force); whereas Asians are overrepresented (5 percent of the labor force).

14. Most new businesses start with small amounts of capital. Three quarters of startups use less than $5,000. Twelve percent of startups use $25,000 or more in initial financial capital. To fund these startups, owners often rely on their own personal savings, assets, and credit sources.

15. Startups owned by Blacks, Latinxs, and Native Americans hire fewer employees per startup in the initial year than do startups owned by non-Latinx Whites. The disparities are large, with Black startups hiring 0.13 (67 percent) fewer employees per startup, Latinx startups hiring 0.07 (36 percent) fewer employees, and Native American startups hiring 0.10 (56 percent) fewer employees on average than White-owned startups. In contrast, startups owned by Asians have 0.09 (49 percent) more employees on average than White-owned startups.

16. Exploring what contributes to these racial and ethnic differences in initial employment levels among startups, we find that undercapitalization and low levels of human capital are barriers faced by Black, Latinx, and Native American startups.

17. Asian-owned startups have the highest level of startup capital, which is associated with the highest level of early-stage employment among startups owned by any major racial or ethnic group.

Overall, the analysis of the new administrative data set on the universe of US startups that we create, the Comprehensive Startup Panel, provides several findings that shed light on fundamental, and surprisingly unanswered, questions regarding the job creation potential and survival likelihood of entrepreneurs. The main theme is that job creation rates per startup and survival rates are lower and less optimistic than the numbers presented by the federal government, which focus on new employer businesses. Even when we switch to a restrictive definition of a startup that excludes almost all sole proprietor startup entities or when we count the owner's job, we continue to find less optimistic numbers. Also, our investigation of racial disparities in first-year job creation reveals that some minority groups face significant barriers to entrepreneurship and hiring their first employee. Two important corollaries from this analysis are that policymakers and would-be entrepreneurs need to manage expectations about potential job creation, survival, and growth in this regard and recognize that many entrepreneurs only want to create a job for themselves. The second is that policymakers should recognize important race-based entrepreneurial gaps.

The analysis and findings also contribute more generally to the rapidly growing literature on entrepreneurship. This emerging field has struggled with finding adequate data and with agreeing on definitions of entrepreneurship. The new Comprehensive Startup Panel data set that we generate allows substantial flexibility in how one defines entrepreneurship and facilitates the exploration of many theoretical and empirical questions around entrepreneurial job creation, survival, and growth. The new data set and the findings presented here provide a jumping-off point for future research on entrepreneurship, especially research focusing on evaluating policies and further exploring inequality.

2 Businesses and Startups in the United States

Perhaps the first, most basic question we should begin with is to ask ourselves, What exactly is a business startup? We often think about some of the famous startups in Silicon Valley, which began as a couple of people tinkering with a big idea in their garage. But even before we get to the garage in Menlo Park full of computers, electronics, and a Ping-Pong table, the initial ideas and work may have started even earlier—say, in a dorm room. Many restaurant owners provide stories of how their businesses started in their own kitchens as they experimented with different recipes, which were then shared with friends and family. Or the business started when the hobbyist suddenly realized that they could get paid to do what she enjoys doing. But when does an idea, experiment, or hobby make the leap from the "entrepreneur" to the "business," with a dedicated space, purchased equipment, and employees?

Should we measure startups from the moment they generate their first sale or revenue? Or from the moment they generate their first job? Or perhaps when they first request a business tax identifier? Or even when an initial investment in the startup is first made? The number of startups that are identified and measured will change depending on your answer to this question. Perhaps more important, the answer might depend on your research question, and might be largely constrained by data availability. The most successful startups go on to create a large number of jobs and serve as important sources of innovation in the economy. However, many more remain as nonemployers, generating at most a single job or an alternative source of income for the owner, and one that might not last long. Our goal is to go to the data and use the data to count, measure, and study startups. You might already sense that this is easier said than done.

Before turning to the question of what is a startup, then, it may help to start with a different question: What is a business? This seemingly simple question is surprisingly difficult to answer in some cases. For someone who owns a restaurant or shop, the answer is relatively simple. But in other cases the answer can get more complicated. An example is a consultant who secures some income from advising and guiding others in a specialized field. If that person were to receive their primary income from that activity, we could perhaps confidently declare it a "consulting business." But is it still a consulting business if that person also has a regular wage or salary job outside of advising and guiding others? Is it a business if you devote all your waking hours to it but do not have any sales?

For the most part in this book, we use one of the most comprehensive definitions possible of what constitutes a business and the definition used by the US Census Bureau. It is based on the presence of a revenue tax liability. The key concept is that an entity is defined as a business when it first generates sufficient revenues, creating a tax liability that it then fulfills with the Internal Revenue Service. The Census Bureau therefore identifies the presence of a business from its tax filings. This definition includes businesses with employees (if they file payroll taxes) and businesses without employees (if they file only income taxes).[1] Although the initial business ideas might start before the first tax liability is created, and entrepreneurs could work on those ideas for several months or even years, the revenue or employment threshold creates a distinct demarcation point for the business entity that allows its systematic measurement in administrative data.[2] We use this definition as the start of a business throughout the analysis but discuss other alternative definitions, such as when an entity first applies for an employer identification number (EIN) or when a person first obtains a patent, in later chapters.

In this chapter, we also use the US Census Bureau's Business Register data to show the number of businesses in the United States. The underlying administrative data capture both businesses hiring employees and businesses with no employees, which make up the largest share of businesses in the United States. The administrative data also capture the legal form of the organization, including whether it is incorporated or unincorporated. We present tabulated numbers of businesses using this Census Bureau data set, which captures the universe of businesses. We compare these numbers to ones on self-employed business owners from household survey data that are used extensively in research on entrepreneurship, such as the Current

Population Survey (a joint project of the Census Bureau and the Bureau of Labor Statistics; see, e.g., Fairlie and Fossen 2020; Levine and Rubinstein 2016, 2018; and Wang 2019). We then transition to the more difficult measurement of startups. Documenting the start of a business is crucial. This chapter also includes a discussion of how we create our Comprehensive Startup Panel data set and how it can be accessed for future research. The goal is to introduce this data source and provide some technical information on how it was created.

How Many Businesses Exist in the United States?

We present data showing the number of businesses in the United States. The starting point for the discussion is the US Census Bureau's *Business Register*. The Business Register is a comprehensive database on all US business establishments; it is developed and maintained by the US Census Bureau, with data going back to the 1970s. The Business Register captures the universe of private businesses in the United States.[3] Table 2.1 reports the total number of businesses in the United States for selected years.

There were a little over 20 million businesses in the United States in 1997. The number of businesses grew steadily to 25.6 million in 2005 and more than 31.7 million in 2018. Many of these businesses, however, are not traditional stores or restaurants and instead represent contracting, consulting, and side and gig businesses. We return to this issue later when we define startups and when we refine which types of startups are included or not in an alternative definition.

The Business Register's main distinction is between nonemployer and employer businesses. Nonemployer business entities make up the bulk of business entities or units—more than three quarters in most years. Nonemployer

Table 2.1
Number of businesses in the United States

	1997	2000	2005	2010	2015	2018
Total	20,217,791	21,435,875	25,560,601	27,130,253	29,483,274	31,774,072

Source: US Census Bureau, Business Dynamic Statistics (https://www.census.gov/programs -surveys/bds.html) and Nonemployer Statistics (https://www.census.gov/programs -surveys/nonemployer-statistics.html).

businesses are defined as those having no paid employees (i.e., no payroll) and are subject to federal income taxes. Most nonemployers are self-employed individuals operating very small unincorporated businesses that may or may not be the owner's principal source of income. In some cases, nonemployer businesses receive payments as independent agents and contractors. For nonemployers, each distinct business income tax return filed by a nonemployer business is counted as a firm. A nonemployer business may operate from its owner's home address or from a separate physical location.

Nonemployer businesses have multiple legal forms of organization, including C corporations, S corporations, individual proprietorships (also referred to as "sole proprietorships," which are unincorporated businesses owned by an individual or self-employed person), and partnerships (unincorporated businesses owned by two or more persons who have a shared financial interest in the business). Businesses choose the legal form they operate under. We later show that the future performance of the business, including its likelihood of hiring employees, its survival, and its receipts, differs substantially across the different types of legal form. The demographic characteristics of the business owners are also very different. We take advantage of these distinctions in chapter 6 to create alternative measures of job creation and survival.

Table 2.2 reports the number of nonemployer businesses for selected years.[4] The number of nonemployer businesses in the United States was 15.4 million in 1997, 20.4 million in 2005, and 26.5 million in 2018. The growth in total number of businesses in the United States was driven almost entirely by the growth in nonemployer businesses.

The US Census Bureau also tracks the number of employer businesses in the Business Register. The key distinction between employer and nonemployer businesses is whether they have employees as reported in their

Table 2.2
Number of nonemployer businesses in the United States

	1997	2000	2005	2010	2015	2018
Non-employer businesses	15,439,609	16,529,955	20,392,068	22,110,628	24,331,403	26,485,532

Source: US Census Bureau, Nonemployer Statistics (https://www.census.gov/programs-surveys/nonemployer-statistics.html).

payroll filing.[5] Employer businesses have an EIN. These firms can have full- and part-time employees, including salaried officers and executives of the corporation who were on the payroll in the pay period that included March 12. Employees on sick leave, holiday, or vacation during that week are included. Proprietors and partners of employer businesses are not included if they are not on the payroll of the firm. In some cases, firms have an EIN but no current employees as of that pay period. This can happen for a variety of reasons, such as seasonality (e.g., summer or winter jobs) or the use of volunteers, or because the firm starts operations after the week of March 12. There is a nontrivial number of employer firms with an EIN but no current employees as of that pay period that are still included in the employer data if they have positive annual payroll; that is, they hired workers after the week that included March 12.

Although these data are reported by the federal government through a variety of different products, we focus on those reported in the Business Dynamics Statistics (BDS) series, which provide annual measures of the number of employer businesses and establishments for the United States. The BDS is based on the Longitudinal Business Database (LBD), and numbers from it are similar to the US Census Bureau's County Business Patterns (CBP) and Statistics of US Business (SUSB) programs.[6] Table 2.3 reports the number of employer firms and establishments.

The number of employer businesses was 4.8 million in 1997. The number grew to 5.2 million in 2005, dropped back to 5.0 million in 2010, and then grew to 5.3 million in 2018. Employer businesses constitute roughly 20 percent of the total number of businesses in the United States. Nonemployers are the dominant form of business entity when it comes to business type. However, when it comes to size (as measured by receipts), nonemployers account for only a relatively small share of the economy.

Table 2.3
Number of employer businesses and establishments in the United States

	1997	2000	2005	2010	2015	2018
Employer firms	4,778,182	4,905,920	5,168,533	5,019,625	5,151,871	5,288,540
Employer establishments	6,076,988	6,295,525	6,677,154	6,671,187	6,909,168	7,098,769

Source: US Census Bureau, Business Dynamics Statistics (https://www.census.gov/programs-surveys/bds.html).

The number of establishments is also reported in table 2.3. A firm is defined as a business organization consisting of one or more domestic establishments that are specified to be under common ownership or control. The firm and the establishment are one and the same for single-establishment firms. Employer businesses might have multiple establishments. Establishments are single physical locations where business is conducted or where services or industrial operations are performed. They include separate stores, factories, or warehouses of the same business. The number of employer establishments is greater than the number of firm units by a ratio of roughly 1.3 to 1.

Most employer businesses have only one establishment, and the modal multi-unit has two establishments. But, as is the case in the comparison with nonemployer firms, the bulk of economic activity, as measured by revenue or employment, is concentrated among the select set of firms with more than two establishments.

We focus on the business and not the establishment. This distinction is especially important when examining startups because new establishments could simply represent the opening of another store or factory of an existing firm, which can rely on an existing business plan, branding, or goodwill. To define a startup, we must also include only new businesses. Recent research has shown that startups disproportionally contribute to job creation in their first few years, outpacing the job creation of the largest firms (Haltiwanger, Jarmin, and Miranda 2013), and that they also are important sources of innovation and productivity growth (Acemoglu et al. 2018; Haltiwanger et al. 2017).

Business Owners in the United States

An alternative commonly used national measure of business activity is the number of business owners in the United States. The US Bureau of Labor Statistics (BLS), for example, reports estimates in the Self-Employed Series from the underlying Current Population Survey (CPS) data.[7] The measure of business ownership in the CPS captures all business owners, including those who own incorporated or unincorporated businesses and those who are employers or nonemployers.[8] Although some business owners own large businesses with multiple establishments, the predominant business types tend to be nonemployers and small, single-unit entities. We briefly

Table 2.4

Number of business owners in the United States

	2000	2005	2010	2015	2018
Business owners	14,673,000	15,718,000	14,872,000	14,991,000	15,558,000

Source: US Bureau of Labor Statistics, Current Population Survey (https://www.bls.gov /webapps/legacy/cpsatab9.htm).

present some of the underlying figures on business ownership before turning back to our measure of startups.

Table 2.4 reports estimates of the number of business owners in the United States from the BLS. The number of business owners was 14.7 million in 2000 and climbed to 15.7 million by 2005 before dropping down to 14.9 million in the post–financial crisis period. But the number of business owners had increased to 15.6 million by 2018.

The number of business owners is much smaller than the total number of businesses in the United States (the total number of businesses was more than 27 million in 2010 and more than 31.7 million in 2018), which raises the question as to why these estimates differ so much. First, the CPS estimates of the number of business owners are based on household survey data and enumerate individual business owners. The Business Register includes all nonemployer business operations that file tax forms as individual proprietorships, partnerships, or any type of corporation, and all employer businesses filing EINs. This means that the Business Register does not rely on self-reporting to define what constitutes a business, as opposed to the CPS estimates. A hobbyist who reports income received from the hobby in an IRS income tax filing is counted in the Business Register data as a business, while that same individual filling out the survey may look at (and report) the hobby differently. Second, the CPS estimates include only individuals owning businesses as their main work activity, with a substantial commitment of hours.[9] The nonemployer statistics sourced from the Business Register include all nonemployer firms with receipts of $1,000 or more, which may include side or "casual" businesses owned by wage-and-salary workers, unemployed persons, retired workers, or investor owners. According to the Census Bureau's Survey of Business Owners (SBO), roughly 30 percent of business owners report working fewer than twenty hours per week in the business (US Census Bureau 2013). Third, the CPS estimates include all business owners, whereas the Business Register excludes agriculture and a few other types of businesses (which actually might decrease the discrepancy). Finally, estimates of the number of businesses can differ from the number of business owners because there can be: (1) multiple owners of businesses, (2) individuals who own multiple businesses, (3) definitional differences in scope, such as workers in occupations like sales and real estate, and (4) differences in the reference period for capturing business ownership and other measurement issues (for more discussion, see Bjelland et al. 2006; Fairlie and Robb 2008; Headd 2003; and Headd and Saade 2008).

These differences in reporting and defining businesses (and their owners) will matter when we consider the characteristics of businesses, profile startups, and the demographics of the owners. Though both measurement approaches have their advantages and disadvantages, we take an agnostic view as to which measure best captures the "true" count of businesses that exist in the United States. For our analysis, however, we focus primarily on the administrative records (Business Register) approach because of the universal, systematic, longitudinal, and unbiased coverage of data it offers and the ability to link the data to other Census Bureau data sets. This allows us to return universe-based statistics, take a deeper dive into the full life cycle of an individual business from inception to death, and document the dynamics of that business over time.

The Age Distribution of Businesses in the United States

Data on the number of businesses are readily available. Finding data on startups is more difficult. Startups are of particular interest because of their job-creating potential (Haltiwanger, Jarmin, and Miranda 2013). In addition to creating jobs, business formation is associated with the creation of new industries, innovation, improvement in sector productivity, and economic growth (Acemoglu et al. 2018; Audretsch, Keilbach, and Lehmann 2006; Foster et al. 2018; Haltiwanger et al. 2017; Parker 2018; Reynolds 2005). Startups are also becoming a common proxy for entrepreneurship. Surprisingly, there is no universally agreed-upon or official definition of "entrepreneur" in government data or research (Decker et al. 2014; Parker 2018). The US BLS publishes statistics on entrepreneurs that are defined as new employer establishments. We use a similar approach of defining entrepreneurs as new businesses or business startups.

Data on startups are also useful for measuring the beginning of a business and following it over time. There is no issue with left censoring in the data when you can identify the startup year and track the business from that point in time. Left censoring in the data for older firms can create problems for analyzing some questions.

Before turning to a discussion of measuring startups in the economy, we examine the age distribution of businesses in the United States. A source of data on businesses that is based on the same underlying business data and includes (1) nonemployer businesses, (2) employer businesses, and (3) information on age of the business is the Census Bureau's SBO. Unlike the administrative data presented above, the SBO is a survey in which firms report electronically by using Census Taker, the Census Bureau's secure online interactive application, or complete and return a hard-copy form by mail.[10]

Using published SBO 2007 data, we report the age distribution of businesses in figure 2.1. Slightly more than 10 percent of businesses are less than one year old. The share of firms that reach the one-year mark drops to 7 percent. By four years, the share drops to 4 percent. Most businesses are older, but their numbers are aggregated into different age groups. Often individuals do not remember precise dates back in time for business starts (and other information), so survey takers need to sacrifice less accurate reporting of more precise categories (i.e., the exact year of business founding) in favor of more accurate reporting of less precise categories. The administrative data that we use below, of course, avoid these questionnaire response problems. The estimates essentially indicate an increasing rate of decline. The five- to seven-year-old category captures 12 percent of businesses and the eight- to seventeen-year-old category captures 22 percent of businesses. Simply averaging by the number of age years within each category, we find that each age-in-years in the five to seven years age group captures slightly less than 4 percent of the total and each age-in-years in the eight to seventeen years age group captures 2 percent of the total. The eighteen to twenty-seven years age group captures 13 percent overall, but roughly 1 percent for each age-in-years group.

The businesses from the older age groups are only the ones that survived up to that point. This is an often overlooked issue. But any comparisons made between new businesses and older businesses should be interpreted from the standpoint of survivor bias. The firms surviving to five, ten, or

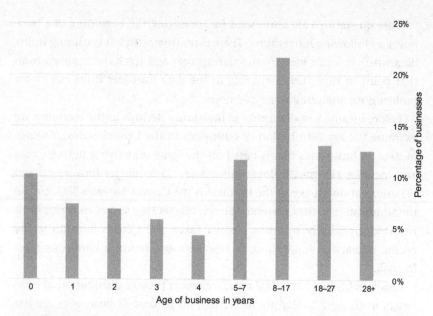

Figure 2.1
Age distribution of businesses. *Source*: Published data from the Survey of Business Owners, 2007 (US Census Bureau 2013, https://www.census.gov/programs-surveys/sbo/data/tables.html).

fifteen years out are very different from the average startup. This is true even for businesses surviving only two, three, or four years out.

Figure 2.2, also from the SBO, demonstrates the problem by displaying the percentage of employer businesses as a share of all businesses (employer and nonemployer) by business age. Having versus not having employees (or employer versus nonemployer status) is a useful measure of success because employer businesses are larger scale, more growth-oriented, and have higher revenues on average. The goal here is simply to show how easy it is to detect survivor bias in the data.

Only 9 percent of new businesses have employees. The percentage jumps considerably for businesses that are one year old. For this group, 19 percent have employees. By only four years out, 28 percent of businesses have employees, and for the oldest age group of businesses, the percentage that have employees increases to 48 percent. Are older firms just more likely to have employees than startups? No. As we show in

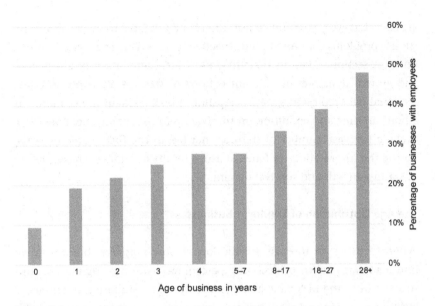

Figure 2.2
Percentage of businesses with employees by age of business. *Source*: Published data
from the Survey of Business Owners, 2007 (US Census Bureau 2013).

later chapters, the story is more complicated, with many startups exiting
each year and the ones surviving being more successful than the average
startup.

What do we learn from these mostly illustrative estimates from SBO data?
First, these data indicate that startups make up a sizable portion of all businesses. Second, it is clear that most startups do not survive, shutting down
quickly, based on the declining percentages by age of businesses. Third, this
"retrospective" method of measuring startups and their survival is, however,
problematic because of recall bias by owners. Also, businesses change ownership and the new owner may not know the year of founding. Survey data
are limited in this regard. In examining the underlying data, we found
that 6 percent of owners reported not knowing the start year, and an
additional 2.5 percent left the question blank even though they answered
other questions on the survey.

We proceed by looking at administrative panel data on startups. Shifting
the focus from surveys to administrative records removes problems with
sample attrition and item nonresponse. Furthermore, administrative data

are collected every year and do not suffer from potential recall bias or nonre-sponse problems common in retrospective surveys. Panel data also improve on cross-sectional data in that they allow an examination of entry, exit, and growth dynamics of different cohorts of startups. By contrast, cross-sectional data represent a static snapshot of businesses in the economy at a point in time and condition on survival up to that point; therefore, they exclude the vast number of startups that fail in the first couple of years. Losing the information on failed startups results in an incomplete picture of startup growth and survival dynamics.

The Age Distribution of Employer Businesses

When focusing on the age distribution of only employer businesses we find a similar pattern of declining percentages with age. Figure 2.3, constructed from the BDS database, displays the age distribution of employer businesses. Nine percent of employer businesses are less than one year old. The share of firms that are one year old drops to 7 percent. By four years

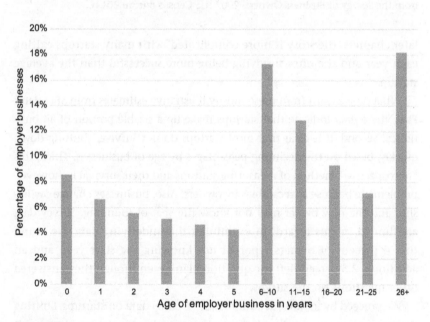

Figure 2.3
Age distribution of employer businesses. *Source*: Census Bureau, Business Dynamics Statistics (https://www.census.gov/programs-surveys/bds.html).

old, the percentage drops to 5 percent. Averaging the older age categories by number of age-in-years included, the percentage drops to 3.5 percent for businesses aged six to ten years and 1.5 percent for businesses aged twenty-one to twenty-five years. These patterns for employer businesses are consistent with high exit rates for young firms.

Concerns over Identifying the Starting Year

One limitation with the age distribution reported in figure 2.3, however, is that the age of employer firms is determined by the first time the business has employees. This definition of the age of a business does not account for the possibility of the business existing in previous years as a nonemployer business, thus potentially hiding the nonemployer origin of a large number of employer businesses and their contribution to jobs in the economy (Haltiwanger et al. 2009). The BDS data used to create this figure capture only employer businesses.[11]

The BDS, underlying the LBD, and related establishment-level data are often used in government publications and research on startups. For example, the federal government releases two often cited and influential statistics on job creation and survival rates by employer startups: six new jobs per startup and a 50 percent survival rate after five years (US SBA 2017). These numbers are based on *employer* businesses or establishments and ignore a business's previous existence as a nonemployer startup. Furthermore, previous research on job creation among businesses focuses almost exclusively on employer firms (e.g., Decker et al. 2014; Garcia-Macia, Hsieh, and Klenow 2016; Glaeser, Kerr, and Kerr 2015; Glaeser, Kerr, and Ponzetto 2010; Haltiwanger, Jarmin, and Miranda 2013; Kulick et al. 2016; Tracy 2011). One important reason is that data on nonemployer startups are difficult to work with and are fraught with some of the conceptual issues we hinted at earlier in the chapter. Series of nonemployer businesses by firm age are not regularly published by the Census Bureau. Among OECD countries, the United States is one of the few countries that do not report nonemployer business creation rates (see OECD 2017a, figure 4.1, for example).

The exclusion of nonemployer histories creates a significant data gap. The classic studies of entrepreneurship, such as Knight (1921), Schumpeter (1934), and more recently Kihlstrom and Laffont (1979), Jovanovic (1982), and Evans and Jovanovic (1989), which have helped establish entrepreneurship as an independent field in economics, do not limit the definition of entrepreneurship by employer status or legal form of organization. Furthermore, many employer businesses started life as nonemployers, and nonemployer firms constitute the majority of both startups and total firms in the United States.

How we define the year of birth of a business is partly a result of data availability. The year of birth of a business defined by the hiring of the first employee can be different from the year of birth of a business defined by the first sale or revenue.[12] Alternative definitions will necessarily lead to alternative measures of survival and growth. In general, incorporating the nonemployer history of firms by using a revenue-based definition of birth will shed light on important early entrepreneurial dynamics that are crucial to understanding the relationships between and among entrepreneurship, job creation, and survival. Ignoring nonemployers is also likely to miss the changing dynamics of the worker-employer relation and the growth of the contracting and gig economy.

A graphical illustration is helpful to support these arguments. Consider the new employer businesses in figure 2.4 (in gray).

Firms A, B, C, and D all become new employer businesses in the same year. Firm A and firm C are still operating in year 5, whereas firm B exits in

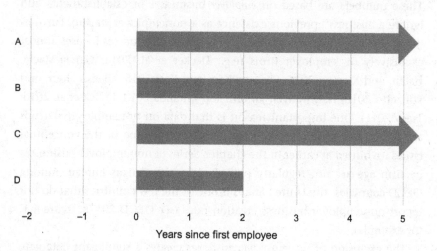

Figure 2.4
Employee-based approach to measuring startup year.

year 4 and firm D exits in year 2. Arrows denote that the business survives through year 5.

It is possible, however, that some of these new employer firms started as nonemployer firms first. We discuss this in more detail in following chapters but note here that many nonemployer businesses transition to employer businesses. Even well-known businesses that have grown to become employer businesses may have started as nonemployers.

From a revenue perspective, the same businesses will appear to start in a different year. In figure 2.5 we denote years with revenues but no employees in gray.

In this case, both firm C and firm D actually started earlier as nonemployer businesses and made the transition to employer businesses in a later year. The transition to employer business is when those businesses would be captured in the widely used BDS/LBD employer data as *new* employer businesses.

Similarly, we can examine these patterns from the point of view of nonemployer startups. In figure 2.6, gray denotes years without employees and black denotes years with employees.

In this case, firms E and F do not make the transition to new employer businesses, but firms G and H do. Firm G would be identified as a new employer firm in year 2, and firm H would be identified as a new employer firm in year 3.

Years since first employee

Figure 2.5
Revenue-based approach to measuring startup year.

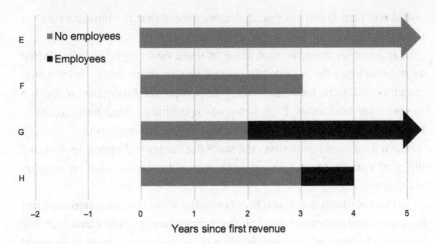

Figure 2.6
Nonemployer firms and transition from nonemployer to employer.

The three graphical representations highlight the challenges in identifying startup years and cohorts. First, without examining previous nonemployer status, firms C and D would be attributed to the same startup cohort as all the other firms shown. When we incorporate their nonemployer spell, however, we find that both firms actually started in earlier years and belong to an earlier startup cohort. Second, survival rates will differ in potentially dramatic ways. Figure 2.4 shows that firm D, for example, survived two years. But figure 2.5, which takes into account firm D's previous nonemployer spell, shows that it survived four years. Third, job creation by birth year will also change. The jobs created in later years by firm G would be attributed in year 2 for the main startup cohort. Finally, more generally, the exclusion of firms E through H in the calculation of job creation and survival rates will result in different job creation levels per startup and different survival rates relative to basing measurement on new employer status.

Creating a New Panel Data Set of Startups

We combine and analyze a new compilation of administrative panel data on the universe of business startups in the United States. The new Comprehensive Startup Panel uses the presence of revenues in a year to identify a business birth and combines two existing Census Bureau panel data sets:

(1) the Longitudinal Business Database, a panel of all nonfarm employer establishments beginning from 1976, and (2) the Integrated Longitudinal Business Database (ILBD), a panel of nonemployer establishments, containing a quinquennial cross section of firms starting from 1977 to 1992 and the annual panel dimension starting in 1994. The combination of data sets allows us to measure job creation and survival among *all* startups in the economy that generate revenue. The ILBD contains links to the employer universe in the LBD that are generated either through the tax ID (EIN or PIK, protected identification key) or through name and geography matching of the business.

A careful examination of job creation and survival among the universe of startups requires identifying transitions between nonemployer and employer status.[13] The employer and nonemployer administrative data are sourced from different administrative filings, making it difficult for the Census Bureau to always and easily identify these transitions. Businesses in the United States are required to file separately income and payroll (employment) taxes. However, businesses may or may not use the same tax identifiers when filing their income and payroll reports.[14] Since the transition to employer status can be identified only by linking the income filing to the payroll filing, this can lead to broken linkages between the two. To resolve this problem, the ILBD links the employer and nonemployer businesses units by a variety of identifiers, including the EIN, the PIK, and the name and state of the owner or business.[15] These enhanced linkages are tracked in the ILBD through a longitudinal business identifier, the ILBDNUM.

Beta versions of the ILBD have been used in previous work (e.g., Davis et al. 2007; Fairlie and Miranda 2017; Fairlie, Miranda, and Zolas 2019) to study transitions between nonemployer and employer business units. These analyses were conducted for only one or two years, or for a subset of industries, or were not focused on startups. A beta version of the ILBD was first introduced by Davis et al. (2007) to study transitions between nonemployer and employer business units for a subset of industries in 1992 and between 1994 and 2000. Subsequently, Fairlie and Miranda (2017) created another beta version to look specifically at startup activity. They used the 1997 nonemployer startup cohort to examine transitions to employer businesses. Most recently, Fairlie, Miranda, and Zolas (2019) also provide a description of the new data set and present some examples of what can be done with the data using only the first 1997 "beta" cohort. With each revised file, Census Bureau economists incorporate and resolve insights and data challenges identified in previous versions. The new version we use is no different in this regard and incorporates the latest data fixes and insights. These had to do with improvements in the definition of business reactivations, exits, and transitions from nonemployer to employer firms.[16]

We combine the underlying confidential and restricted-access ILBD and LBD microdata for several startup cohorts (i.e., the 1995 to 2011 startup cohorts). The new Comprehensive Startup Panel data set created here follows each startup cohort from one to seven years after the startup year (which in most cases does not cover a full calendar year). Thus, follow-up years of data cover the years 1996 to 2018. The combination of the ILBD and the LBD then allows us to explore the connections between the two universes, including transitions between the two.[17] The resulting startup panel data set provides annual information that allows all businesses, employer and nonemployer, to be followed over time. Because the underlying data contain links between the employer and nonemployer universes, it is possible to accurately identify the point of startup for business units, and to follow each annual cohort of startups over time. A business entity can be included in the startup cohort for a given year only if it is not found in any of the previous seven years of the nonemployer or employer universe.[18] Additionally, mergers and acquisitions of existing firms are not identified as startups but instead are treated as a continuation of the initial business if the firm retains its original identifier.

Startups that switch their original employer firm identifier for whatever reason (either through an ownership change, reorganization, or acquisition) are classified as exits.[19] The simplification is taken because ownership changes, reorganizations, and merger and acquisition activity are active areas of research and present their own challenges when it comes to defining firm survival among startups. For example, if a startup with one establishment undergoes a reorganization or change in legal form, should that count as an exit of the initial business? Can we clearly distinguish a firm expansion from an acquisition? Should acquisitions be considered exits of the initial firm? There are also data limitations since our data do not distinguish the acquiree from the acquirer, and reasonable researchers might disagree on how to define. Ideally, the startup firms we want to capture and retain in the data in this context are ones with one establishment and organically grow to having multiple establishments. For all of these reasons here we take the simpler approach of measuring exits and recognize that results do not differ much if we change our definition.[20]

The Comprehensive Startup Panel includes every business that files taxes or a tax report.[21] One concern is that the Comprehensive Startup Panel data set contains a large number of business activities whose participants have no intention of hiring employees and represent consulting, contracting, gig, or hobby activities. But these data provide a useful view of the universe of business units. These data also allow identification of the more growth-oriented businesses by conditioning on a few administrative variables, depending on the research question. The data contain information on the legal form (i.e., sole proprietor, partnership, or corporation), the type of tax identifier (i.e., EIN or PIK), revenue, and industry of activity, in addition to information on startup year, employment, payroll, exits, and geographic location. We explore these issues in detail later by examining populations with and without sole proprietor businesses that do not have EINs.

Most of the analysis presented in the book focuses on the job creation and survival of startups.[22] We do not focus on examining revenues as an outcome metric. This is a consequence of the fact that the Census Bureau places particular emphasis on describing economic activity based on employment counts and payroll dollars. The Census Bureau's Business Register is thus based on payroll filings, whereas revenue comes from income filings. Businesses are not required to use the same tax identifiers (EIN) when filing these different forms. As a result, the revenue values filed under an income tax form can become unlinked from the payroll and employment values filed under the payroll tax form. Further complicating measurement, revenue filings can cover the activity of different establishments than those covered by payroll filings. This is often the case with complex holding companies. Unlinked records are also fairly common among small sole proprietors, where the sole proprietor might file under the business name for the payroll filing and under the owner's name for the income filing. Additionally, information on revenues is incomplete for employer businesses (i.e., in the LBD) and regular coverage begins only with 1997 onward. Future work focusing on revenue as a business outcome will need to address these issues.

Accessing the Comprehensive Startup Panel Data Set

The new Comprehensive Startup Panel data, which contain the underlying ILBD and LBD data, and the compilation code are confidential and restricted access. They are accessible to researchers approved to access the data following application through Federal Statistical Research Data Centers (FSRDCs).[23]

To be clear, the Comprehensive Startup Panel data set is not a distinct data product at the Census Bureau. Instead, the Comprehensive Startup Panel data set is a *package* that can be requested and is updated as the underlying data are updated. It consists of the ILBD, the LBD, and an SAS code that links the ILBD and LBD together, as well as necessary transitions. It includes all startups starting in 1995 and a number of identifiable characteristics of the startups, such as their industry, legal form, geography (zip or FIPS—Federal Information Processing Standard—codes), number of employees, payroll (none for nonemployers), and revenues. The SAS code we developed can be run at an FSRDC, for example, and the Comprehensive Startup Panel data set will be created and ready for analysis. Our Comprehensive Startup Panel database can be used to study all the questions addressed in this and subsequent chapters of the book.

How Many Startups Are There?

Using our Comprehensive Startup Panel, we find that on average, 4.1 million businesses are started each year in the United States. Among these startups a disproportionate share consists of nonemployer startups. We find that 3.7 million are nonemployer startups, representing 89 percent of all startups. Employer startups are also a large group in the United States, however, numbering 439,000 per year. If we exclude the large number of nonemployer sole proprietorships without EINs, as discussed in detail in chapter 6 there are a total of 1.2 million startups per year.

Startups also represent a large share of the total stock of business in the US economy. During our sample period, the stock of businesses in the United States was on average around 26 million, indicating that startups constitute roughly 16 percent of all business entities. We examine the job creation potential of these startups in the next chapter.

Startups by Major Industry Group

Startups are not concentrated in just a few industries or sectors of the economy but instead are quite diverse. Table 2.5 reports the distribution of startups in the United States across major industry groups or sectors of the economy. We exclude from the analysis agricultural farms (since these are not covered by the Economic Census and are excluded from the LBD) and government entities. The largest share of startups is in the Professional, Scientific, and Technical Services sector and the Other Services sector, each of which accounts for roughly 13 percent of all startups. This sector is followed closely by two sectors, each with 11–12 percent shares of the total: (1) Utilities and Construction (two sectors treated as one group on this book)[24] and (2) Retail Trade. Additional sectors that have relatively large shares of startups are Health Care and Social Assistance (10 percent) and Administrative and Support and Waste Management and Remediation Services (9 percent).

Among the notable sectors, Transportation and Warehousing, which includes taxi driving, is represented by four percent of startups. The Accommodation and Food Services sector, which includes restaurants and hotels, is represented by only 3 percent of startups. As expected, sectors such as Manufacturing and Wholesale Trade, which have large returns to scale favoring large businesses, are represented by only a very small share of startups. Creating a new manufacturing business, for example, takes a large investment of capital and financial risk. We wouldn't expect many entrepreneurs to jump into manufacturing, and indeed, there are only roughly 70,000 startups on average in manufacturing in the entire country per year.

Overall, startups concentrate in service-oriented businesses, which is consistent with their smaller size. Startups do not concentrate in industries that favor large-scale establishments and operations. They do not concentrate in numbers in sectors of the economy that require large financial investment but instead concentrate in smaller-scale operations that require less financial capital. Startups are also concentrated in major industry groups that produce nontradable goods and services.

Conclusions

Our compilation of administrative data on the universe of US startups discussed in this chapter yields a new and exciting Comprehensive Startup

Table 2.5

Startups by major industry group, average per year

Major industry group (sector)	Number of startups	Percent of all startups
Agriculture, Forestry, Fishing and Hunting	51,265	1.3
Mining	10,088	0.3
Construction; Utilities[a]	449,941	11.6
Manufacturing	70,412	1.8
Wholesale Trade	87,706	2.3
Retail Trade	426,294	11.0
Transportation and Warehousing	162,824	4.2
Information	75,353	1.9
Finance and Insurance	126,706	3.3
Real Estate and Rental and Leasing	267,471	6.9
Professional, Scientific, and Technical Services	515,706	13.3
Management of Companies and Enterprises	11,559	0.3
Administrative and Support and Waste Management and Remediation Services	359,118	9.2
Educational Services	107,471	2.8
Health Care and Social Assistance	375,588	9.7
Arts, Entertainment, and Recreation	165,412	4.3
Accommodation and Food Services	120,059	3.1
Other Services (except Public Administration)	504,882	13.0
Not elsewhere specified	205,706	5.3
Total number of startups	4,093,559	100.0

Note: a. To avoid the disclosure of confidential information, throughout this book we report the Utilities sector and Construction sector together as one group rather than separately.

Source: Authors' calculations from the newly compiled Comprehensive Startup Panel data set (1995–2018).

Panel data set for studying questions about entrepreneurship, job creation, and other subjects. The advantages of our Comprehensive Startup Panel for studying these questions include having access to the universe of startups (both nonemployer and employer businesses), information on job creation (employees and payroll), and panel data, and the ability to follow annual startup cohorts over time. The data are administrative, so there is little attrition and no survey item nonresponse.

The Comprehensive Startup Panel data set provides a broad view of business starts. Linking the universe of nonemployer firms to the universe of employer firms allows us to track survival among all business startups in the US economy. Firms that start as nonemployer businesses and make the transition to employer businesses in a subsequent year will be assigned to their nonemployer startup cohort, affecting their corresponding business age. When a business first hires employees, we can look back to determine whether it had a prior nonemployer history. For all the illustrative examples of startups provided in figures 2.3 through 2.5, we can identify the start dates, startup cohort year, and age of the business.

There are more than four million startups each year in the United States. These new businesses represent a large share of all businesses in the country. Although many of these startups are in service areas of the economy, they are widely spread across industrial sectors. We turn next to measuring job creation among these startups.

3 Job Creation by Startups

In this chapter, we examine job creation among startups. The topic is especially important for policy debates over supporting entrepreneurs since a common goal of these programs is to create jobs. Public policies that foster entrepreneurship, such as incubators, training programs, loan programs, tax breaks, and investor incentives, are popular around the world (OECD 2017b). In the United States, for example, the US Small Business Administration (SBA) alone administers several programs to support small businesses, including loan guarantees, training, federal contracting, and other programs.

Expenditures are often made, however, without measurement of the benefits in terms of the number of businesses, number of jobs, or total payroll created relative to the costs of these programs. Such measures are important for getting a sense of what the broader public benefits are from various programs. In other words, what is the return on investment for these programs? The evidence on the effectiveness of programs to spur entrepreneurship is also mixed. Relevant to any benefit-to-cost calculation is knowing how many jobs the average entrepreneur creates. Answering this question is not easy and depends in large measure on how we define a firm and at what point after its creation we choose to measure its performance.

Congress and the federal government recognize the importance of measuring job creation for policy evaluation. In 2018, Congress passed the Ryan-Murray bill to improve government performance. The Foundations for Evidence-Based Policymaking Act established a fifteen-member commission to study how best to strengthen and expand the use of data to evaluate the effectiveness of federal programs and tax expenditures. Additionally, the US Government Accountability Office (GAO) recently recommended that the SBA use job creation and other outcome-based measures to evaluate the effectiveness of its programs (Congressional Research Service 2020). Also, Small Business Development Centers (SBDCs), which are partly funded by the SBA, measure job creation resulting from their training and assistance centers around the country from surveys of participants (Chrisman 2016). Despite the lack of solid evidence on job creation, public policies to foster entrepreneurship continue to grow.

Exploring the fundamental nature of entrepreneurship also depends on carefully measuring job creation among entrepreneurs. On the one hand, entrepreneurship is about creating innovative products, services, and jobs (i.e., Schumpeterian entrepreneurship); on the other hand, it is primarily about having job independence, contract work, consulting work, schedule flexibility, or being part of the gig economy (Hamilton 2000; Hurst and Pugsley 2011; Katz and Krueger 2016; Levine and Rubinstein 2016). Is entrepreneurship fundamentally about creating *jobs*, creating *a job*, or both? Your answer might depend on your stated policy goal; however, the variety and rich diversity of entrepreneurs, their motivations, and their aspirations should be recognized.

In this chapter, we use the new compilation of administrative data on the universe of business startups in the United States to answer the important question of how many jobs are created by the average entrepreneur. We also answer the equally important question of whether these jobs last over time. We are interested in how job creation starts out and then changes over the first several years of a business's existence.

We measure entrepreneurial job creation using *every* startup in the United States as measured by the presence of revenue or employees. We thus start by using the broadest definition possible of a startup and then consider more restrictive definitions in later chapters. The classic studies of entrepreneurship, such as Knight (1921), Schumpeter (1934), and more recently Kihlstrom and Laffont (1979), Jovanovic (1982), and Evans and Jovanovic (1989), which have helped establish entrepreneurship as an independent field in economics, do not limit the definition of entrepreneurship by employer, incorporation, or any other status. We follow this approach in this chapter to provide a more complete view of job creation that includes both employer and nonemployer startups. Estimates of job creation that are based on new *employer* businesses do not factor nonemployer startups into the calculation. Nonemployer firms constitute the majority of both startups and total firms in the United States. Incorporating them into the calculation offers a broader view that explicitly recognizes that a large fraction of employer firms start as nonemployer businesses.

We then examine several additional aspects of job creation. First, we compare the total number of jobs created by startups to those created by existing firms. We examine how many new jobs in the economy are created by startups. Second, we examine the number of jobs created by the average startup. Third, we examine how much these jobs pay on average compared to jobs at nonstartups. We also examine how job creation changes over time with the age of the startup and the startup cohort. Finally, we perform a statistical regression analysis to better discern how startup job creation differs by industry and evolves over time, with other factors controlled for.

In this chapter, we do not explicitly analyze the exit rates of startups. Job creation levels per startup after the initial year, however, implicitly account for exit rates because a startup that no longer exists cannot create jobs in that year. For example, any startups that did not survive five years after their initial year have zero job creation by definition. We explore issues around exits in the next chapter. Additionally, we do not explore the issue of how to account for the owner's job in this chapter. In a broader sense, job creation measures might be higher because entrepreneurs create jobs for themselves, and those jobs are not counted as employee jobs in the data. We focus on the standard definition of job creation—the number of employees hired per startup—in this chapter and return to the discussion of an alternative measure of total job creation in chapter 6. Employees of startups are paid wages or salaries, whereas owners might be losing or making very little money in the first couple of years. On the other hand, many nonemployer startups have no intention of hiring employees; their primary goal is to create a job for the owners.

Startups Create Many New Jobs in the Economy

On average, 4.1 million businesses are started each year in the United States. Each annual cohort of more than four million startups creates an average of 3.0 million salaried jobs in the first year after startup. Figure 3.1 displays total job creation for the entire startup cohort following job creation from the first year after startup to seven follow-up years after startup.[1] The total number of jobs at startups declines from a peak of 3.0 million to 2.6 million by the fifth follow-up year and to 2.3 million by the seventh follow-up

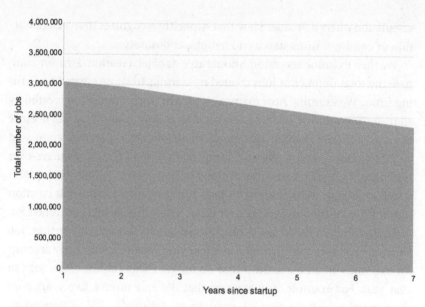

Figure 3.1
Number of jobs created per startup cohort. *Source*: Authors' calculations from the newly compiled Comprehensive Startup Panel data set (1995–2018).

year. We refer to job creation as the total number of employees per startup cohort in that year.

The number of jobs declines linearly from the first year through the seventh follow up year. The average startup cohort includes 4,093,000 businesses. At the highest point of job creation this startup cohort employs 3,046,000 workers in that year. The decline each year after that high point is steady, averaging roughly 100,000 fewer jobs per year. The total number of employees was 2,590,000 at five years after startup and 2,344,000 at seven years after startup. Keep in mind that due to our strict definition of firm exits, we are likely undercounting the "true" job creation potential of startups.

The 3.0 million jobs created by startups in the first year represent roughly three percent of total employment by all US businesses. Figure 3.2 displays the share of total US employment created by startups in each year since startup. To calculate the startup employment share, total employment is averaged across all of the years following each cohort. Total US employment ranged from 112 million to 118 million over the corresponding years.[2] In the first follow-up year, job creation among startups represents

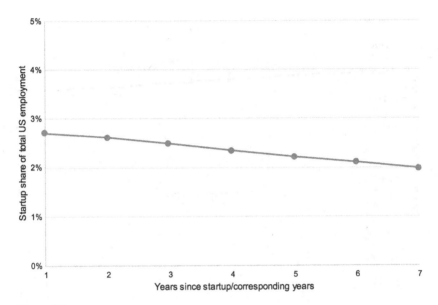

Figure 3.2
Share of total US employment created by startups. *Sources*: Authors' calculations from the newly compiled Comprehensive Startup Panel data set (1995–to 2018) and the US Census Bureau's Business Dynamics Statistics database (1996–2018).

2.7 percent of total employment by all firms. After five years the share of total US employment by the average startup cohort is 2.2 percent, declining to 2.0 percent after seven years.

Startups Create New Jobs, Older Firms Lose Jobs

Although startups represent a small share of total employment, they represent a large percentage of net job creation each year, especially in the first two follow-up years of existence. Figure 3.3 displays net job creation by startups and all other firms over time. Net job creation for all other firms is negative in every year, averaging 1.9 million job losses per year. Without the job creation contributions of startups through their first seven years of existence, net job creation would be negative in the United States.[3]

These statistics indicate the importance of young firms to job creation in the United States. Using the Census Bureau's Business Dynamics Statistics (BDS) database and focusing on the 2005 cohort, Haltiwanger, Jarmin, and

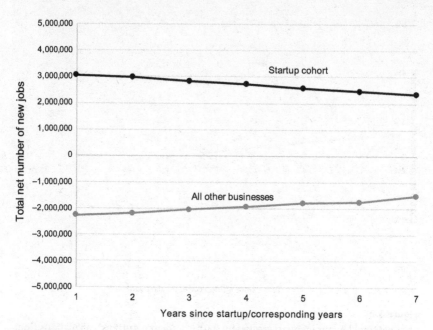

Figure 3.3
Net job creation by startups and all other businesses. *Sources*: Authors' calculations
from the newly compiled Comprehensive Startup Panel data set (1995–2018) and the
Census Bureau's Business Dynamics Statistics database (1996–2018).

Miranda (2013) find that new (i.e., age zero) employer firms create 3.5 million net new jobs, compared with a loss of one million net jobs for firms
of all other ages (i.e., age one year and older) combined. These findings are
similar to our estimates for the initial year contribution to job creation for
the average startup cohort (which includes all startups).

But How Many Jobs Are Created per Startup?

We turn to examining the following questions: (1) How many jobs are
created by each entrepreneur? and (2) Do these jobs last over time? The
answers to these questions are fundamental to how we think about entrepreneurship from policy, economic welfare, and theoretical perspectives.
Figure 3.4 displays the number of jobs created by the average startup over
seven follow-up years. As noted earlier, here we focus on jobs created for
employees and not the owner, but we return to the owner's job later. The

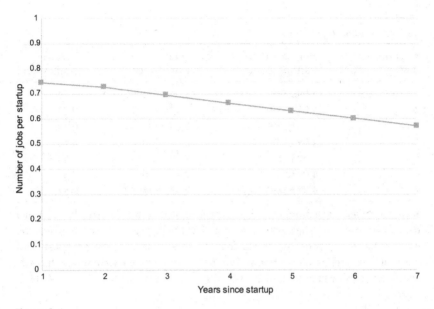

Figure 3.4
Number of jobs created per startup. *Source*: Authors' calculations from the newly compiled Comprehensive Startup Panel data set (1995–2018).

average entrepreneur creates 0.74 jobs for others in the first year after startup. Average employment per startup does not disappear quickly: it is 0.63 five years after startup and 0.57 seven years after startup. All startups in a cohort are included in the denominator, even if they exit, to focus on the expected value of job creation per startup.

Administrative panel data on the universe of startups is essential for this calculation because we do not have slippage in job creation through survey response attrition or survival bias. A major problem with volunteer panel surveys is that participants drop out over time, and the likelihood of dropping out is probably correlated with outcomes such as job creation or survival. This might lead to biased estimates. We avoid this problem because the Comprehensive Startup Panel is derived from administrative records, not from surveys of business owners.

We report the total number of jobs and average number of jobs for the average startup cohort in table 3.1. The numbers in table format complement figures 3.1 and 3.4. The 4.1 million startups in the US economy create an average of 0.74 jobs, or 3.0 million total jobs in the first follow-up year.

Table 3.1
Job creation among startups

Years since startup	Number of startups (year 0)	Total employment	Average employment
1	4,093,559	3,046,724	0.74
2	4,093,559	2,976,871	0.73
3	4,093,559	2,846,435	0.70
4	4,093,559	2,715,700	0.66
5	4,093,559	2,589,553	0.63
6	4,093,559	2,465,776	0.60
7	4,093,559	2,343,941	0.57

Source: Authors' calculations from the newly compiled Comprehensive Startup Panel data set (1995–2018). The startup year (year 0) is the first calendar year in which the business has revenues or payroll. The following year (year 1) captures the first complete calendar year of information on number of employees and survival in the data. Startup cohorts include 1995 to 2011, and follow-up years include 1996 to 2018.

By the fifth follow-up year both the total number of jobs and average jobs per startup have declined, but not substantially.

These patterns of job creation by the average startup reveal two important findings. First, job creation levels per entrepreneur are relatively low. Startups create an average of roughly three quarters of a job each. This finding parallels findings from the employer universe, where relatively few young firms, those that grow rapidly, contribute the most jobs (Haltiwanger et al. 2017). Second, although total levels of job creation might be viewed as relatively low, the jobs created by entrepreneurs do not disappear right away. The number of jobs created by the average startup declines by only 0.17 jobs, from 0.74 jobs to 0.57 jobs, seven years later. This is despite the large amount of exit among the startup cohort, the implication being that surviving businesses make up for most of the job loss from business exits. On net, job creation by startups is relatively long-lasting. When viewed from this broader perspective, the levels of job creation are considerably lower than the six jobs per employer startup often cited in federal statistics (e.g., US SBA 2017). We discuss this comparison in more detail below. But the key difference is that startups without employees are included in these calculations, whereas the higher numbers include only new employer firms (which might have started in previous years as nonemployers).

Are These Just Low-Paying Jobs?

From administrative payroll records, we can also approximate how much employees are paid on average at each startup. In the Comprehensive Startup Panel, information is reported on total payroll and total number of employees at each startup. Using the ratio of the two we can calculate average payroll (earnings) per employee. The average earnings per employee are $34,700 in the first year after startup. Earnings per employee increase from there as the startup ages. Figure 3.5 displays average payroll per employee by year since startup. All payroll statistics are adjusted for inflation and reported in 2015 dollars. Earnings per employee increase steadily in each follow-up year. By the fifth follow-up year, earnings per employee are $38,600, rising to $40,000 by year 7.

The rise in the average pay per employee in this analysis should be viewed with appropriate caution given the limitations of the data. First, the number of employees measured in the administrative data is a point-in-time measure (number of employees in the pay period that includes the week of

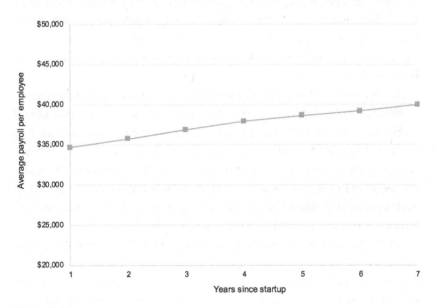

Figure 3.5
Average payroll per employee by startups. *Source*: Authors' calculations from the newly compiled Comprehensive Startup Panel data set (1995–2018).

March 12), whereas payroll is an annual measure (total payroll for the year). Changes in the number of employees after March 12 are not captured in our pay-per-employee estimates. Inasmuch as adjustments are symmetric across years, then the trend estimates are accurate. If, however, patterns in the startup year differ from those in other years with respect to employment adjustment, then the slope might be affected. Second, in interpreting these estimates one should take into consideration survival effects. Firms that exit early on might hire lower-skilled workers and pay lower wages than surviving firms. The rise in pay per employee might be purely the result of a composition effect. With this caution in mind, the pattern over time provides evidence that employees earn less in the startup phase of a new business. It is also consistent with higher exit rates for startups with lower pay per employee. As time progresses the more successful startups have more ability to pay their employees and increase pay. The link between wage and business dynamics early in the life cycle of firms is an area of research that is underdeveloped, and many questions remain. Competitive forces might also come into play. As the startup ages and the excitement and promise of the initial years wane, workers might expect to start reaping the fruit of their efforts and demand higher wages. More generally, productivity gains from learning-by-doing and investments in equipment, coupled with growing demand and brand loyalty, will lead to higher wages (Burton et al. 2018; Foster et al. 2016).

Average salaries at startups are lower than at more established businesses. Establishment-level data from the US Census Bureau indicate that over a similar time period, all business establishments in the United States paid an average of roughly $45,000 per employee. The finding of lower wages paid at young firms relative to older firms is in line with previous work focusing on employer businesses (Brown and Medoff 2003; Haltiwanger et al. 2012). Additionally, it is related to a large earlier literature showing that smaller businesses pay less than larger firms (Oi and Idson 1999).

Although we have information on average payroll per employee in the startup panel data set, we do not have information on worker characteristics. We also do not have information on their labor supply (i.e., whether they work part-time or full-time) or on their fringe benefits, such as employer-based health insurance and other benefits. The absence of information on employee characteristics may be especially important because a simple comparison of the average earnings per employee among startups and the average earnings per employee among older firms does not adjust for differences in employee characteristics. Employees at startups might have less work experience, for example, and that might be one reason why wages are lower (Ouimet and Zarutskie 2014). Observed wage differences between startups and more established firms may therefore reflect differences in whom firms hire rather than in how much they pay. Furthermore, by definition, employees at startups have less tenure at the firm, and tenure is highly correlated with higher wages. Everyone at a startup in the first year of operation has no tenure at the firm. Overall, these differences in employee characteristics and selection could be more responsible for wage differences than underlying differences between startups and more established firms in their productivity or ability to pay higher wages (Abowd, Kramarz, and Margolis 1999).

In a recent study using Danish data, Burton, Dahl and Sorenson (2018) explore these issues in depth. To address the problems noted above, they estimate age and size effects separately as categories; focus on new hires to the firm, which removes problems with differences in firm tenure; match observationally equivalent employees at smaller and younger firms with employees at larger, more established firms; and include fixed effects for detailed industry classifications. They find that younger firms pay more than older ones (though less than 5 percent more) and that smaller firms pay less than larger ones (roughly 10–15 percent less) after adjusting for differences in employee characteristics and other methodological concerns. Combining both the younger age and smaller size of startups, they find that startups pay less than the average established firm. These findings and those from other studies imply that adjusting for characteristics of employees might be important for a careful comparison of wages between startups and other businesses. Linking the startup panel to the Census Bureau's administrative jobs database would allow careful analysis of these issues using US data.[4]

Contributions to Total Payroll

Payroll can also be viewed in terms of the total created by startups. Figure 3.6 displays total payroll by the average startup, which also includes nonemployer startups. Total payroll for the average startup is $25,800 in the

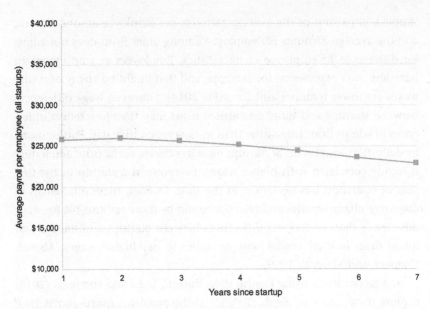

Figure 3.6
Total payroll created per startup. *Source*: Authors' calculations from the newly compiled Comprehensive Startup Panel data set (1995–2018).

first year after startup. In the fifth follow-up year the startup cohort creates an average of $24,400 in total payroll per business. The lower total payroll per startup relative to earnings per employee simply reflects the finding, discussed earlier, that the average startup hires only 0.63 employees in the fifth follow-up year.

The trends for total payroll reflect the total number of jobs associated with the startup cohort. The average startup cohort creates more than $100 billion in payroll in the first year after startup. The sheer number of jobs created by startups multiplied by average earnings per employee contributes substantially to the US economy. Figure 3.7 displays total payroll created by the average startup cohort. In the first year after startup, the entire startup cohort creates a total of $106 billion in total payroll. Total payroll remains at this level for a couple of years and then starts to decline slowly after that. In the fifth year after startup total payroll is $100 billion, and in the seventh year after startup total payroll is $94 billion. Combining the results in figures 3.4, 3.5, and 3.6, we find that the declining contribution to jobs and payroll from the startup cohort, coupled with the increase in the pay per employee, reflects the large number of exits among young

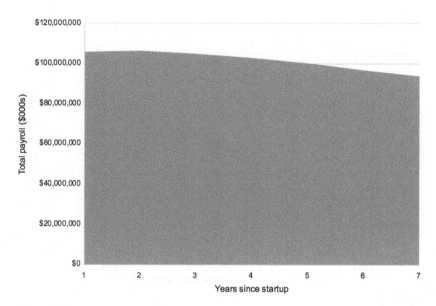

Figure 3.7
Total payroll created per startup cohort. *Source*: Authors' calculations from the newly compiled Comprehensive Startup Panel data set (1995–2018).

firms. Surviving firms make up for a large number of jobs lost and pay higher wages per employee.

Another way of analyzing these large contributions to the US economy is to accumulate total payroll over time for the startup cohort. Instead of examining how much is created in each follow-up year, we examine the cumulative amount over time. Using this lens for a contribution, we see that the average cohort pays out a total of $290 billion through the first two follow-up years combined.[5] Figure 3.8 displays the cumulative payroll of the average startup cohort through the fifth follow-up year. By the end of the third follow-up year the startup cohort has paid out $395 billion to employees. Over the period from startup to five years post startup, employees are paid $598 billion. These are clearly large amounts of money that startups generate as contributions to the US economy.

Job Creation by Major Industry Group

Does job creation differ substantially across major industry groups or sectors of the economy? We examine this question next. Table 3.2 reports the

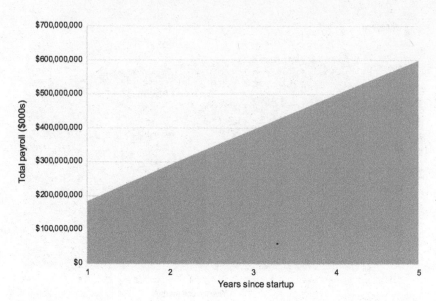

Figure 3.8
Cumulative payroll created per startup cohort. *Source*: Authors' calculations from the newly compiled Comprehensive Startup Panel data set (1995–2018).

average number of employees at follow-up year 1 and follow-up year 5 by major industry group. There are large differences in job creation by industry. Using job creation numbers in the first follow-up year (year 1), for example, average job creation per startup ranges from highs of 4.82 in Accommodation and Food Services and 3.89 in Manufacturing to lows of 0.27 in Real Estate and Rental and Leasing and 0.29 in Agriculture.[6] For other notable sectors, as expected, Wholesale Trade had a relatively high average level of employment at 1.41. Construction startups created 0.56 jobs per business, which is lower than the average job creation for all startups (at 0.74).[7] Retail Trade startups created a higher level, at 0.70 jobs per startup. In general, service sectors, especially the catch-all category of Other Services, have low average job creation per business, reflecting the nonemployer character of many of the startups in this industry group.

Table 3.2 also reports job creation numbers per startup by major industry group for follow-up year 5. The patterns are mostly similar across major industry groups, with declining average employee levels per startup from year 1 to year 5. There are some slight deviations from this pattern for a few major industry groups, but in general, average levels of employment across

Table 3.2
Startup job creation by major industry group

Major industry group	Number of startups	Average employment in year 1	Average employment in year 5
Agriculture, Forestry, Fishing and Hunting	51,265	0.29	0.22
Mining	10,088	1.53	1.53
Construction; Utilities	449,941	0.56	0.48
Manufacturing	70,412	3.89	3.10
Wholesale Trade	87,706	1.41	1.30
Retail Trade	426,294	0.70	0.53
Transportation and Warehousing	162,824	0.49	0.42
Information	75,353	0.88	0.79
Finance and Insurance	126,706	0.70	0.62
Real Estate and Rental and Leasing	267,471	0.27	0.22
Professional, Scientific, and Technical Services	515,706	0.46	0.44
Management of Companies and Enterprises	11,559	2.06	1.55
Administrative and Support and Waste Management and Remediation Service.	359,118	0.83	0.75
Educational Services	107,471	0.49	0.57
Health Care and Social Assistance	375,588	0.90	0.97
Arts, Entertainment, and Recreation	165,412	0.39	0.32
Accommodation and Food Services	120,059	4.82	3.25
Other Services (except Public Administration)	504,882	0.32	0.26

Source: Authors' calculations from the newly compiled Comprehensive Startup Panel data set (1995–2018). The startup year (year 0) is the first calendar year in which the business has revenues or payroll. The following year (year 1) captures the first complete calendar year of information on number of employees and survival in the data. Startup cohorts include 1995 to 2011, and follow-up years include 1996 to 2018.

sectors are set in the first year and continue through subsequent follow-up years.

Regression Analysis of Job Creation by Startups

In this chapter, we presented job creation numbers by year after startup and industry group. Both of these measures are important for how we view startup job creation. They also have implications for policy. One concern, however, is that we are not controlling for other relevant factors when interpreting the numbers. For example, startups in certain industries could be concentrated in specific parts of the country. If those parts of the country have high job creation rates on their own, then the industries might show up as having higher job creation rates. The underlying problem is related to the question of whether there are confounding factors influencing our estimates of job creation by follow-up year and sector.

To address this problem, we estimate regression models. Multivariate regression models are useful for controlling for confounding factors to isolate the independent effects of follow-up year and industry. In the regressions, we control for geographic areas. By controlling for these geographic areas, we can remove confounding effects from regional variation in business policies or local economies that might be correlated with industry. We also control for the differences in job creation across startup cohorts. We do not find major differences across startup cohorts and do not focus on that question here.[8] Controlling for different startup cohorts and their correlation with the business cycle provides an improved estimate of job creation by follow-up year.

Using our regression model, we explore the factors associated with job creation among the universe of startups. To investigate this question, we estimate the following equation:

$$Y_{it} = \alpha + \sum_{s=2}^{7} \delta^s D_i^s + \sum_{k=1}^{18} \beta^k I_i^k + \gamma_t + u_i + \epsilon_{it} \tag{3.1}$$

where Y_{it} is employment at firm i in year t, D_i^s is a set of dummy variables for years since startup for firm i (the excluded or reference year is the first year after startup), I_i^k is a set of dummy variables for industry groups, γ_t are fixed effects capturing each annual startup cohort, and $u_i + \epsilon_{it}$ is a composite error term. The main parameters of interest are δ^s, which captures job creation in follow-up year s relative to the omitted first follow-up year, and β^k, which captures job creation for industry group k. Standard errors are clustered at the firm level to account for multiple observations per startup.

To estimate equation (3.1), we include the full sample of firm–year observations even after exits. In the case of exits, we set employment to zero and include observations for all subsequent years for that firm. We thus treat a nonsurviving startup as having no employment, which is similar to the idea of net job creation per startup over time. We are essentially averaging in the zeros for startups that did not survive. Because we have administrative data on all startups over time, we can rule out the concern that sample attrition is masking exits. This would be a problem with survey data and needs to be addressed. In addition, the use of data on the universe of startups for the cohorts starting from 1995 to 2011 and following them through 2018 creates a massive sample size of more than 550 million observations. The sample size makes it easy to find statistical significance on regression coefficients.

Table 3.3 reports estimates of the regression represented by equation (3.1).[9] The sample size for this regression is more than 500 million observations, and the level of analysis is firm–year. Even clustering at the business level, the standard errors on all reported coefficient estimates are extremely small, and all coefficients are statistically significant at the 0.01 level (and even the 0.001 level).

After controlling for startup cohort years, sectors, and zip codes, we find that job creation decreases slightly after the first year after startup and continues to decline slightly through the seventh follow-up year. The regression estimates indicate that job creation decreased by 0.02 jobs from the first follow-up year after startup to the second follow-up year, and by 0.17 jobs from the first follow-up year to the seventh follow-up year. As noted above, 0.74 jobs are created by the average entrepreneur at the first follow-up year. These estimates are similar to those implied by the patterns displayed in figure 3.4. The declining pattern across years since startup is not driven by differences in industries, startup cohorts, or geography. The regression controls for these factors.

Table 3.3 also reports coefficients by industry group. Job creation levels differ substantially across sectors. In all regressions reported here and below, Other Services is the left-out category and has an average employment level of 0.32 jobs at year 1 and 0.26 jobs at year 5. A few sectors have employment levels that are two to three jobs higher on average:

Table 3.3
Regressions for number of employees using all startup years

	Employment coefficient
1 year since startup	(Excluded category)
2 years since startup	−0.019***
	(0.001)
3 years since startup	−0.050***
	(0.001)
4 years since startup	−0.082***
	(0.001)
5 years since startup	−0.112***
	(0.001)
6 years since startup	−0.143***
	(0.001)
7 years since startup	−0.173***
	(0.001)
11-Agriculture, Forestry, Fishing and Hunting	−0.035***
	(0.004)
21-Mining	1.042***
	(0.051)
22–23-Construction; Utilities	0.212***
	(0.002)
31–33-Manufacturing	2.914***
	(0.028)
42-Wholesale Trade	0.952***
	(0.007)
44–45-Retail Trade	0.277***
	(0.002)
48–49-Transportation and Warehousing	0.135***
	(0.004)
51-Information	0.546***
	(0.015)
52-Finance and Insurance	0.335***
	(0.006)
53-Real Estate and Rental and Leasing	−0.048***
	(0.002)
54-Professional, Scientific, and Technical Services	0.144***
	(0.002)
55-Management of Companies and Enterprises	2.305***
	(0.118)
56-Administrative and Support and Waste Manage and Remediation Services	0.487***
	(0.006)

Table 3.3

(continued)

	Employment coefficient
61-Educational Services	0.273***
	(0.010)
62-Health Care and Social Assistance	0.633***
	(0.005)
71-Arts, Entertainment, and Recreation	0.063***
	(0.004)
72-Accommodation and Food Services	3.198***
	(0.011)
81-Other Services (except Public Administration)	(Excluded category)
Sample Size	556,700,000

Notes: Each observation is a firm–year combination, and all possible follow-up years are included. The dependent variable is the number of employees in that year for the startup and equals zero if the startup does not exist in that year. Standard errors are reported in parentheses below coefficient estimates and are clustered at the firm level. * $p < 0.10$, ** $p < 0.05$, *** $p < 0.01$.

Source: Sample includes the universe of startups from the newly compiled Comprehensive Startup Panel data set (1995–2018). Startup cohorts include 1995 to 2011, and follow-up years include 1996 to 2018.

Accommodation and Food Services (+3.20), Manufacturing (+2.91), and Management (+2.31). Sectors with the lowest job creation levels in addition to Other Services, which is the third-lowest level, are Real Estate (–0.05) and Agriculture (–0.04). The sector Arts, Entertainment, and Recreation has an average employment level slightly higher than Other Services (+0.06).

Conclusions

We create and analyze a new compilation of administrative data covering the universe of startups in the United States. Our analysis of this new Comprehensive Startup Panel data set produces findings on entrepreneurship and job creation that have important implications for policy, economic welfare, and our understanding of entrepreneurship. Entrepreneurs make major contributions to total job creation in the United States. We find that on average, each annual cohort of startups creates a total of 3.0 million jobs in the first year after startup and employs a total of 2.6 million workers five years later. These high levels of job creation are likely even higher in the later follow-up years due to our strict definition of startup exits. Without the job creation contributions of startups through their first several years of existence, job creation by all businesses would be negative in most years in the United States. Without these jobs created by startups, net job creation would be negative and total nearly two million job losses per year.

The findings build on several influential studies on job creation among small businesses. These studies focus on identifying the share of jobs created by small or young businesses relative to large or older businesses. Starting with the seminal study by Birch (1979) showing that small businesses are the principal driver of job creation in the US economy, there has been considerable interest in job creation among entrepreneurs. Recent evidence indicates that young and high-impact businesses (defined as having high rates of growth in sales and employment) disproportionately contribute jobs in the economy (Haltiwanger, Jarmin, and Miranda 2013; Kulick et al. 2016; Tracy 2011). Additionally, young businesses are important to the speed of recovery after a recession (Pugsley and Sahin 2019). A few recent studies also examine the relationship between and growth patterns of nonemployer and employer businesses. These studies find, for example, that nonemployers have startup rates that are nearly three times the startup rates of employer firms; a significant number of new employer firms start as nonemployer firms; and, if nonemployer startups hire, the bulk of hiring occurs in the first few years of existence (Acs, Headd, and Agwara 2009; Davis et al. 2007; Fairlie and Miranda 2017).[10] The previous literature, however, does not focus on the full universe of startups and the entire history of a firm's employer status to measure entrepreneurial job creation and survival.

Our findings also contribute more generally to the rapidly growing literature on entrepreneurship and complement two key contributions to the field (Brown, Hamilton, and Medoff 1990; Davis, Haltiwanger, and Schuh 1998). This emerging field has struggled with finding adequate data and agreement on definitions of entrepreneurship. We create a new compilation of administrative data that captures the universe of business startups in the United States. The new Comprehensive Startup Panel data set allows exploration of many questions around entrepreneurial job creation, survival, and growth, and affords substantial flexibility in how one defines entrepreneurship. Additionally, the massive number of observations—an average of 4.1 million startups *each* year—allows unprecedented detail in analyzing different types of entrepreneurs (as we do in subsequent chapters). The administrative panel data also eliminate concerns over survivor, recall, and attrition biases. The new compilation of administrative data on the universe of startups created, described, and examined here may be useful for future research.

4 Startup Survival

One of the most important concerns for every entrepreneur is whether the startup can survive. The answer to this question is a complicated one. It often depends on avoiding unforeseen events such as recessions, a new competitor, changes in consumer preferences, natural disasters, loss of a key employee, or an increase in rent or another important input. No one can predict the future with certainty. Many business ventures would not have started had the owner have been able to predict these changes. On the other hand, unforeseen events can work in the other direction, resulting in better conditions for success. The bottom line is that millions of entrepreneurs take a leap of faith each year in starting their businesses without knowledge of what is going to happen.

There is certainly a perception that many or even most new businesses will fail. Even with this perception, however, entrepreneurs continue to start businesses. Overconfidence among entrepreneurs is even seen as a positive characteristic and not a negative one. It is part of American folklore—the entrepreneur taking incredible risks to create something new and innovative, with the risks being worth the potential reward of success. The history of the United States is full of examples of these entrepreneurs—Thomas Edison, Henry Ford, Google cofounders Larry Page and Sergey Brin—and their successes, with little regard for all the entrepreneurs who failed in their attempt at business success.

In this chapter, we use the new Comprehensive Startup Panel data set to answer a fundamental question about entrepreneurship and survival. We provide one of the first answers to the question of how many entrepreneurial firms survive each year after startup. The question is of obvious importance not only for entrepreneurs contemplating starting a business but also for policymakers who devise programs to assist entrepreneurs.

A better understanding of survival rates among startups is valuable for conducting benefit-cost estimates of various business development programs.

The federal government releases an often cited and influential statistic on startup survival rates—50 percent of startups survive after five years (US SBA 2017). The statistic is cited widely, even showing up in TV commercials and on web pages devoted to helping entrepreneurs. But the underlying data used to create this number include only new *employer* businesses or establishments and do not include nonemployer startups, nor do they look backward in time for a startup's previous existence as a nonemployer startup. This is important because estimates of survival rates among *employer* startups will greatly overestimate survival rates among *all* startups. After all, as we have shown in previous chapters, nonemployer firms constitute the majority of both startups and total firms in the United States.

Another challenge with this approach was also discussed in chapter 2. Employer firms will be misclassified as new businesses if they actually started several years earlier with no employees. For example, a high-tech firm that starts without employees and takes a couple of years to hire its first employee will not be classified as a startup until that first employee is hired. Thus the classification potentially provides a misleading measure of the year of startup. Additionally, all the startups without employees that do not survive until they hire an employee disappear from measurements of survival, resulting in an overestimate of survival rates. The inclusion of nonemployer startups is important for measuring survival rates over time because many nonemployer firms exit before ever hiring an employee. In general, ignoring the nonemployer history of firms is likely to miss important early entrepreneurial dynamics related to survival.

We first examine survival rates by startups. We explore the data for the universe of startups in terms of the total number surviving each year after startup and then focus on the percentage surviving each year. We also examine survival numbers and rates by major industry groups, separating construction firms from retail businesses, for example. We also estimate regressions to control for potentially confounding factors such as geographic area, year-of-startup economic conditions, and business policies.

A Large Number of Startups Exit Quickly

Using the universe of startups, we explore the third fundamental question: How many entrepreneurial firms survive each year after inception?

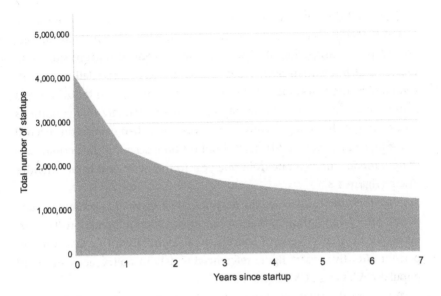

Figure 4.1
Number of survivors per startup cohort. *Source*: Authors' calculations from the newly compiled Comprehensive Startup Panel data set (1995–2018).

Figure 4.1 shows the total number of startups (both employer and non-employer) in the United States surviving over the seven-year follow-up period from the representative startup cohort. In all our analyses of survival rates, we do not distinguish between business closures and failures. We return to this question below but for now focus on all exits. Because of data limitations, and to follow federal government convention, we focus on survival of the original business entity. We define a surviving firm as one that is present in either the employer or nonemployer universe (i.e., it reported positive payroll or revenue in tax filing) in a given year.[1] Of the 4.1 million startups, a large number disappear in each follow-up year. After one year, only 2.4 million of the 4.1 million survive. As noted in previous chapters, the startup year (year 0) is the first calendar year in which the business has revenues or payroll. The following year (year 1) captures the first complete calendar year of information for these businesses and their survival in the data. After two years, only 1.9 million startups survive. But after this initial shakeout, the increase in exits starts to slow down. After five years 1.4 million startups remain in operation and after seven years 1.2 million startups remain in operation out of the initial average cohort size of 4.1 million startups.

Figure 4.2 displays survival rates in percentages of the average startup cohort to facilitate comparisons with widely circulated survival rates among new employer firms. Slightly fewer than 60 percent of startups survive to year 1, and fewer than 50 percent survive to year 2. We define the survival rate as the percentage of startups surviving to a given follow-up year instead of using an annual contemporaneous survival rate that conditions on existing in that year for consistency with published sources on survival of startups (e.g., US SBA 2017). We hold off on discussing the annual contemporaneous survival rate from one year to the next until later, when we discuss figure 4.3.

After the initial shakeout, the decline in the survival rate starts to slow down. After five years, 33 percent of startups remain in operation. The survival rate for the universe of startups is substantially lower than the "50 percent after five years" figure referenced widely in policy, academic, and popular circles (e.g., US SBA 2017).

We report the total number of surviving startups and the survival rate for the average startup cohort in table 4.1. The numbers in table format

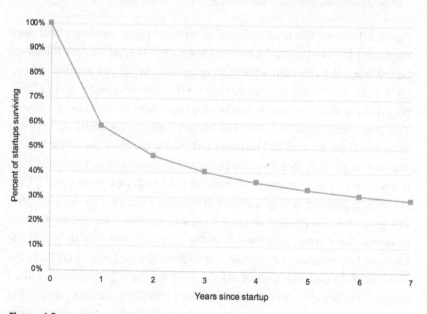

Figure 4.2
Survival rates among startups. *Source*: Authors' calculations from the newly compiled Comprehensive Startup Panel data set (1995–2018).

Table 4.1
Survival among startups

Years since startup	Startups (year 0)	Surviving startups	Survival rate
0	4,093,559	4,093,559	1.00
1	4,093,559	2,403,988	0.59
2	4,093,559	1,908,629	0.47
3	4,093,559	1,652,579	0.40
4	4,093,559	1,481,268	0.36
5	4,093,559	1,361,906	0.33
6	4,093,559	1,267,456	0.31
7	4,093,559	1,193,518	0.29

Source: Authors' calculations from the newly compiled Comprehensive Startup Panel data set (1995–2018). The startup year (year 0) is the first calendar year in which the business has revenues or payroll. The following year (year 1) captures the first complete calendar year of information on number of employees and survival in the data. Startup cohorts include 1995 to 2011, and follow-up years include 1996 to 2018.

complement the information graphed in figures 4.1 and 4.2. The 4.1 million startups in the US economy drop to 2.4 million in the first follow-up year (i.e., a 59 percent survival rate). By the fifth follow-up year the number of survivors drops to 1.4 million, representing 33 percent of the cohort. Survival drops rapidly among the startup cohort and is much lower than estimates based on new employer businesses, which we discuss in more detail in following chapters. In this chapter, we focus on survival among the universe of startups.

Another way to view survival is the annual or contemporaneous probability of surviving to the next year. This is different from the survival rate from startup to the specified follow-up year. Figure 4.3 shows the annual survival rate for each follow-up year to the next.[2] For example, the figure shows that the rate of surviving to year 2 among all startups that survived to year 1 is 88 percent. Overall, the results show that once firms get past the initial years, the probability of survival in each proceeding year increases, similar in some ways to the life expectancy of most animals in the wild. Like animals, the first year of life for a business is often the most difficult and dangerous. But as the business navigates early perils and finds its footing, its chances of survival increase and level off pretty quickly.

The sheer number of exits among business entities in the United States each year is striking. When viewed through this lens, starting a business

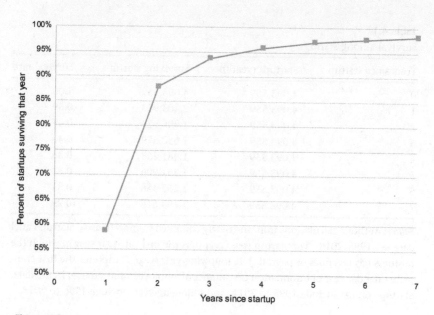

Figure 4.3
Annual survival probability among startups. *Source*: Authors' calculations from the newly compiled Comprehensive Startup Panel data set (1995–2018).

is risky. It creates disruptions in the economy, but this is not necessarily a negative but rather the result of experimentation and may even be referred to as "creative destruction," as popularized by Joseph Schumpeter, who believed that entrepreneurial innovation was a necessary destructive force to stimulate economic growth (Schumpeter 1934). It is beyond the scope of this analysis to evaluate the trade-offs between economies in which there are high entry and exit rates of businesses compared with ones in which there are fewer startups and more established, older firms. Suffice it to say that high business- and job-turnover rates are a common feature of modern market economies.

Survival Rates by Major Industry Groups

Although overall exit rates are high among the universe of startups, perhaps there are sectors of the economy in which startups tend to fare better. High overall rates of exit might reflect an averaging of very high exit rates among a few risky sectors, with relatively low exit rates among other sectors that are less risky. For example, construction firms and restaurants might be viewed as being riskier, with a higher propensity to exit, whereas professional service or manufacturing firms might be viewed as less risky. Alternatively, some sectors might naturally experience more (less) turnover because of ease (difficulty) of entering and exiting. To investigate this question, we explore survival rates by major industry groups.

The results suggest that all industry groups have fairly high exit rates. We focus on one-year survival rates first and then move to the five-year window. Figure 4.4 displays one-year survival rates by major industry group. The one-year survival rate captures the percentage of startups that survive from the startup year (year 0) to the first follow-up year (year 1). Even though we examine only a one-year period, survival rates across each sector are consistently low. Among some notable sectors, such as Construction, only 57 percent survive after one year. Part of the high initial exit rate for this group might be related to experimentation, but part of it may be due to a realization that the business will not succeed. Storefront industries such as retail businesses and restaurants also have low survival

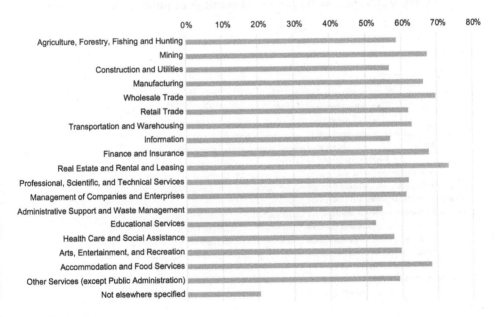

Figure 4.4
One-year survival rates of startups by major industry group. *Source*: Authors' calculations from the newly compiled Comprehensive Startup Panel data set (1995–2018).

rates in the initial year. The broader industries capturing these types of businesses have survival rates of 62–68 percent. Real Estate and Rental and Leasing has the highest one-year survival rate among broad categories at 73 percent.

Moving forward to five years after startup, we might expect more variation in the survival rates across sectors since some of the first-year factors that seem to have an impact on survival in year 1 may no longer apply. However, we find that every industry group experiences a large drop in survival rates. No type of business activity is immune to exiting. Figure 4.5 displays five-year survival rates by major industry group. In notable sectors such as Construction, only 32 percent of startups survive to the five-year mark. Startups in Retail Trade have only a 31 percent survival rate, and startups in Accommodation and Food Services have only a 35 percent survival rate over five years. The highest survival rate of any major industry group is Real Estate and Rental and Leasing, but even for this group of startups only 51 percent survive five years later.

Expanding to all years after startup, the patterns are relatively smooth for every sector (i.e., we do not see discontinuous jumps in survival rates

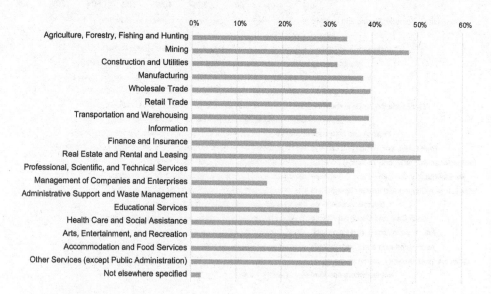

Figure 4.5
Five-year survival rates of startups by major industry group. *Source*: Authors' calculations from the newly compiled Comprehensive Startup Panel data set (1995–2018).

over each follow-up year). Table 4.2 reports survival rates by year following startup for all major industries. All industry groups experience high exit rates in the first year, fifth year, and every year between or after. The patterns generally follow those displayed for all startups.

Regression Analysis for Survival among Startups

Similar to the analysis for job creation rates by follow-up year and sector, we are concerned about confounding factors for survival rates. To address these concerns, we estimate regression models controlling for potentially confounding factors such as year of startup. To investigate this question we estimate equation (3.1), where Y_{it} is now survival of firm i in year t (equal to 0 or 1). Equation (3.1) is reported in chapter 3. Note that survival $Y_{it} = 1$ in the startup year for all businesses, and thus all follow-up years are compared to this initial year. Standard errors are clustered at the firm level to account for multiple observations per startup. Regressions are estimated with a linear probability model.

To estimate equation (3.1) we include the full sample of firm–year observations even after exits. In the case of exits, we set survival equal to zero and include observations for all subsequent years for that firm. Alternatively, we could estimate a hazard model for the length of the survival spell, but the typical advantages of hazard models, such as addressing left and right censoring of spells and having multiple spells, do not apply here. To simplify estimation with the restricted and confidential data with a large sample, we estimate the regressions with a linear probability model (ordinary least squares) using all possible observations over the eight-year window for each startup. Similar to the employment regressions, the administrative data on startups rule out the concern that sample attrition is masking exits, and statistical significance benefits from the massive sample sizes of 557 million observations.

Table 4.3 reports estimates of the regression represented by equation (3.1). The sample size for this regression is roughly 550 million observations and the level of analysis is firm–year. Even clustering at the business level, the standard errors on all reported coefficient estimates are extremely small and all coefficients are statistically significant at the 0.01 level (and even at the 0.001 level).

After controlling for startup years and sectors, we find that survival rates decrease sharply in the first couple of years and then taper off. The

Table 4.2
Startup survival rates by major industry group

Major industry group	Number of startups	Survival rate, year 1	Survival rate, year 2	Survival rate, year 3	Survival rate, year 4	Survival rate, year 5	Survival rate, year 6	Survival rate, year 7
Agriculture, Forestry, Fishing and Hunting	51,265	0.59	0.48	0.42	0.38	0.34	0.32	0.29
Mining	10,088	0.67	0.60	0.58	0.52	0.48	0.45	0.42
Construction; Utilities	449,941	0.57	0.45	0.39	0.35	0.32	0.30	0.28
Manufacturing	70,412	0.66	0.54	0.47	0.42	0.38	0.35	0.32
Wholesale Trade	87,706	0.70	0.57	0.50	0.44	0.40	0.36	0.33
Retail Trade	426,294	0.62	0.48	0.40	0.35	0.31	0.28	0.26
Transportation and Warehousing	162,824	0.63	0.51	0.45	0.42	0.39	0.38	0.37
Information	75,353	0.57	0.42	0.35	0.30	0.28	0.25	0.23
Finance and Insurance	126,706	0.68	0.56	0.50	0.44	0.40	0.37	0.35
Real Estate and Rental and Leasing	267,471	0.73	0.64	0.59	0.54	0.51	0.48	0.46
Professional, Scientific, and Technical Services	515,706	0.62	0.49	0.44	0.39	0.36	0.34	0.32
Management of Companies and Enterprises	11,559	0.61	0.39	0.22	0.19	0.17	0.14	0.13
Administrative and Support and Waste Management and Remediation Services	359,118	0.55	0.42	0.35	0.32	0.29	0.27	0.26

Educational Services	107,471	0.53	0.40	0.33	0.30	0.28	0.27	0.26
Health Care and Social Assistance	375,588	0.58	0.45	0.38	0.34	0.31	0.29	0.27
Arts, Entertainment, and Recreation	165,412	0.60	0.49	0.44	0.40	0.37	0.35	0.33
Accommodation and Food Services	120,059	0.68	0.54	0.45	0.40	0.35	0.32	0.29
Other Services (except Public Administration)	504,882	0.59	0.48	0.43	0.39	0.36	0.34	0.31
Not elsewhere specified	205,706	0.20	0.07	0.04	0.03	0.02	0.02	0.02

Source: Authors' calculations from the newly compiled Comprehensive Startup Panel data set (1995–2018). The startup year (year 0) is the first calendar year in which the business has revenues or payroll. The following year (year 1) captures the first complete calendar year of information on number of employees and survival in the data. Startup cohorts include 1995 to 2011, and follow-up years include 1996 to 2018.

Table 4.3
Regressions for the probability of survival using all startup years

	Survival coefficient
Startup year	(Excluded category)
1 year since startup	−0.417***
2 years since startup	−0.540***
3 years since startup	−0.603***
4 years since startup	−0.645***
5 years since startup	−0.675***
6 years since startup	−0.698***
7 years since startup	−0.717***
11-Agriculture, Forestry, Fishing and Hunting	−0.012***
21-Mining	0.070***
22–23-Construction; Utilities	−0.020***
31–33-Manufacturing	0.027***
42-Wholesale Trade	0.041***
44–45-Retail Trade	−0.023***
48–49-Transportation and Warehousing	0.017***
51-Information	−0.041***
52-Finance and Insurance	0.044***
53-Real Estate and Rental and Leasing	0.124***
54-Professional, Scientific, and Technical Services	0.007***
55-Management of Companies and Enterprises	−0.030***
56-Administrative and Support and Waste Management and Remediation Services	−0.045***
61-Educational Services	−0.051***
62-Health Care and Social Assistance	−0.027***
71-Arts, Entertainment, and Recreation	0.012***
72-Accommodation and Food Services	0.027***
81-Other Services (except Public Administration)	(Excluded category)
Sample size	556,700,000

Notes: Each observation is a firm-year and all possible follow-up years are included. The dependent variable equals one if the startup survived to that year. Standard errors are clustered at the firm level and are not reported because they are small and do not show at the three decimal level. * $p<0.10$, ** $p<0.05$, *** $p<0.01$.

Source: Sample includes the universe of startups from the newly compiled Comprehensive Startup Panel data set (1995–2018). Startup cohorts include 1995 to 2011, and follow-up years include 1996 to 2018.

survival rate is 0.42 (or 42 percentage points) lower in the first follow-up year after startup. Two years after startup, survival rates have dropped by 54 percentage points. After five years post startup, the survival rate drops 72 percentage points relative to startup levels. Controlling for startup-year and sectoral differences does not change the finding of a strong downward trend in survival rates over years since startup.

In contrast to job creation rates by sector, survival rates do not differ substantially by industry group. Other Services is the omitted category and has a survival rate of 59 percent in year 1 and 36 percent in year 5. Regression-adjusted survival rates by sector mostly differ by three percentage points or less in either direction from this omitted category. Only a few sectors differ notably from this level. The main exceptions are that the survival rate is twelve percentage points higher for Real Estate and five percentage points lower for Educational Services. But overall, the differences are not large, and survival probabilities are largely independent of industry.

Survival versus Success

Business exits are a common feature of business life. Businesses operate in an uncertain and very dynamic environment, and whether they succeed or not is a matter of the owners' foresight, their ability to innovate and respond to new challenges, and a good amount of luck. As we have seen, however, most exits tend to happen shortly after a business is started, but this is not always the case. Many exits are associated with small businesses, and many of these are old. Large and medium-size firms are often well established or have assets that make them valuable targets of acquisition by other firms. They might choose to merge with another firm instead for strategic reasons. Complete shutdowns of large firms are unlikely, with reorganizations, divestitures, or spinoffs being much more likely.

When thinking about small-business exits, however, we typically think of exits that are associated with a business having insufficient revenues to cover costs, and thus going out of business. Additionally, exits are often a consequence of an entrepreneurial decision. Ultimately, entrepreneurs can close businesses for many different reasons. For example, the business might no longer be profitable (maybe it never reached profitability), and the owners want to cut their losses, or maybe they want to pursue other activities (e.g., as salaried employees, or to try their luck at a different venture), or maybe there are no survivors that want to or can take over the business once a key founder/owner has decided to retire or perhaps is deceased.

The administrative data used in this chapter do not include direct measures describing the reasons for the exit.[3] Additional data sources could be brought to bear and linked to these data to shed light on the nature of these exits, but these questions lie well beyond the scope of this book. Mergers and acquisitions, the acquisition or divestiture of business establishments, present challenging issues when it comes to tracking businesses and accounting for firm exit. Should we define exits based on ownership changes? After all, the original management team is likely not in place anymore. Or should we consider an exit to have happened only when the establishment ceases to exist? The answer once again is likely to depend on your research question and data availability. Understanding business exit remains an important area in need of further research in the field.

Conclusions

The analysis of our new Comprehensive Startup Panel that includes the universe of US startups provides several findings that shed light on fundamental, and surprisingly unanswered, questions regarding survival among startups. We find that survival rates are extremely low among the universe of startups, with a large shakeout occurring in the years immediately after startup. After one year only 59 percent of startups survive, and after two years only 47 percent survive. The decline in survival rates starts to taper off somewhat, and after five years the survival rate is 33 percent. Surprisingly, survival rates are largely consistent across industry groups, in this differing from job creation, which varies substantially across sectors. All industrial sectors have high exit rates, and popular businesses such as those in the Accommodation and Food Services industry, which includes restaurants and hotels, have survival rates of only 35 percent five years after startup.

The findings build on the previous literature that examines entrepreneurial survival rates (e.g., Audretsch 1991; Audretsch and Mahmood 1995; Phillips and Kirchhoff 1989; Robb and Farhat 2013; US BLS 2017; US SBA 2017). Recent estimates from the BLS (2017) indicate that 48 percent of new employer establishments survive after five years. None of these previous studies, however, used the full universe of startups and the entire history of employer status to measure entrepreneurial survival. Using this full history and universe of startups clearly changes the conclusions regarding survival. Survival rates are low among all startups in the economy. In chapter 6, we refine the analysis to include only more growth-oriented startups, but we continue to find low survival rates (although not as low as shown here).

The findings also have implications for job creation. In a broader sense, job creation is higher because entrepreneurs create jobs for themselves and those jobs are not counted as employee jobs in the data. Although the "entrepreneurs create jobs for themselves" argument is often made in the policy arena, the results presented here indicate that business ownership jobs do not last very long. We find extremely high exit rates among startups. A survival rate of only 33 percent (i.e., one out of three) after five years is not optimistic for the "creating a job for the owner" argument. On the other hand, gaining entrepreneurial experience, even if for a short period of time, can open up new job opportunities that would otherwise be unrealized. Regardless, these types of considerations should enter the economic welfare calculus for entrepreneurship policies.

5   The Dynamics of Job Creation and Survival among Startups

The previous two chapters painted separate pictures of job creation and survival among startups. In this chapter we start to peek under the hood by combining the two. Of particular interest is the dynamic pattern of job creation and survival. Startup activity is anything but predictable, and each startup follows a different path. Of most relevance here is that there is likely to be rich variation in job creation and survival patterns across startups. Some firms might grow quickly, with growth then flattening out over time, such as a restaurant with one location whose owner has no ambition to expand. On the other hand, we are all aware of very successful local restaurants that expand and open additional locations before becoming very successful local, national, or even international chains. And we have seen what we think is surely the beginning of a great new restaurant, only to find it closed a year later. In other cases, rapid expansion is the primary cause for the downfall of a restaurant. And these are just a few of the possible patterns of growth and survival among new restaurants.

In this chapter we explore some new questions related to the underlying dynamics of job creation and survival among startups. First, we explore the question of why the average number of jobs per startup cohort remains relatively constant over the years after startup. Referring back to table 3.1, we find that the average number of employees per startup is 0.74 in the first year after startup and 0.57 in the seventh year after startup. Despite the relatively flat levels, patterns in the average number of jobs created per startup potentially conceal a substantial amount of heterogeneity in the underlying dynamics of job creation by startups. In particular, the stable pattern might hide complex underlying dynamics, each of which describes very different outcomes. For example, the uniform levels could potentially be explained by a large percentage of startups surviving, with most of these startups growing slowly but steadily over time. The result would be a relatively consistent pattern in the average number of jobs created per startup over the first several years after startup. Alternatively, the uniform levels could be explained by a small percentage of startups surviving, with a small percentage of survivors growing very rapidly. This underlying pattern would also lead to a relatively flat growth pattern in jobs per startup cohort overall. A third explanation has either a large percentage of startups surviving and a small percentage of the survivors growing rapidly or a small percentage of startups surviving and a large percent of survivors growing steadily. All these are potential candidates that warrant closer inspection.

We also examine different key transitions in the employment process. Hiring employees represents one of the major thresholds that entrepreneurs encounter when growing their businesses. The step from nonemployer to employer entails additional registration and legal requirements; managing health insurance, workers' compensation, and unemployment insurance issues; and taking on the burden of making payroll. Filing for an employer identification number (Form SS-4), preparing federal wage and tax statements (Form W-2), verifying employee eligibility (Form I-9), and navigating state new hire reporting programs, workers' compensation insurance programs, unemployment insurance tax registration programs, and disability insurance in some states may be especially daunting to small business owners considering hiring their first employee. But perhaps the most important consideration for the owner is whether current and future revenues are large enough to cover the extra expenses of having employees. Because of the importance of this transition from having no employees to hiring employees, we carefully examine the timing of when nonemployer startups take the leap to employer status.

Three questions of interest pertaining to the decision by entrepreneurs to hire their first employee are examined here. First, what are the dynamic patterns of hiring employees among startups in their first few years of existence? Second, which entrepreneurs take the leap? In other words, what are the demographic and human capital characteristics of entrepreneurs that are associated with making the decision to hire the first employee in the first several years of operation? For instance, are female, minority, or immigrant owners less likely to cross the employer threshold? Or are more educated entrepreneurs more likely to hire their first employee in the first years of existence? Finally, what dynamic business conditions are associated with the hiring of the first employee? Is there a sales or business asset milestone that firms often reach before hiring their first employee? Do nonemployer firms typically have intellectual property, such as patents, copyrights, and trademarks, before hiring their first employee?

We explore these questions here by examining the underlying dynamics of startup job creation and survival. Answers to these questions shed new light on movements between nonemployer and employer states and on firm survival.

Why Does the Number of Jobs per Startup Remain Constant?

We first explore the question of why the average number of jobs per startup cohort shows only a slight decline, remaining relatively constant throughout the years after startup. Patterns in the average number of jobs created conceal a substantial amount of heterogeneity in the underlying dynamics of job creation by startups, which might hold the answer. We explore four potential explanations for the relatively flat pattern: (1) a large percentage of startups survive and these startups grow slowly, (2) a large percentage of startups survive and a small percentage of the survivors grow rapidly, (3) a small percentage of startups survive and a large percentage of survivors grow steadily, and (4) a small percentage of startups survive and a small percentage of survivors grow very rapidly.

Because such a large percentage of startups exit in the first few years of operation, we can likely rule out the first two explanations owing to the relatively flat level of job creation over time. To examine this directly, however, figure 5.1 displays job creation per *surviving* startup and job creation per *all* startups over time. Job creation levels per *surviving* startup grow rapidly over time. In the first year after startup, the average surviving startup employs 1.27 workers (excluding the owner).[1] Five years after startup, the average surviving startup hires an average of 1.90 employees. Seven years later, surviving startups hire an average of 1.96 employees each, representing a substantial growth rate over time. This is a stark contrast to the relatively flat rate described earlier for all startups (also shown in figure 5.1). These results are consistent with the strong "up or out" pattern of startup dynamics first noted among employer startups in Haltiwanger, Jarmin, and Miranda (2013), in which startups that survive are likely to grow significantly in size.

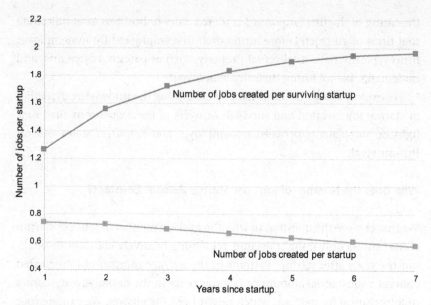

Figure 5.1
Number of jobs created per startup and surviving startup. *Source*: Authors' calculations from the newly compiled Comprehensive Startup Panel data set (1995–2018).

The large number of exits from the initial cohort of startup firms hides the large growth rates among the surviving firms. These firm exits explain the anemic overall contribution to jobs as the cohort ages. From the startup year to five years later the number of jobs per initial startup remains below 0.8 workers.

Regression Analysis of Job Creation Conditioning on Survival

Given the strong pattern of employment growth among surviving startups, we examine the determinants of job creation conditional on survival. Are the characteristics associated with job creation per startup different when focusing on only *surviving* startups? To investigate this question we estimate the regression represented by equation (3.1) in chapter 3 but only include surviving startups in the estimation sample. We condition on survival in that year, thereby dropping all firms that have exited by then. For example, for a startup that exits in year 5, we would only include follow-up years 1–4 for that business in the estimation sample. For a startup that survives throughout the analysis window of seven follow-up years, we include all of those years in the estimation sample. We are thus estimating a model that measures net job creation per *surviving* startup similar to the top line displayed in figure 5.1.[2]

Table 5.1 reports estimates for the conditional model. The same sets of variables and controls are included in the regression, and the same left-out categories are used (year 1 and the Other Services industry). Because we condition on surviving startups up to that year in the data, the sample size is now smaller, and the sample mean of the dependent variable is larger Regression estimates from the survivor sample of startups indicate a different time series pattern for job creation than for the unconditional model that includes all observations. Conditioning on survival, the number of jobs per startup increases steadily from the first full year of the business. Two years after startup, average employment increases by 0.30 compared to the first year after startup. Five years after startup, average employment increases by 0.69, and seven years after startup employment increases by 0.77. This is due to the removal of startups that exited by the time of that follow-up year and thus are not included in the sample (or denominator) anymore. This also is the rate after we control for other potentially confounding factors, such as cohort year and sector.

The patterns across major industry groups generally follow the same patterns as the unconditional sample estimates. We continue to find that the sectors with the highest levels of conditional job creation are Accommodation and Food Services (+6.33), Manufacturing (+5.74), and Management of Companies and Enterprises (+4.69). This should be interpreted as an overall level shift of the growth pattern summarized in the regression. Sectors with the lowest levels of job creation conditional on survival in addition to Other Services, which is the third-lowest level, are Agriculture and Real Estate. These sectors have growth rates that are on average 0.04 and 0.27 jobs per startup below the level of Other Services.

Most of the coefficients are much larger in absolute magnitude than the coefficients from the unconditional model based on the full sample. The finding that the sector coefficients from the conditional and unconditional samples line up reasonably well suggests that differences in survivor rates are not driving the overall differences by major industry group. This is consistent with the finding from table 3.2 that survival rates do not differ substantially across industry groups. The unconditional model includes

Table 5.1
Regression for number of employees using only surviving startup years

	Employment coefficient
1 year since startup	(Excluded category)
2 years since startup	0.302***
	(0.002)
3 years since startup	0.488***
	(0.003)
4 years since startup	0.609***
	(0.003)
5 years since startup	0.689***
	(0.004)
6 years since startup	0.745***
	(0.004)
7 years since startup	0.771***
	(0.004)
11-Agriculture, Forestry, Fishing and Hunting	−0.037***
	(0.008)
21-Mining	1.829***
	(0.096)
22–23-Construction; Utilities	0.516***
	(0.004)
31–33-Manufacturing	5.742***
	(0.056)
42-Wholesale Trade	1.789***
	(0.014)
44–45-Retail Trade	0.681***
	(0.004)
48–49-Transportation and Warehousing	0.246***
	(0.008)
51-Information	1.352***
	(0.033)
52-Finance and Insurance	0.581***
	(0.011)
53-Real Estate and Rental and Leasing	−0.270***
	(0.003)
54-Professional, Scientific, and Technical Services	0.297***
	(0.003)
55-Management of Companies and Enterprises	4.689***
	(0.230)
56-Administrative and Support and Waste Management and Remediation Services	1.237***
	(0.015)
61-Educational Services	0.759***
	(0.024)
62-Health Care and Social Assistance	1.485***
	(0.010)

Table 5.1
(continued)

	Employment coefficient
71-Arts, Entertainment, and Recreation	0.108***
	(0.007)
72-Accommodation and Food Services	6.327***
	(0.022)
81-Other Services (except Public Administration)	(Excluded category)
Sample size	261,200,000

Notes: Each observation is a firm-year and all surviving follow-up years are included. The dependent variable is the number of employees in that year for the startup, and is removed from the sample if the startup does not exist in that year. Standard errors are reported in parentheses below coefficient estimates and are clustered at the firm level. * $p<0.10$, ** $p<0.05$, *** $p<0.01$.

Source: Sample includes the universe of startups from the newly compiled Comprehensive Startup Panel data set (1995–2018). Startup cohorts include 1995 to 2011, and follow-up years include 1996 to 2018.

a value of zero employees after a startup exits. Since exit rates are similar across sectors, including them will simply result in a uniform shift downward in absolute magnitude in coefficients.

The regression results confirm what we report in figure 5.1: average job creation per startup grows very quickly among surviving startups and continues to increase over time. Controlling for macroeconomic conditions and sectors through the regressions does not change this conclusion. To put it simply, surviving startups tend to grow fast on average.

Movement between No Employment, Employment, and Exit

Another important type of underlying heterogeneity in the dynamics of startups is the movement between not having employees, having employees, and exiting. Only a small share of all startups hire employees in the initial year, but many nonemployer startups later transition to hiring employees over time. The startup panel provides a rare look at these patterns. Because of the previous focus of research and of federal government statistics on only new employer businesses, these movements have not been previously examined in detail.

Figure 5.2 displays the evolution of startups over time across the trichotomy of (1) not hiring employees, (2) hiring any employees, and (3) exit. The percentages of the startup cohort that hire employees, do not hire any employees, and exit in the startup year and over the seven follow-up years are reported. Transitions from nonemployer to employer status and vice versa are possible in this chart. Eleven percent of the startup cohort hire employees in the initial year, with the rate declining steadily over time. By the seventh follow-up year, 7 percent of the startup cohort hires employees. In contrast, 89 percent of the startup cohort have no employees in the initial year, and by the seventh follow-up year 22 percent have no employees. The declines in the percentages of startups hiring employees and not hiring employees are primarily driven by the large percentage of startups that exit early on. By the seventh follow-up year, 71 percent of the startup cohort have exited.

The up-or-out dynamics that were observed by Haltiwanger et al. (2009) are evident here for the Comprehensive Startup Panel cohort. The patterns, however, are much more intense once we consider nonemployers. Figure

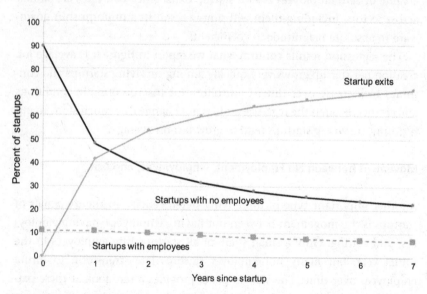

Figure 5.2
Share of startup cohort that is nonemployer, employer, or exit. *Source*: Authors' calculations from the newly compiled Comprehensive Startup Panel data set (1995–2018).

5.2 tells us that startups without employees exit at extremely high rates and overwhelm the exits from employer startups through their sheer magnitude. By year 7 exit rates are tapering off.

Focusing solely on surviving startups, we observe a continuous compositional shift away from businesses with no employees toward businesses with employees as a result of nonemployer exits over time. At startup, there are 8.25 nonemployer firms for every employer firm. In the first follow-up year, this drops to 4.4 nonemployer firms for every employer firm and then steadily decreases for each additional year since startup. After seven follow-up years, there are 3.3 nonemployer firms for every employer firm. Naturally, these startups with employees did not all start with employees. In fact, 29 percent of startups with any employees in our panel's eight-year time window and that also survived through year 7 started with no employees.

We return to this issue of how many surviving startups with employees had no employees at startup in the next chapter. The statistic clearly indicates that many startups start with no employees and that the transition from nonemployer to employer is an important part of the early-stage process of business growth. We would even expect many entrepreneurs to start their businesses first without employees to try out the idea and wait to see whether the business takes off before hiring employees. An entrepreneur starting a construction business, for example, might work on a few smaller projects alone at first to gauge demand and build some experience and reputation. We turn to focusing the analysis directly on the transition from nonemployer to employer among startups.[3]

The Leap of Hiring the First Employee

Perhaps the most important transition startups make is from having no employees to having employees (i.e., the nonemployer-to-employer transition). It is a big decision when the owner of a small shop, for example, hires his or her first employee. In this case, the owner of a startup has to make a commitment to payroll and figure out more complicated hiring issues. The legal issues and additional investment make the decision particularly difficult. We examine this transition carefully focusing on the timing of when nonemployer startups take the leap to employer status.

To provide a sense of the complication of this decision we turn to the SBA's web page titled "Business Guide—Hire and Manage Employees." The SBA lists ten important steps to hiring employees and setting up payroll.[4]

1. Get an Employer Identification Number (EIN).
2. Find out whether you need state or local tax IDs.
3. Decide if you want an independent contractor or an employee.
4. Ensure new employees return a completed W-4 form.
5. Schedule pay periods to coordinate tax withholding for the IRS.
6. Create a compensation plan for holiday, vacation, and leave.
7. Choose an in-house or external service for administering payroll.
8. Decide who will manage your payroll system.
9. Know which records must stay on file and for how long.
10. Report payroll taxes as needed on a quarterly and annual basis.

And these are just the logistical, legal, and tax issues involved in hiring employees by startups. This list does not factor in additional concerns, such as having enough business revenues to pay these employees, handling personnel issues, and being able to manage these employees in the business. Surely, the decision is a difficult one for most entrepreneurs.

We examine three main questions related to the decision by entrepreneurs to hire their first employee that have not been examined in detail in the previous literature. First, what are the dynamic patterns of hiring employees among startups in their first few years of existence? Second, what are the demographic and human capital characteristics of entrepreneurs that are associated with making the decision to hire their first employee in the first several years of operation? Are female, minority, or immigrant owners less likely to cross the employer threshold than their counterparts? Are more educated entrepreneurs more likely to hire their first employee in the first years of existence, or do they wait? Finally, what dynamic business conditions are associated with hiring the first employee? Is there a sales or business asset milestone that firms often reach before hiring their first employee? Do nonemployer firms typically have intellectual property, such as patents, copyrights, and trademarks, before hiring their first employee?

In this chapter, we use data from two sources: (1) our Comprehensive Startup Panel, which provides longitudinal data on the universe of nonemployers matched to employers over time, and (2) the Kauffman Firm Survey (KFS), which provides panel data on detailed owner and business characteristics and follows a sample of roughly five thousand growth-oriented startups over the first several years of existence. The KFS sample is drawn from a random sample of the Dun & Bradstreet business directory list of new businesses (which can be thought of as a subset of the universe of businesses). The KFS asks the startups in its panel detailed survey questions each year.[5] Using these data, this chapter provides a detailed longitudinal study of the determinants of nonemployers hiring their first employee.

We examine the dynamic patterns of hiring employees among startups. We start by examining patterns of hiring among nonemployer startups in the universe of nonemployers provided in the startup panel. Table 5.2 reports the distribution of all nonemployer startups (averaged across cohorts) and the hiring of their first employee across the seven follow-up years. Other outcomes are the startups not hiring their first employee by the end of the seven-year period or exiting before hiring an employee during the seven-year period.

Table 5.2
Distribution across follow-up years in which nonemployer startup hired its first employee

	Percent	Number
Hired first employee at:		
1 year after startup	1.6	57,118
2 years after startup	0.5	19,029
3 years after startup	0.3	11,618
4 years after startup	0.2	8,324
5 years after startup	0.2	6,500
6 years after startup	0.1	5,265
7 years after startup	0.1	4,412
Did not hire employee by end of study period	24.2	884,724
Exited before hiring employee by end of study period	72.7	2,657,541
Total number of nonemployer startups		3,654,529

Source: Authors' calculations from the newly compiled Comprehensive Startup Panel data set (1995–2018). The startup year (year 0) is the first calendar year in which the business has revenues or payroll. The following year (year 1) captures the first complete calendar year of information on number of employees and survival in the data. Startup cohorts include 1995 to 2011, and follow-up years include 1996 to 2018.

This distribution tells us a few different things. First, it provides detail on when nonemployer startups hire their first employee. For example, it answers the question of what percentage of businesses hire their first employee in the first year after startup versus the second year after startup. Usually, this happens very early on in the life cycle of a startup.

We find that on average, there are 3.7 million nonemployer startups each year in the United States. Among all nonemployer startups, 1.6 percent hire their first employee in the first year after startup, with a much lower percentage of nonemployer startups hiring their first employee after that year. Only 0.5 percent hire an employee in the following year. In fact, if a nonemployer firm is going to hire an employee ever, it is more likely to do it in the first year than in all of the remaining years that we follow. A large percentage of nonemployer startups (24.2 percent) do not hire their first employee by the end of the seven-year follow-up period. Finally, 72.7 percent of nonemployer startups exited over the sample period before ever hiring their first employee.

It is important to note here that businesses may fail to report revenue for some years only to start reporting again. In this sense, exits are not necessarily a permanent status. When that is the case, we do not consider them exits in our calculations. For our purposes, we define a business to have exited only when there is no business activity at the end of our seven-year period (and thus is not in the business universe that year). We might expect some of these exits to reverse in later years. In this regard, the exit rates we report here may be overestimated. However, as we saw earlier, the vast majority of exits happen early and tend to be permanent in nature.

A very large percentage of these nonemployer businesses are consulting, contracting, or small-scale business activities, whereas others may be more oriented toward growth. In earlier work using only the 1997 startup cohort, we examined hiring and exit rates for different types of nonemployer startups based on their legal form and type of tax identifier (EIN versus SSN). We found that certain nonemployers have much higher rates of eventually offering employment, depending on their legal form (Fairlie and Miranda 2017). For example, we examined only EIN cases for nonemployer startups. These are businesses that are identified through filing for an EIN even though they do not have employees. We also examined incorporated nonemployer startups. In both cases, transition rates from nonemployer to employer were much higher, but as before, most of the transitions occurred in the first few years, and there continued to be a very high exit rate (or nonexistence rate in year 7). See Fairlie and Miranda (2014) for more discussion on these findings. In the next chapter we discuss a new but related method of refining the nonemployer startup group to calculate "upper bounds" on job creation levels and survival rates for the startup panel.

The hiring patterns we observe in the first several years after startup reveal interesting facts. Many nonemployer startups hire their first employee in the first three years of existence. After that initial period of time, and through seven years, only a few additional firms make the switch from nonemployer to employer status. In other words, the up-or-out dynamic is evident and strong. It is not entirely clear why this is so. Maybe the intention of the owner always was to keep the business as a nonemployer business; or maybe the owner(s) would like to expand their business to hiring an employee but are not able to do so because of costs, administrative issues, or other concerns. It might also be that the entrepreneurs were simply experimenting with the intention to quickly shut down the business if expectations were not met. What we can see in the data is that if a business does not hire an employee in the first few years, it is very unlikely to ever hire an employee.

Dynamic Business Milestones Associated with Hiring the First Employee

We now turn to exploring the dynamic business factors associated with hiring decisions. An important question is whether there are milestones that nonemployer startups often reach before hiring their first employee. For example, do nonemployer firms often wait until they have large enough annual revenues to take on the extra expenses of hiring employees? Do startups wait to build up assets or acquire intellectual property before hiring their first employee?

Answering these questions requires longitudinal data on startups with measures of both employment and milestone variables year by year instead of a single point in time. Although the startup panel has the ability to be linked to other data sets to answer some of these questions directly, we use the KFS panel data set to explore all of these questions. The KFS follows a sample cohort of startups in 2004 over several years and provides detailed information on owner and business characteristics (Ballou et al. 2008; Robb et al. 2010). In the KFS data, we are able to select only nonemployer startups in which the startup has not previously hired an employee for comparative purposes. It is, however, important to recognize that the KFS sample is drawn from Dun & Bradstreet data (which include businesses with a credit report) and as such it is skewed toward more growth- and employment-oriented startups even when focusing only on nonemployer startups. Fairlie and Miranda (2017) provide more details.

Table 5.3 reports an estimate of the annual probability of hiring the first employee among nonemployer firms by revenue class, business assets, and intellectual property ownership. Perhaps surprisingly, the likelihood of hiring the first employee is not strongly related to total business revenues, an early indication that maybe these businesses have a clear growth orientation from the beginning. That the probability of hiring an employee is higher for firms with $0 in annual revenue is indicative that for many of these firms, their nonemployer status is only an interim situation before they hire their first employee. The probability of hiring an employee decreases by 8.1 percentage points for nonemployer firms with annual revenues between $1 and $10,000. The likelihood of becoming an employer firm remains steady as revenues increase until the $100,001 or more level. For revenues of $100,001 or more, the probability of hiring the first employee in the next year increases by nine percentage points from nonemployers with revenues of $25,001–$100,000.[6] Even this change is not large if one considers the potential importance of higher revenues to offset the increased costs of hiring employees.

Table 5.3 also reports estimates by business asset levels. Assets include cash, accounts receivable, equipment, machinery, product inventory, and vehicles. Nonemployer startups may wait until their business assets hit a certain level to offer financing or collateral for raising money to hire employees. As with revenue levels, however, there is no clear evidence that the probability of a nonemployer firm hiring its first employee over the following year increases substantially with business asset levels. The probability that a nonemployer business with $0 in total business assets hires its first employee over the following year is 22.0 percent. For nonemployers with $100,001 or more in total business assets, the probability is not much higher. Nonemployers with $25,001–$100,000 in total business assets have a probability that is four percentage points higher.

Both business revenues and assets are tangible measures that provide a glimpse of the current resources of the firm, but future potential resources or intangible assets of the firm may be more important in making the decision to become an employer firm. In particular, a milestone for many

Table 5.3
Annual rates of hiring first employee among nonemployer startups, Kauffman Firm Survey

	Hire first employee	
Milestone	Percent	N
All nonemployer observations	23.4	6,092
Total revenues (annual)		
Zero	26.7	1,750
$1–$10,000	18.6	1,313
$10,000–$25,000	19.8	710
$25,000–$100,000	21.4	1,369
$100,000 or more	30.4	777
Total business assets		
Zero	22.0	667
$1–$10,000	19.7	2,130
$10,000–$25,000	24.6	1,013
$25,000–$100,000	28.2	1,342
$100,000 or more	24.2	920
Patents		
No	23.3	5,867
Yes	31.9	168
Copyrights		
No	23.2	5447
Yes	28.1	535
Trademarks		
No	22.4	5,382
Yes	35.6	586
Any intellectual property?		
No	22.4	4,951
Yes	31.2	940

Source: Authors' calculations from the Kauffman Firm Survey, covering 2004–2011. The sample includes annual observations for firms that had not yet hired their first employee from the KFS startup cohort.

nonemployer startups might be when they obtain intellectual property, such as a patent, trademark, or copyright. Patents, trademarks, and copyrights might be useful for nonemployer firms considering hiring employees because they provide a potential source of future revenues even if the firm is experiencing low current revenues. For nonemployer firms with patents, the probability of hiring the first employee increases by 8.6 percentage points. Obtaining copyrights and trademarks is also associated with an increase in the likelihood of becoming an employer firm: the increase is roughly five percentage points for copyrights and thirteen percentage points for trademarks. Combining all types of measurable intellectual property, the estimates indicate that having at least one type is associated with roughly a nine percentage point higher rate of hiring the first employee.

In a similar type of exercise that focuses on household innovations by linking US Patent and Trademark Office (USPTO) patent data to the full nonemployer database, we find a similar jump in the transition rates to employer status among nonemployer firms that owned at least one patent (Miranda and Zolas 2018).

To identify the independent associations between these milestones and the decision to hire the first employee, we estimate several regressions for the probability of hiring employees.

The observational unit in the regressions is the business year, and only startups that have not previously hired an employee up to that year are included in the sample. The regression analysis allows us to control for potentially correlated factors such as owner characteristics, industry, and regional controls. We do not report results here and instead refer the reader to Fairlie and Miranda (2017). After controlling for other factors, there does not appear to be a strong, clear relationship between revenues and the probability of hiring the first employee. Most of the coefficients on revenue levels are negative, indicating that nonemployer businesses with zero revenues have relatively high probabilities of hiring their first employee in the sample period (the left-out or comparison category is zero revenue). There is some evidence, however, that the largest revenue class has a higher probability of hiring the first employee than the previous revenue classes, indicating a somewhat U-shaped relationship. Again, this might have something to do with the original intent of the entrepreneur, which we do not directly observe in the data. A direct relationship between revenue and transitions rates is consistent with one of the author's findings in Davis et al. (2007). In this work, however, we did not expressly focus on nonemployer startups. Additional work is necessary to reconcile these findings. The skewed nature of the KFS sample toward growth-oriented businesses is a likely explanation.

The estimates for business assets, however, indicate a positive relationship with the annual employment probability. An increase in the probability of hiring the first employee occurs when firms have business assets of $10,001 to $25,000. After that level there is no further increase, but firms with at least $10,001 in business assets have a six to nine percentage point higher probability of hiring the first employee over the sample period, all else equal.

Ownership of intellectual property also has a positive association with making the nonemployer-to-employer transition during the sample period. Intellectual property, which includes patents, copyrights, and trademarks, is associated with a seven percentage point increase in the annual probability of hiring the first employee. When we estimate regression specifications that include all three types separately, we find that the strongest relationship is between trademarks and the annual probability of hiring the first employee.

Revenues and business assets are positively correlated, which might weaken their estimated relationships with employment probability. Using several regression specifications we can confirm that business assets have a positive association with the probability of hiring the first employee, but revenues do not have a clear relationship. It may be more important for nonemployer firms to build up assets to use or borrow against to hire their first employee rather than rely on large revenues in the previous year. Alternatively, the presence of assets might be indicative of the financial strength of the entrepreneur and her willingness to risk capital before she knows whether the venture is truly successful.

Although all these dynamic business milestones are measured when the business has no current employees, there remains the concern that the estimated effects are not causal. The positive relationship between business assets and hiring the first employee might simply represent the unobserved growth plan of the business and not that higher assets *cause* nonemployer firms to take the leap to being an employer firm. The same concern arises for intellectual property. Although it is measured for the business prior to hiring its first employee, estimates of the relationship might capture other unobserved factors. Distinguishing between temporary nonemployer businesses that are simply in a holding pattern with regard to their starting operations as employers and the more permanent nonemployer businesses that are born with the intention of being nonemployer businesses is one way to address the issues of causality and one future research should consider.

Distribution of Employment among Startups

The results displayed in figure 4.1 indicate rapid growth in average employment levels among surviving startups. An important question is whether the strong upward trend in average employees per surviving startup can be attributed to a few very fast-growing survivors ("gazelles") or to a larger number of steadily growing survivors. To investigate this question, we return to the Comprehensive Startup Panel and examine the transition across employment size classes over time for all startups that survive to year 1. For this analysis we look at broad employment groups in year 1 and track how firms change employment groups by year 5. Table 5.4 reports the year 5 distribution (of survivors) for each year 1 employment group, as well as the share of each year 1 employment group that exits by year 5. We see a significant share of firms exiting by year 5 for each year 1 employment group—and this is even conditional on surviving the initial shakeout between year 0 and year 1.[7] We also see only modest employment growth overall by firms surviving to year 5. Firms are by far most likely to remain in the same broad employment group, and they are more likely to move to a lower employment bin than to a higher one.

Despite the transition patterns in table 5.4, we still see an upward shift in the size distribution of startups from year 1 to year 5. Table 5.5 shows the share of surviving startups in each of our four broad employment categories

Table 5.4

Employment size transitions among startups

| Employment at year 1 | Among surviving startups (%) | | | | Among all startups (%) | |
| | Employment at year 5 | | | | Status at year 5 | |
	0	1 to 9	10 to 99	100+	Survive	Exit
0	95.5	4.1	0.4	0.0	43.8	56.2
1–9	14.8	76.3	8.9	0.1	61.5	38.5
10–99	6.6	19.8	70.8	2.8	64.9	35.1
100+	3.8	2.0	18.8	75.4	65.6	34.4

Notes: Percentages represent shares with respect to the corresponding rows (i.e., shares of the year 1 employment categories).

Source: Authors' calculations from the newly compiled Comprehensive Startup Panel data set (1995–2018).

Table 5.5
Employment size distribution among year 5 surviving startups

Employment	Year 1 (%)	Year 5 (%)
0	79.5	78.6
1–9	17.0	16.9
10–99	3.3	4.2
100+	0.2	0.3

Notes: Both columns represent the set of startups that survived to year 5. The two columns show the employment distributions based on the startups' employment in each year.
Source: Authors' calculations from the newly compiled Comprehensive Startup Panel data set (1995–2018).

in year 1 and year 5. Conditioning on survival allows us to compare the distributions in the two years using the same set of firms.[8] We find that the share of startups in the two smallest employment groups decreased in year 5, while the share in the two largest groups increased. This upward shift occurs despite what we find in table 5.4 because although the startups that grow represent a small share of firms in their year 1 employment group, these startups represent a relatively larger share of their year 5 employment group. For example, while only 8.9 percent of startups with one to nine employees in year 1 transitioned to ten to ninety-nine employees in year 5, these startups represent 36 percent of the firms with ten to ninety-nine employees in year 5. And even though only 2.8 percent of startups with ten to ninety-nine employees in year 1 transitioned to 100+ employees in year 5, these startups make up 35 percent of the firms with 100+ employees in year 5. These patterns are consistent with the growth dynamics evidenced in Haltiwanger et al. (2012). They show that firm growth is highly skewed with relatively few firms disproportionally contributing to overall job creation. By contrast, most firms remain small or exit. These up-or-out dynamics appear to be reinforced here by using the universe of startups in our Comprehensive Startup Panel. Further research into the underlying growth patterns and accompanying entrepreneurial motivation is necessary to fully understand high growth firms among this universe.

Together these findings tell a story of a very tumultuous life for business startups. Many firms enter every year, but many of those do not survive past the first few years. These businesses exhibit very low rates of hiring any employees. Despite the large exit rates, because of the large volume of entrants, those that do survive and hire employees contribute significantly to job creation and growth. Perhaps most dramatic is the amount of business experimentation that these numbers suggest. Understanding the motivation for the formation of these businesses, their success, and their growth remains an underexplored area of research.

Conclusions

Average patterns of job creation and survival presented in the two previous chapters conceal a substantial amount of heterogeneity in the underlying dynamics of job creation and survival by startups along several dimensions explored here. We explore several hypotheses for why the average number of jobs for a startup cohort declines only slightly, remaining relatively constant over years, and find that although startups have extremely high exit rates, the resulting job losses from these exits are nearly offset by the opposing pattern of strong average employment growth among surviving startups and the large number (but small share of the total) of nonemployer startups that eventually hire employees. Selection and growth drive a continual upward shift in the employment size distribution of survivors. Turning to heterogeneity across startup types, we find that some startups make sizable contributions to employment several years after startup. Examining heterogeneity across industries, we find that a few industry groups are job creators—Manufacturing and Accommodation and Food Services, for example, have average employment levels that are much higher than those of other sectors.

From the analysis of longitudinal data, several interesting patterns emerge regarding the dynamics of nonemployer startups hiring their first employee. Among businesses hiring employees, a large percentage of nonemployer startups hire their first employee in the first three years of existence, with only a small percentage hiring their first employee in the few years after that period. Hiring patterns over time are roughly similar to what is seen in the KFS sample of nonemployer startups, which show higher rates of employment because of the more growth- and employment-oriented businesses included in the KFS data. Using the longitudinal data from the KFS, another important question we examined is whether there are milestones that nonemployer startups often reach before hiring their first employee.

Surprisingly, we do not find clear evidence of a strong relationship between the revenues of nonemployer firms and the decision to hire their first employee in the KFS sample. Additional research is neceded to determine whether this finding holds in administrative data. The evidence, however, is less ambiguous that higher levels of business assets are associated with nonemployer businesses making the transition to employer firms. It may be important for nonemployer firms to build up assets to use or borrow against to hire their first employee. Ownership of intangible assets, such as intellectual property, also has a positive association with making the nonemployer to employer transition during the sample period. Intellectual property, which includes patents, copyrights, and trademarks, is associated with a seven percentage point increase in the annual probability of hiring the first employee. The importance of patents in the nonemployer to employer transition is confirmed by more recent administrative data. Intellectual property may be valuable for securing future revenues for hiring employees and is perhaps indicative of the commercial viability of a business idea. Determining causality in the hiring decision is an area ripe for additional research.

The findings presented in this chapter build on previous research. In addition to the previous research on the impact of small businesses on employment in the United States, a few recent studies examine the relationship and growth patterns between nonemployer and employer businesses. Acs, Headd, and Agwara (2009), for example, find that nonemployers have a startup rate of 35 percent, which is nearly three times the startup rate of employer firms. Using matched data from the Census Bureau, Davis and et al. (2007) find that a significant number of new employer firms start as nonemployer firms. The link between nonemployer and employer status and how it is related to reaching business milestones and owner characteristics, however, has not previously been examined in detail. The limited prior research on the topic is largely a consequence of data limitations. Very few data sets provide information on the time at which a business hires its first employee, information on owner and business characteristics, or longitudinal information on business conditions or milestones. These limitations are finally being overcome.

Heterogeneity across industries has also been understudied. The finding that some industry groups are job creators with average employment levels that are one to two jobs higher is important. Further research should focus on why startups in some industries tend to grow rapidly while startups in other industries do not. The extent to which these differences are driven by industry-specific market frictions or imperfections or by the business models inherent in them is an area warranting further examination. Evidence from Hurst and Pugsley (2011) focusing on employer businesses suggests some industries are more likely to attract lifestyle entrepreneurs, that is, entrepreneurs with no particular desire for growth or innovation. In this regard, nonpecuniary motives (such as being one's own boss or having flexible hours) may be even more important among the universe of nonemployer startups. To what degree should policy target and support these types of businesses? What are the types of barriers that might prevent otherwise successful businesses from succeeding? What is the role of experimentation in future entrepreneurial success and growth? Answering these questions requires a firm understanding of the drivers of success and growth that these types of new data sets can facilitate.

6 Refining Our Definition of an Entrepreneur

What is an entrepreneur? Sometimes the word conjures up the image of a computer genius launching multiple high-tech startups in Silicon Valley, striving to be the next Google or Instagram. What about restaurant owners? Are they entrepreneurs? Some restaurants grow to become national chains even when the owner does not expect it. Does someone in construction who starts working independently remodeling kitchens or working on small projects count as an entrepreneur? What if that same business grows into another Bechtel, one of the largest construction firms in the world? We would certainly call that person an entrepreneur, right?

From these examples, we learn three things. First, entrepreneurs are not limited to one industry but can be found in all types of industries and sectors. Restaurants, local construction firms, and even hair salons all have the potential to grow into national and sometimes international successes. Second, we should not base our definition of an entrepreneur on whether the business is successful or not. Certainly the founders of all those high-tech startups in Silicon Valley that ultimately were not successful are still considered to be entrepreneurs. At the outset of a startup, it is very difficult to identify which ventures will succeed and which ones will not succeed. In other words, we do not want to label someone an entrepreneur only if his business survives and becomes very successful. Entrepreneurs often fail. Finally, we should not define entrepreneurs by their original intentions for the startup business. We can get into trouble if we only designate people entrepreneurs according to whether their intention is to grow enough to launch an IPO. Many entrepreneurs also start out small with no intention of substantial long-term growth, only to discover that their business idea has wings. Should we not consider an entrepreneur someone who opens up a small store in the community? We need to incorporate a broad definition of entrepreneur to avoid these pitfalls.

In this chapter, we explore heterogeneity among startups based on the presence of employees, having an employer identification number (EIN), and the organizational structure of the business. Businesses are not all created at similar scale. Some startups are created without employees and some are created with employees. Some nonemployer startups have already registered for an EIN. Furthermore, startups can be created as sole proprietorships, partnerships, or incorporated businesses. There is likely to be substantial heterogeneity across these organizational structures, and a careful analysis of job creation and survival based on these distinctions is important.

The analysis of heterogeneity is important because of implications for understanding the fundamental nature of entrepreneurship. As noted in earlier chapters, there is some tension between the idea that entrepreneurship is primarily about creating innovative products, services, and jobs (i.e., Schumpeterian entrepreneurship) and the idea that it is instead primarily about job independence, schedule flexibility, and contract, consulting, and gig work. From the entrepreneur's perspective, is the goal to create jobs or just create a job for the entrepreneur? And is the goal to create a long-term job or just a temporary job, which is related to taking risks (Kihlstrom and Laffont 1979; Knight 1921) or diversifying risk (i.e., through multiple job activities)?

We focus on two broad questions about the definition of an entrepreneur. First, do nonemployer startups create jobs in the initial year or two or more years later, and if so, do they make a sizable contribution to job creation in the United States? The previous literature has not been able to answer this question because of data limitations. Second, we explore the related question of whether the low levels of job creation per entrepreneur and the low firm survival rates found in previous chapters are simply the result of an overly inclusive definition of entrepreneur. If we restrict the population of startups to be less inclusive and require a stronger signal of commitment by entrepreneurs at startup, do we continue to find low levels of job creation and low survival rates?

In the analyses of job creation and survival dynamics presented in previous chapters, we used the most inclusive definition of entrepreneurship possible—the universe of business startups in the US economy. To explore the heterogeneity across business types when starting a business, we begin by focusing on the main distinction between startup types, namely, whether they are nonemployers or employers at the time of startup. The distinction arises primarily because of how the two types of businesses are tracked in Census Bureau data. As noted in chapter 2, nonemployer businesses have revenue but no employees and are generally tracked by their protected identification key (PIK), while employer businesses have employees and are tracked by their EIN (although some nonemployers might also have an EIN). Using the new Comprehensive Startup Panel data set, however, we can identify whether the first observation in the administrative startup panel data is a nonemployer or employer business entity.

In this chapter, we also examine an alternative, less standard measure of job creation per startup. We add the owner to employment to create a measure of total jobs created per startup. Owing to the large percentage of sole proprietor startups that are unlikely to have a goal of hiring employees, this calculation creates an alternative measure of job creation per startup that incorporates the owner's job. Admittedly, the owner's job is not directly comparable to jobs created for employees and comes with considerable risk in terms of zero or even negative earnings, but the exercise is useful for thinking about broader policy implications. Ultimately many entrepreneurs might want simply to create a job for themselves. We do not want to entirely ignore those jobs when we discuss broader issues around job creation.

Previous Focus on Employer Startups

Previous research and statistics on entrepreneurs, startups, and small businesses published by the US Census Bureau, the US Bureau of Labor Statistics (BLS), and US Small Business Administration (SBA) focus almost exclusively on new *employer* businesses or new *employer* establishments. As noted in earlier chapters, new employer businesses are primarily identified by the first year they have employees and the subsequent records they file in fulfillment of their legal responsibilities. Since nonemployers do not have the same responsibilities, it is natural to limit the initial analysis to what is available rather than attempt to look back for potential nonemployer startup histories, a task that, as should be clear by now, carries its own challenges. Published numbers and numbers calculated from these sources indicate higher levels of job creation and survival rates than for the full and complete startup universe. On its well-publicized "Frequently Asked Questions about Small Business" web page, the SBA reports that the average number of employees per new employer firm is roughly six.[1] The SBA also reports that an average of 79 percent of new employer establishments survive one year later and that roughly 50 percent of all new employer establishments survive five years or longer. These reports are based on Census Bureau data, including the Business Dynamics Statistics (BDS) series and the related Statistics of US Businesses (SUSB) data set.[2]

Recently, the BLS started publishing aggregate data on its web page "Entrepreneurship in the U.S. Economy," based on the Business Employment Dynamics (BED) series.[3] Statistics on the number of establishments that are less than one year old are used to measure "entrepreneurs." When averaged over many cohort years, these data indicate that 48 percent of new employer establishments survive at least five years. Job creation can also be calculated from reported BED data and indicate that new employer establishments hire an average of 5.7 employees in the first year. Unfortunately, only the first year's hiring data are published by the BLS.[4]

The US Census Bureau publishes statistics on the number of firm startups based on the BDS data set. Job creation numbers and survival rates can be calculated for new employer businesses.[5] The BDS is created from the underlying Longitudinal Business Database (LBD), which includes only payroll-positive businesses. The startup year for firms in the BDS is defined as the first year with positive employment. Thus in this case, and with recent research analyzing the underlying data, entrepreneurial activity is represented primarily as new *employer* businesses (e.g., Decker et al. 2014). But the focus of the BDS is on new employer businesses and not necessarily on new employer establishments, which is an advantage of using the BDS over the BED. By using information from multiple years and the age of businesses, researchers can track cohorts over time. We calculate that a new cohort of employer businesses creates an average of 6.1 jobs in the first year and 4.7 jobs in the fifth year after startup.[6] This calculation is based on the initial cohort of entrants and does not exclude exiting businesses from the denominator. Survival rates for the average cohort of employer business is 76 percent after one year, 65 percent after two years, and 46 percent after five years.

For comparison, a nongovernment source of data on startup survival rates is the Kauffman Firm Survey (KFS). The KFS follows a sample of roughly 5,000 nonemployer and employer startups from the 2004 cohort. For this sample of startups, roughly 90 percent survive one year and 55 percent survive five years after startup (Robb and Farhat 2013). The underlying sampling frame of the KFS, however, is skewed toward including employer and other high-growth-oriented firms, which may also explain why these survival rate estimates are much higher than those for the universe of startups.[7]

But Nonemployer Startups Create Lots of Jobs

In light of the previous focus on employer startups, it is important to understand what is lost (or at least captured only later) by not including nonemployer startups. Figure 6.1 displays the number of nonemployer and employer startups per year in the United States. Of the 4.1 million startups per year in the country, the bulk are started with no employees. There are 3.7 million nonemployer startups each year. The number of businesses starting with employees is much smaller—around 439,000 per year.

Even though there are 3.7 million nonemployer startups each year, these businesses might create very few total jobs in the economy. An important

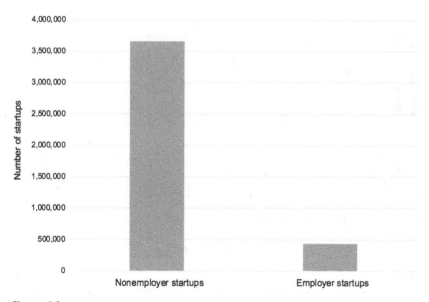

Figure 6.1

Number of startups by classification. *Source*: Authors' calculations from the newly compiled Comprehensive Startup Panel data set (1995–2018).

question, then, is whether nonemployer startups create jobs in the years following startup, and if so, how many jobs they create. Figure 6.2 displays the number of jobs created by the average employer startup and the average nonemployer startup over time. Note that nonemployer startups that do eventually hire an employee are classified as employer firms in those years but they are not classified here as employer startups. Job creation per nonemployer startup is substantially lower than job creation per employer startup in the follow-up years, as expected. The average employer startup creates 6.53 jobs in the first year after startup; that number falls to 4.61 jobs in the seventh year after startup (without conditioning on survival). Seven years after startup, the average business that started without employees has slightly fewer than 0.1 employees.

Although these statistics appear to indicate that employer startups generate essentially all jobs among startups, this is not the case because of the sheer number of nonemployer startups. There are many more nonemployer startups than employer startups, representing roughly 90 percent of all startups. The total number of existing nonemployer businesses (i.e.,

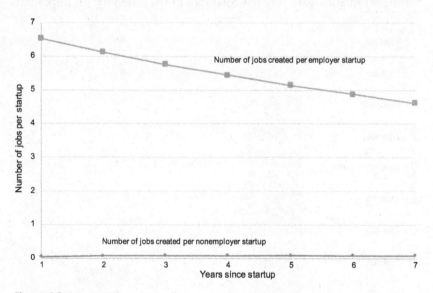

Figure 6.2
Number of jobs created per startup by employer and nonemployer startups. *Source*: Authors' calculations from the newly compiled Comprehensive Startup Panel data set (1995–2018).

not necessarily startups) also dwarfs the total number of existing employer businesses. Nonemployer businesses represent more than three quarters of all businesses in the United States.[8]

Examining total jobs created by all employer startups versus all nonemployer startups reveals a somewhat different pattern than that seen with jobs created per startup. Figure 6.3 displays the total number of jobs created by employer and nonemployer startups over time. The total number of jobs created by nonemployer startups steadily increases relative to the total number of jobs created by employer startups over time. Even only one year after startup, nonemployer startups hire 181,000 employees. Employer startups hire many more workers, 2.9 million, in the first follow-up year, but the differential narrows over time. Seven years after startup, we find that nonemployer startup hiring grows to 319,000 employees and employer startup hiring drops to 2.0 million employees.[9] Thus the share of total job creation by nonemployer startups increases from 6 percent one year after startup to 14 percent (or one out of seven) seven years after startup.

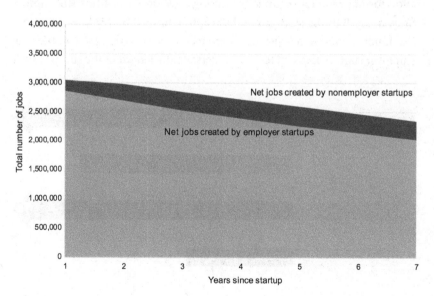

Figure 6.3
Number of jobs created per nonemployer and employer startup cohort. *Source*: Authors' calculations from the newly compiled Comprehensive Startup Panel data set (1995–2018).

The Timing of Startup Is Defined Differently

The focus on new employer startups changes the timing of startup. Returning to the discussion in chapter 2, an illustrative figure is useful. Figure 6.4, which repeats figure 2.5, shows the startup timelines for four example startups. Firm A starts with employees and survives throughout the sample time period. Firm B starts with employees and survives a couple of years. Firm C starts as a nonemployer business and become an employer business after a couple of years and survives. Firm D starts as a nonemployer and switches to employer status and survives for a couple of years.

These patterns have implications for accurately capturing the size of startup cohorts. Using the Comprehensive Startup Panel data set, we find that roughly 20 percent of new employer firms have a history as a nonemployer business. Thus these firms started in an earlier year than what would be recorded for them as a new employer firm. These patterns also have implications for job creation and survival rates. Specifically, average job creation for firms A and B in the startup year could be different from average job creation for new employer firms. Measuring new employer firms will capture firms A and B in the startup year but capture firms C and D later. There are also implications when calculating survival rates. Survival based on the new employer startup date will tend to understate the length of the survival spell

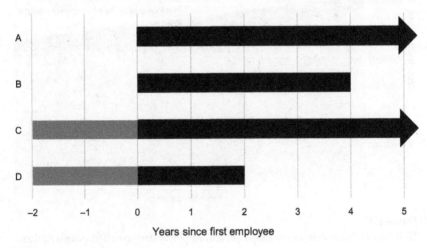

Figure 6.4
Revenue-based approach to defining startup year.

for those firms. The time during which the firm was a nonemployer will not be counted. On the other hand, as shown in previous chapters, very large numbers of nonemployer startups never make it to the employer stage. The focus on new employer firms will thus overstate survival rates if the goal is to calculate survival rates among all startups in the economy.

The question of what start date to use is essentially about the definition of a business. If we use the broader definition of a business to include the universe of nonemployers and employers, then a startup should be defined by the first year that the business exists, even if it begins initially as a sole proprietorship. From this perspective, work that relies on definitions that limit startups to only employer businesses will necessarily identify new businesses at a potentially later stage of development and exclude the large class of nonemployer business startups.

What Is an Entrepreneur? Arguments for Creating a Comprehensive Startup Panel

The inclusion of nonemployer startups is important for conceptual reasons. A large part of the entrepreneurship literature takes an individual approach to analyzing entrepreneurship. For example, classic studies of the entrepreneur, such as Knight (1921), Schumpeter (1934), and more recently Evans and Jovanovic (1989), do not limit the definition of entrepreneurs to include only those undertaking business ventures with employees. Additionally, most previous empirical studies of entrepreneurship using a vast range of different data sets do not distinguish between entrepreneurs with and those without employees (for a few examples, see Blanchflower and Oswald 1998; Cullen and Gordon 2007; Evans and Leighton 1989; Fairlie 1999; Fairlie and Robb 2008; Hamilton 2000; Holtz-Eakin, Joulfaian, and Rosen 1994; Hvide and Oyer 2018; Lafontaine and Shaw 2016; Levine and Rubinstein 2016, 2018; and review in Parker 2018).

Many nonemployer businesses are extremely successful. The latest nonemployer data reported by the US Census Bureau on annual revenue counts are reported in table 6.1. There are over 600,000 nonemployer businesses with annual sales and receipts in the $100,000–$250,000 range. Moving to the half million to $1 million sales level, there are 283,000 nonemployers, and 42,000 nonemployers have more than $1 million in annual sales and receipts. When these categories are put together, nearly one million

Table 6.1
Number of high-revenue nonemployer businesses in the United States

Sales and receipt size	Number of nonemployer businesses
$250,000–$499,999	629,837
$500,000–$999,999	282,819
$1,000,000 or more	42,079

Source: US Census Bureau, Nonemployer data, 2017.

nonemployer businesses have at least a quarter of a million in sales and receipts. These are certainly successful startups, many of which transition to create jobs and whose contribution we might not want to minimize.

Thus, including nonemployer startups will shed light on an important dimension of early-stage entrepreneurial dynamics in the United States. In particular, we can now answer the question of how many jobs are created by the average entrepreneur. Many nonemployer startups become employer firms and make substantial contributions to job creation, sometimes several years after startup. But many also exit quickly and never create jobs. The inclusion of nonemployers in our Comprehensive Startup Panel data set is important for measuring survival rates from this perspective, identifying the startup cohort year, and establishing the business age for those young employer firms that began as nonemployer startups. Among firms hiring their first employee (using the LBD definition of an employer startup), roughly 80 percent of these firms are employer startups and 20 percent are nonemployer startups from previous years, according to our Comprehensive Startup Panel.

Selecting More Growth-Minded Nonemployer Startups

Our Comprehensive Startup Panel data set includes all business startups; however, we might worry that it is too inclusive in terms of what we commonly think of as a business. We explore an alternative definition of a startup that excludes secondary jobs and smaller-scale self-employment activities. These types of business activities might not be viewed in all cases as startups. Using markers for growth orientation we can be more selective in choosing which startups are included in the analysis.

Using this restriction, we examine whether the low levels of job creation per startup and survival rates found above are simply the result of an overly inclusive definition of entrepreneurial activities (i.e., using the entire startup universe). If we restrict the population of startups to be less inclusive and require a stronger signal of commitment by entrepreneurs at startup, do we continue to find low levels of job creation and survival?

There are essentially two data-driven primary classifications of business entities by the US Census Bureau, four legal form subclassifications within the nonemployer universe, and one additional subclassification based on having an EIN or not. These classifications are the following:

1. Employer startups
2. Nonemployer startups
   2.1. Incorporated: Business granted a charter recognizing it as a separate legal entity having its own privileges and liabilities distinct from those of its members.
   2.2. S Corporation: A form of corporation where the entity does not pay any federal income taxes, and its income or losses are divided among and passed to its shareholders (and reported on their own individual income tax returns).
   2.3. Partnership: Unincorporated business where two or more persons join to carry on a trade or business, with each having a shared financial interest in the business.
   2.4. Sole proprietorship: Unincorporated business with a sole owner. Has an EIN at startup, but no employees.
   2.5. Sole proprietorship: Unincorporated business with a sole owner. Does not have an EIN at startup.

Instead of excluding all nonemployer startups, we want to use this information to narrow down the definition of an entrepreneur. The goal is to propose an alternative definition of entrepreneurship that might serve as a reasonable upper bound on job creation per entrepreneur and survival rates. We include all nonemployer startups that are incorporated, S corporations, partnerships, or sole proprietorships with EINs, but exclude sole proprietorships without an EIN.[10] In other words, we include only categories 2.1–2.4 and exclude category 2.5 from the list above.

In each of these cases there is a much stronger business registration requirement than for sole proprietorships without an EIN. Also, consultants and contract workers will typically show up as sole proprietors. These work arrangements are technically classified as business entities in the data because of their treatment in the Tax Code, but they do not fit the theoretical concept of an entrepreneur or the conventional view of a business owner. Owners receive a Form 1099 from a business for contract or consulting work but do not have additional business ownership responsibilities. They also typically would not apply for and receive an EIN if the goal is to make money and not grow enough to hire employees. Unfortunately, using this approach will still result in the loss of some growth-oriented sole proprietorships that eventually hire employees.

The SBA provides a guide on choosing a business structure on its web page for entrepreneurs titled "Choose a Business Structure."[11] Under the category of sole proprietorships, the guide discusses the advantages and disadvantages of a sole proprietorship compared to other, more involved organizational structures. One advantage that the guide notes is that sole proprietorships are easy to form and give the owner complete control of the business. In contrast, one of the noted disadvantages is that owners can be held personally liable for the debts and obligations of the business. Because there is no separate business entity created with sole proprietorships, the owner's business assets and liabilities are not separate from the owner's personal assets and liabilities. Another disadvantage noted by the SBA in this guide is that it can be more difficult to raise financial capital for the business because banks are often hesitant to lend to sole proprietorships, and sole proprietorships cannot sell stock.

Overall, however, the SBA notes on its web page that "Sole proprietorships can be a good choice for low-risk businesses and owners who want to test their business idea before forming a more formal business." In this spirit, we want to be careful about removing this group of businesses when calculating job creation and survival numbers. We keep this in mind in the analysis below.

The approach of using organizational structure of the startup is in line with recent work that refines the definition of the entrepreneur. For example, Guzman and Stern (2016) use characteristics at founding, such as how the firm is organized (e.g., as a corporation, partnership, or LLC, and whether the company is registered in Delaware), how it is named (e.g., whether the owners name the firm eponymously after themselves), and how the idea behind the business is protected (e.g., through an early patent or trademark application) to identify high-potential startups.[12] They note that although new businesses can be organized as sole proprietorships, more formal registration is a useful prerequisite for growth and includes benefits such as limited liability, tax benefits, the ability to issue and trade ownership shares, and credibility with potential customers. Levine and Rubinstein (2016, 2018) separate the incorporated and unincorporated self-employed in the Current Population Survey (CPS) and National Longitudinal Survey of Youth (NLSY) to identify "entrepreneurs" and "other business owners," respectively. They demonstrate that the incorporated self-employed engage in activities requiring strong nonroutine cognitive abilities, tend to be more educated, score higher on learning aptitude tests, exhibit greater self-esteem, engage in more illicit activities when young, and experience a large increase in earnings relative to wage or salary work. They also find that incorporated business owners are positively selected on human capital and collateral and move with the business cycle, but unincorporated owners do not. With the new Comprehensive Startup Panel data set, we can explore many alternative classifications.

Number of Startups by Classification

Before exploring job creation numbers, we examine the number of startups in each classification. The first column of figure 6.5 displays the total number of startups in a given year, which is 4.1 million on average. Combining the more selective group of nonemployer startups (i.e., nonemployers, excluding sole proprietorships without EINs) and the group of employer startups gives a total of 1.2 million startups in the average cohort in the United States. This new selective definition of a startup nets 743,000 nonemployer startups and 439,000 employer startups. The restriction has removed 2.9 million sole-proprietor-without-EIN startups. Although the newly defined group of startups is much smaller in total number than the universe of startups, we show below that we are not losing a large number of total jobs created in the US economy.

If we focus on more detailed categories, nonemployer sole proprietors that have an EIN (category 2.4 above) account for 220,000 startups (5 percent of all startups) and nonemployer startups that are sole proprietors without EINs (category 2.5) account for 2.9 million startups (71 percent of all startups). The remaining nonemployer categories (2.1, 2.2, and 2.3) account for 520,000 startups (13 percent of all startups).

The major industry group distribution of the selective group of startups differs somewhat from the industry distribution derived using the universe

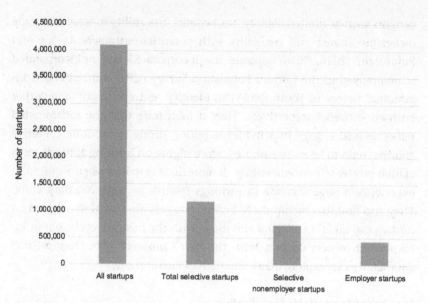

Figure 6.5
Number of startups by classification. *Source*: Authors' calculations from the newly compiled Comprehensive Startup Panel data set (1995–2018).

of startups, but the differences are not large. Table 6.2 reports the major industry group distributions for all startups and for the selective group of startups that excludes sole-proprietor-without-EIN startups. The selective group of startups is more likely to be in Finance and Insurance and Accommodation and Food Services, and much more likely to be in Real Estate and Rental and Leasing. The selective group is less likely to be in Administrative and Support, Health Care and Social Assistance, and Other Services (except Public Administration). Most other major industry groups have similar percentages within each group of startups.

Another way to compare major industries of selective startups to the universe of startups is to calculate the percentage of all startups that are in the selective group by major industry group. This comparison magnifies differences within industries even for those major industry groups that are relatively small. Table 6.2 also reports the percentage of all startups that are selective startups (i.e., startups with an EIN) by major industry group. The percentages vary substantially across industries. For example, 81.7 percent of startups in the Management of Companies and Enterprises industry are

Table 6.2

Startups by major industry group for total and selective definition

Major industry group	Number of startups	Percent of total	Number of selective startups	Percent of selective startups	Selective startup percentage
Agriculture, Forestry, Fishing and Hunting	51,265	1.3	16,676	1.4	32.5
Mining	10,088	0.2	4,088	0.3	40.5
Construction; Utilities	449,941	11.0	127,000	10.7	28.2
Manufacturing	70,412	1.7	32,706	2.8	46.4
Wholesale Trade	87,706	2.1	44,294	3.7	50.5
Retail Trade	426,294	10.4	126,294	10.7	29.6
Transportation and Warehousing	162,824	4.0	48,118	4.1	29.6
Information	75,353	1.8	24,588	2.1	32.6
Finance and Insurance	126,706	3.1	60,824	5.1	48.0
Real Estate and Rental and Leasing	267,471	6.5	161,000	13.6	60.2
Professional, Scientific, and Technical Services	515,706	12.6	142,176	12.0	27.6
Management of Companies and Enterprises	11,559	0.3	9,441	0.8	81.7
Administrative and Support and Waste Management and Remediation Services	359,118	8.8	63,235	5.4	17.6
Educational Services	107,471	2.6	13,353	1.1	12.4
Health Care and Social Assistance	375,588	9.2	72,647	6.1	19.3
Arts, Entertainment, and Recreation	165,412	4.0	31,294	2.6	18.9
Accommodation and Food Services	120,059	2.9	69,882	5.9	58.2
Other Services (except Public Administration)	504,882	12.3	99,000	8.4	19.6
Not elsewhere specified	205,706	5.0	35,118	3.0	17.1
Total number of startups	4,093,559		1,181,735		28.9

Note: Selective group of startups excludes sole-proprietor-without-EIN startups.
Source: Authors' calculations from the newly compiled Comprehensive Startup Panel data set (1995–2018).

found in the selective group of startups, although the size of this group of startups in the US economy is very small. Wholesale Trade, Finance and Insurance, Real Estate and Rental and Leasing, and Accommodation and Food Services each have close to or higher than 50 percent of startups in the selective group. Examples of low shares in the selective group of startups are Educational Services, Arts, Entertainment, and Recreation, Health Care and Social Assistance, and Other Services (except Public Administration). These patterns are consistent with the general scale of businesses. But the main takeaway from this analysis is that the more restrictive definition, which removes sole-proprietor-without-EIN startups, does not alter the industry distribution too much. We continue to find large concentrations, for example, in major industry groups such as Construction, Retail Trade, and Professional, Scientific, and Technical Services.

Job Creation by Startups and Sole-Proprietor-without-EIN Startups

Figure 6.6 displays the total number of jobs created by our selective group of startups, as well as the set of sole-proprietor-without-EIN startups over time. The total number of jobs created by this more restrictive population of startups is 3.0 million in the first year after startup. Total net job creation then declines steadily, dropping to 2.3 million in the seventh follow-up year. Excluding sole-proprietor-without-EIN startups results in the loss of 19,000 jobs in the first follow-up year to 56,000 jobs in the seventh follow-up year (which is 18 percent of the jobs created by all nonemployer startups).

As expected, the bigger effect from excluding sole-proprietor-without-EIN startups is on the measure of job creation per entrepreneur in the startup year and average employment size in future years. The numerator (total number of employees) is smaller, but the real change is a much smaller denominator (total number of entrepreneurs). Figure 6.7 displays the number of jobs created by the average selective startup (a category that excludes sole-proprietor-without-EIN startups) and the average sole-proprietor-without-EIN startup over time. Job creation per selective startup is higher than job creation per all startups in the follow-up years. The average selective startup creates 2.56 jobs in the first year after startup, a number that steadily declines to 1.94 jobs seven years later. Seven years later the average sole-proprietor-without-EIN startup hires 0.02 employees (which is primarily driven by the sheer number of these business entities in the universe of startups).

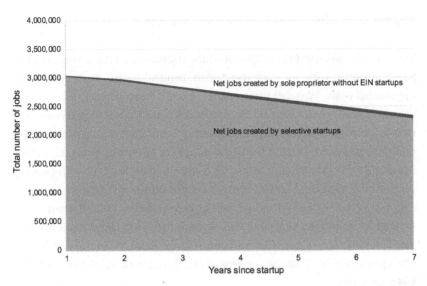

Figure 6.6
Number of jobs created per selective startup cohort and sole-proprietor-without-EIN startup cohort. *Source*: Authors' calculations from the newly compiled Comprehensive Startup Panel data set (1995–2018).

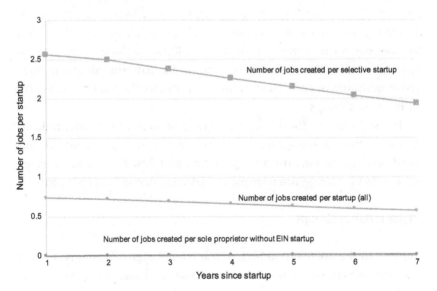

Figure 6.7
Number of jobs created per startup by all, selective, and sole-proprietor-without-EIN startups. *Source*: Authors' calculations from the newly compiled Comprehensive Startup Panel data set (1995–2018).

Regression Results for Selective Group of Startups

We exclude sole-proprietor-without-EIN startups to create the selective group of startups and estimate regressions using all startup years and surviving startup years. We label these results our "All Startup Years" sample. The second excludes exits; that is, the results are conditional on surviving, and thus the sample is labeled "Surviving Startup Year." Table 6.3, specification 1, reports regression estimates using the sample of all startup years, and specification 2 reports regression estimates using the sample of surviving startup years. The conditional sample removes observations for startups after they exit. For example, if a startup survives only to follow-up year 3, then observations for follow-up years 4–7 will be excluded from the estimation sample. The same sets of variables and controls are included in the regressions. The sample size is, of course, smaller, and the means of the dependent variables are larger.

Using the selective group of startups yields the same set of key findings as when we used the universe of startups to estimate the regressions. When we include all startup years for the selective group, we find declining employment levels over years since startup. In contrast, when we include only surviving startup years for the selective group, we find increasing employment levels over years since startup. Growth in the average size for this group is a result of selection as well as job creation from continuing firms. Overall, we find similar patterns (although different magnitudes of coefficient estimates) for years since startup using the universe of startups.

The key findings for the selective group of startups by major industry group are that Manufacturing, Management, and Accommodation and Food Services are job creators. Agriculture and Real Estate tend to create fewer jobs on average when we use the selective definition of a startup.

Major Industry Groups

Turning to the original numbers, which are not regression adjusted, average employment size by major industry group and years since startup generally follows a similar pattern to what we found in chapter 3. Table 6.4 reports average employment size by major industry group and follow-up year. Average job creation is reported for the first follow-up year and fifth

Table 6.3
Regressions for number of employees using all and surviving startup years (selective group of startups)

	Employment coefficient	
	All startup years	Surviving startup years
1 year since startup	(Excluded category)	(Excluded category)
2 years since startup	−0.067***	0.545***
	(0.003)	(0.004)
3 years since startup	−0.181***	0.942***
	(0.003)	(0.006)
4 years since startup	−0.297***	1.267***
	(0.004)	(0.007)
5 years since startup	−0.406***	1.517***
	(0.004)	(0.009)
6 years since startup	−0.514***	1.734***
	(0.004)	(0.011)
7 years since startup	−0.616***	1.893***
	(0.004)	(0.011)
11-Agriculture, Forestry, Fishing and Hunting	−0.604***	−0.932***
	(0.012)	(0.022)
21-Mining	1.912***	2.781***
	(0.125)	(0.199)
22–23-Construction; Utilities	0.339***	0.603***
	(0.007)	(0.011)
31–33-Manufacturing	5.553***	9.200***
	(0.061)	(0.102)
42-Wholesale Trade	1.066***	1.726***
	(0.014)	(0.024)
44–45-Retail Trade	0.540***	1.152***
	(0.007)	(0.011)
48–49-Transportation and Warehousing	0.048***	0.153***
	(0.013)	(0.023)
51-Information	1.202***	2.781***
	(0.046)	(0.090)
52-Finance and Insurance	−0.103***	−0.236***
	(0.013)	(0.021)
53-Real Estate and Rental and Leasing	−0.939***	−1.815***
	(0.004)	(0.007)
54-Professional, Scientific, and Technical Services	0.166***	0.196***
	(0.006)	(0.011)

(continued)

Table 6.3
(continued)

	Employment coefficient	
	All startup years	Surviving startup years
55-Management of Companies and Enterprises	1.714*** (0.140)	3.736*** (0.257)
56-Administrative and Support and Waste Management and Remediation Services	2.819*** (0.036)	5.076*** (0.063)
61-Educational Services	2.761*** (0.080)	4.769*** (0.137)
62-Health Care and Social Assistance	3.262*** (0.024)	4.808*** (0.037)
71-Arts, Entertainment, and Recreation	0.481*** (0.020)	1.036*** (0.036)
72-Accommodation and Food Services	4.543*** (0.019)	7.887*** (0.032)
81-Other Services (except Public Administration)	(Excluded category)	(Excluded category)
Sample size	160,700,000	94,460,000

Notes: For specification 1, each observation is a firm–year combination, and all possible follow-up years are included. The dependent variable is the number of employees in that year for the startup and equals zero if the startup does not exist in that year. For specification 2, each observation is a firm–year combination, and all surviving follow-up years are included. The dependent variable is the number of employees in that year for the startup and is removed from the sample if the startup does not exist in that year. Standard errors are reported in parentheses below coefficient estimates and are clustered at the firm level. * $p < 0.10$, ** $p < 0.05$, *** $p < 0.01$.

Source: Sample includes the selective group of startups, which excludes sole-proprietor-without-EIN startups, from the newly compiled Comprehensive Startup Panel data set (1995–2018). Startup cohorts include 1995 to 2011, and follow-up years include 1996 to 2018.

follow-up year. Job creation mostly falls from year 1 to year 5, partly due to exits.

We can certainly expect estimates of average employment size per startup to be higher if all nonemployer startups are excluded. On the other hand, many nonemployer startups grow and ultimately hire employees many years later. Conditioning on a subset of nonemployer startups seeks to remedy these contrasting forces. We choose to include all nonemployer

Table 6.4

Startup average number of employees by major industry group (selective definition)

Major industry group	Number of selective startups	Average number of employees in year 1	Average number of employees in year 5
Agriculture, Forestry, Fishing and Hunting	16,676	0.88	0.67
Mining	4,088	3.77	3.69
Construction; Utilities	127,000	1.97	1.66
Manufacturing	32,706	8.32	6.60
Wholesale Trade	44,294	2.78	2.53
Retail Trade	126,294	2.36	1.76
Transportation and Warehousing	48,118	1.64	1.40
Information	24,588	2.66	2.39
Finance and Insurance	60,824	1.44	1.26
Real Estate and Rental and Leasing	161,000	0.44	0.36
Professional, Scientific, and Technical Services	142,176	1.65	1.55
Management of Companies and Enterprises	9,441	2.52	1.87
Administrative and Support and Waste Management and Remediation Services	63,235	4.66	4.17
Educational Services	13,353	3.90	4.45
Health Care and Social Assistance	72,647	4.65	4.91
Arts, Entertainment, and Recreation	31,294	2.06	1.66
Accommodation and Food Services	69,882	8.25	5.51
Other Services (except Public Administration)	99,000	1.60	1.28
Not elsewhere specified	35,118	0.25	0.26
Total number of selective startups	1,181,735		

Note: Sample excludes sole-proprietor-without-EIN startups.

Source: Authors' calculations from the newly compiled Comprehensive Startup Panel data set (1995–2018). The startup year (year 0) is the first calendar year in which the business has revenues or payroll. The following year (year 1) captures the first complete calendar year of information on number of employees and survival in the data. Startup cohorts include 1995 to 2011, and follow-up years include 1996 to 2018.

startups except those that are sole proprietors without EINs in the startup year.

Survival Rates among the Selective Group of Startups

As expected, we find that survival rates are higher among the selective group of startups. However, we continue to find extremely high exit rates for these businesses. Figure 6.8 displays survival rates for all startups, selective startups, and sole-proprietor-without-EIN startups. Sole-proprietor-without-EIN startups have lower survival rates. One year after startup, 76 percent of the selective group of startups survive. This is considerably higher than for the universe of startups (59 percent) and the sole-proprietor-without-EIN startup group (55 percent), with a difference of roughly seventeen to twenty-one percentage points, suggesting that some nonemployer startups might be a form of business experimentation. The percentage point difference in survival rates decreases over years since

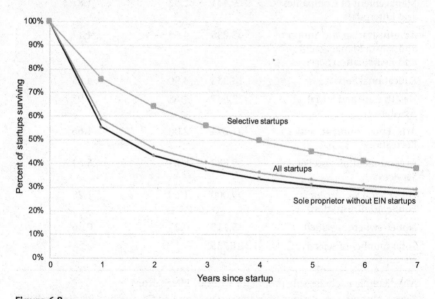

Figure 6.8
Survival rates among all, selective, and sole-proprietor-without-EIN startups. *Source*: Authors' calculations from the newly compiled Comprehensive Startup Panel data set (1995 to 2018).

startup. Five years after startup, the survival rate for the selective group of startups is 45 percent, compared with a survival rate of 33 percent for the universe of startups and 31 percent for sole-proprietor-without-EIN start-ups. By the end of the seven-year period, survival rates for the selective businesses are almost 25 percent higher than those for businesses excluding sole proprietors without an EIN (38 percent survival versus 29 percent). For all measures of startup groups, survival drops off rapidly over years since startup. No group of startups is immune to high exit rates in the early stages of business.

If we focus instead on contemporaneous survival rates, figure 6.9 displays the probability of surviving one more year at each age of the startup.[13] The annual survivor rate for the selective startups starts off higher than for sole-proprietor-without-EIN startups, before they quickly converge around year 5. A lot of the action accounting for the difference in survival thus happens from year 0 to year 1.

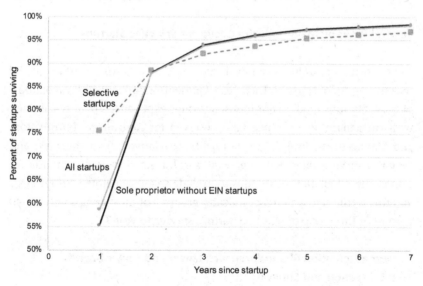

Figure 6.9
Annual survival probabilities among all, selective, and sole-proprietor-without-EIN startups. *Source*: Authors' calculations from the newly compiled Comprehensive Startup Panel data set (1995–2018).

Regression Results for Survival among the Selective Group of Startups

Table 6.5 reports survival regression estimates from the sample of selective startups that excludes sole-proprietor-without-EIN startups. The same
sets of variables and controls are included in the regression. The coefficient
estimates do not change substantially relative to estimates reported in chapter 4 using the full universe of startups. We find the same pattern of a rapid
decline in survival rates and a slight tapering off after that. The main difference is that survival rates are higher for the selective group of startups,
showing up as smaller (in absolute value) negative coefficients on the year
since startup coefficient estimates.

We continue to find only small differences in survival rates across industries. Excluding sole-proprietor-without-EIN startups from the "entrepreneur"
sample used in the regression does not change the general findings regarding
industry differences. The coefficient estimates change for some major industry groups after we restrict the sample, but the overall differences are not large.

Survival Rates by Major Industry Group for Selective Startups

Table 6.6 reports industry survival rates by year following startup for the
selective group of startups. Each year represents a different survival window
of time. Startups in all major industry groups experience low survival rates,
with particularly low survival rates observed for Agriculture, Information,
and Management, Real Estate startups have relatively high short-run and
long-run survival rates. But in general, survival rates are low even after we
restrict the population of startups to exclude sole proprietors without EINs,
and this is true across all major industry groups. For most groups only 30–40
percent of this group of selective startups survive to year 7.

Toward a Definition of Entrepreneurs: Lower and Upper Bounds
on Job Creation and Survival

The inclusion or exclusion of nonemployer or sole-proprietor-without-
EIN startups are important decisions in measuring entrepreneurial job
creation and survival. However, there is no unique or perfect definition.
Instead of taking a stand on whether entrepreneurship is best measured
by considering the universe of startups or by excluding the large number

Table 6.5

Regression for the probability of survival using all startup years (selective group of startups)

	Survival coefficient
Startup year	(Excluded category)
1 year since startup	–0.248***
2 years since startup	–0.365***
3 years since startup	–0.445***
4 years since startup	–0.507***
5 years since startup	–0.554***
6 years since startup	–0.593***
7 years since startup	–0.625***
11-Agriculture, Forestry, Fishing and Hunting	–0.033***
21-Mining	0.053***
22–23-Construction; Utilities	–0.002***
31–33-Manufacturing	0.017***
42-Wholesale Trade	0.015***
44–45-Retail Trade	–0.028***
48–49-Transportation and Warehousing	–0.013***
51-Information	–0.072***
52-Finance and Insurance	0.012***
53-Real Estate and Rental and Leasing	0.085***
54-Professional, Scientific, and Technical Services	0.016***
55-Management of Companies and Enterprises	–0.082***
56-Administrative and Support and Waste Management and Remediation Services	–0.017***
61-Educational Services	–0.002***
62-Health Care and Social Assistance	0.059***
71-Arts, Entertainment, and Recreation	–0.029***
72-Accommodation and Food Services	–0.002***
81-Other Services (except Public Administration)	(Excluded category)
Sample size	160,700,000

Notes: Each observation is a firm–year combination, and all possible follow-up years are included. The dependent variable equals one if the startup survived to that year. Standard errors are clustered at the firm level and are not reported because they are small and do not show at the three-decimal level. * $p<0.10$, ** $p<0.05$, *** $p<0.01$.

Source: Sample includes the selective group of startups, which excludes sole-proprietor-without-EIN startups, from the newly compiled Comprehensive Startup Panel data set (1995–2018). Startup cohorts include 1995 to 2011, and follow-up years include 1996 to 2018.

Table 6.6

Startup survival rates by major industry group (selective definition)

Major industry group	Number of selective startups	Survival rate, year 1	Survival rate, year 2	Survival rate, year 3	Survival rate, year 4	Survival rate, year 5	Survival rate, year 6	Survival rate, year 7
Agriculture, Forestry, Fishing and Hunting	16,676	0.70	0.60	0.54	0.48	0.43	0.39	0.36
Mining	4,088	0.82	0.75	0.71	0.63	0.58	0.53	0.48
Construction; Utilities	127,000	0.76	0.64	0.56	0.49	0.44	0.40	0.37
Manufacturing	32,706	0.79	0.68	0.59	0.52	0.47	0.42	0.39
Wholesale Trade	44,294	0.81	0.70	0.61	0.53	0.48	0.43	0.39
Retail Trade	126,294	0.76	0.62	0.52	0.45	0.40	0.35	0.32
Transportation and Warehousing	48,118	0.77	0.65	0.56	0.50	0.45	0.41	0.38
Information	24,588	0.68	0.53	0.43	0.37	0.33	0.29	0.26
Finance and Insurance	60,824	0.79	0.70	0.63	0.54	0.49	0.44	0.40
Real Estate and Rental and Leasing	161,000	0.81	0.73	0.67	0.62	0.58	0.55	0.52
Professional, Scientific, and Technical Services	142,176	0.78	0.67	0.59	0.52	0.48	0.44	0.40
Management of Companies and Enterprises	9,441	0.65	0.43	0.27	0.23	0.20	0.17	0.15
Administrative and Support, and Waste Management and Remediation Services	63,235	0.74	0.62	0.53	0.47	0.43	0.39	0.36
Educational Services	13,353	0.73	0.62	0.54	0.49	0.45	0.42	0.40
Health Care and Social Assistance	72,647	0.79	0.69	0.62	0.57	0.53	0.49	0.46

Table 6.6
(continued)

Major industry group	Number of selective startups	Survival rate, year 1	Survival rate, year 2	Survival rate, year 3	Survival rate, year 4	Survival rate, year 5	Survival rate, year 6	Survival rate, year 7
Arts, Entertainment, and Recreation	31,294	0.71	0.57	0.48	0.42	0.38	0.35	0.32
Accommodation and Food Services	69,882	0.82	0.67	0.57	0.49	0.43	0.38	0.34
Other Services (except Public Administration)	99,000	0.75	0.63	0.55	0.50	0.45	0.41	0.38

Note: Sample excludes sole-proprietor-without-EIN startups.

Source: Authors' calculations from the newly compiled Comprehensive Startup Panel data set (1995–2018). The startup year (year 0) is the first calendar year in which the business has revenues or payroll. The following year (year 1) captures the first complete calendar year of information on number of employees and survival in the data. Startup cohorts include 1995 to 2011, and follow-up years include 1996 to 2018.

of sole-proprietor-without-EIN startups, we consider the two measures as lower and upper bounds, respectively. We view throwing out all sole-proprietor-without-EIN startups as perhaps too extreme, but also acknowledge that including all these startups is likely to be overly inclusive in terms of thinking about how startups contribute to the economy. Should we consider a consultant, for example, in our calculations of job creation and survival among startups? Linking the startup panel to the universe of wage earners offers an alternative approach to potentially targeting and identifying consultants in a more precise way. This might be particularly fruitful in removing consultants in particular industries. We do not pursue this approach here and simply note that many business entities are started on a part-time basis while the owner holds a salaried job.

Table 6.7 presents the average number of jobs created per entrepreneur using the full universe of startups as a lower bound and the selective group of startups as an upper bound. The lower and upper bounds result in a wide range of values for job creation levels per startup. In the initial year, the lower and upper bounds for employees per entrepreneur are 0.74 and 2.56, respectively. Five years after startup the lower to upper bound range for jobs

Table 6.7
Range of measures for employees per entrepreneur

	Employees per entrepreneur	
Years since startup	Lower bound	Upper bound
1	0.74	2.56
2	0.73	2.50
3	0.70	2.38
4	0.66	2.26
5	0.63	2.15
6	0.60	2.04
7	0.57	1.94

Note: The lower bound includes the universe of startups, and the upper bound excludes sole-proprietor-without-EIN startups.
Source: Authors' calculations from the newly compiled Comprehensive Startup Panel data set (1995–2018). The startup year (year 0) is the first calendar year in which the business has revenues or payroll. The following year (year 1) captures the first complete calendar year of information on number of employees and survival in the data. Startup cohorts include 1995 to 2011, and follow-up years include 1996 to 2018.

per entrepreneur is 0.63–2.15. The pattern holds for all years after startup. The average number of employees (including exits) across all follow-up years ranges from 0.66 at the lower bound to 2.26 at the upper bound.

With respect to survival rates, calculating lower and upper bounds does not result in such a wide range of values but does produce different results. Table 6.8 reports lower and upper bounds for entrepreneurial survival rates obtained using the full universe of startups and selective group of startups. One year after startup, 59–76 percent of entrepreneurial firms survive. This drops rapidly to 47–64 percent in the second year after startup and to 33–45 percent five years after startup. For later follow-up years the survival rates differ by roughly ten percentage points.

Bounding measures of job creation and survival provide interesting results. For job creation per startup, the upper bound of more than two jobs per startup is much higher than our lower bound of slightly more than one-half job per startup. Underlying these very different job creation rates are different lower and upper bound measures of survival. The trends in both job creation per startup and survival rates over years since startup are roughly similar. Our removal of some types of entrepreneurs follows the

Table 6.8

Range of measures for entrepreneurial survival rates

Years since startup	Survival rates (%)	
	Lower bound	Upper bound
0	100	100
1	59	76
2	47	64
3	40	56
4	36	50
5	33	45
6	31	41
7	29	38

Note: The lower bound includes the universe of startups, and the upper bound excludes sole-proprietor-without-EIN startups.

Source: Authors' calculations from the newly compiled Comprehensive Startup Panel data set (1995–2018). The startup year (year 0) is the first calendar year in which the business has revenues or payroll. The following year (year 1) captures the first complete calendar year of information on number of employees and survival in the data. Startup cohorts include 1995 to 2011, and follow-up years include 1996 to 2018.

approach taken in a few recent studies (e.g., including the incorporated self-employed, partnerships, and patent holders). Using this approach, we lose some of the jobs created, but job creation per entrepreneur is now higher and perhaps more in line with what we would expect from entrepreneurs whose businesses have growth potential. Regardless, data availability dictates the approaches we can follow, and it is important to recognize that many new businesses start out as sole proprietorships and grow to become successful businesses. Experimentation is part of the nature of nonemployer startups regardless of legal form or growth marker.

Entrepreneurs Create Jobs for Themselves

The focus we have taken thus far for measuring jobs is in line with the literature and is based on the number of employees in place at the startup. An alternative view of calculating startup job creation is to count the jobs the entrepreneurs create for themselves. These jobs are often not counted as employee jobs in the data. Although the "entrepreneurs create jobs for themselves" argument is often made in the policy arena, an important question is whether the business ownership job lasts very long. Additionally, a worker hired by a startup is paid a wage or salary, whereas the owner might be losing or making very little money in the first couple of years. On the other hand, many nonemployer startups have no intention of hiring employees. The goal is primarily to make a living or to supplement income through a self-employed business activity. Contract workers and consultants, for example, count as participating in business activities with the goal of providing income for the owner, but not necessarily with the goal of creating jobs for others.

Given these concerns, we add the owners of nonemployer startups to job creation and jobs per entrepreneur counts to create an alternative measure of the total number of jobs (including owners) per startup. Table 6.9 reports the new measure of total jobs created per startup in addition to the lower bound measure of job creation per startup. We use the lower bound as a starting point because it includes the universe of startups to capture all types of business activities, which is consistent with the idea of many sole proprietor startups having a primary goal of creating a job for themselves. We also assume for these calculations that each startup has one owner as an approximation for simplification and because of the very large percentage

Table 6.9
Employees per entrepreneur and total jobs per startup including the owner

Years since startup	Employees per entrepreneur (lower bound)	Surviving owners	Total jobs per startup (including owner's job)
1	0.74	0.59	1.33
2	0.73	0.47	1.19
3	0.70	0.40	1.10
4	0.66	0.36	1.03
5	0.63	0.33	0.97
6	0.60	0.31	0.91
7	0.57	0.29	0.86

Note: The lower bound includes the universe of startups.

Source: Authors' calculations from the newly compiled Comprehensive Startup Panel data set (1995–2018). The startup year (year 0) is the first calendar year in which the business has revenues or payroll. The following year (year 1) captures the first complete calendar year of information on number of employees and survival in the data. Startup cohorts include 1995 to 2011, and follow-up years include 1996 to 2018.

of startups that are sole proprietorships, which have only one owner by definition. However, we note that these measures provide an undercount because there are partnerships and some corporations among these types of new ventures (although a small share of the total). Using this alternative measure, we find that total jobs per startup is 1.33 in the first year after startup. By the second follow-up year, the number of total jobs drops to 1.19. Five years after startup the total number of jobs when we include the owner's job drops even further, to 0.97. At the end of our follow-up period, there are 0.86 total jobs, including the owner's, per startup.

Including the owner's job in our calculations shifts the initial average employment size and incorporates an additional measure of job destruction in these metrics—the owner jobs lost by exiting firms. In the first year after startup, almost by definition, the owner's job accounts for most of the total jobs. But by the fifth follow-up year the share drops, as many of these businesses exit. In year 5 the owner's job represents 53 percent of total jobs per startup, and by year 7 the owner's job represents 51 percent of total jobs per startup.

Refocusing job creation from standard measures based on employee counts per startup to add the owner's job results in higher job creation early in the startup process and faster job loss. The high exit rates discussed in detail in chapter 4 account for much of the decline. Table 6.9 also reports counts of surviving owners and shows that these numbers drop quickly over time with the age of the startup. Thus, even with this alternative view of job creation and average employment size, we continue to find relatively low levels of total job creation per startup.

Conclusions

In this chapter, we examine the definitions used to create our measures of job creation and survival. In particular, we explore what types of startup activities should be included or excluded to capture a more commonly used idea of an entrepreneur. The goal is to answer the three fundamental questions about entrepreneurship, job creation, and survival: (1) How many jobs are created by the average entrepreneur? (2) Do these jobs last over time? And (3) How many entrepreneurial firms survive each year after startup? But defining entrepreneurship is difficult and requires assumptions about which startups to include and which ones not to include.

Using the broadest definition possible (or a lower bound measure), we find that the average entrepreneur creates 0.74 jobs at startup and employs 0.63 workers five years later and 0.57 workers seven years later on net and after discounting jobs lost to exits (that is, not conditioning on continuers). We also find that survival rates are extremely low among the universe of startups, with a large shakeout occurring in the years immediately after startup. After one year, only 59 percent of startups survive, and after two years only 47 percent survive. The decline in survival rates starts to taper off, and after five years the survival rate is 33 percent.

But does this all-inclusive definition of entrepreneurship explain why both job creation and survival rates are so low? Because of concerns over including all nonemployer business entities, we also experiment with more restrictive definitions. To create an upper bound measure, we turn to examining different classifications of business startups. We first examine nonemployer versus employer startups and find that nonemployer startups make substantial contributions to job creation: an average of nearly 319,000 jobs seven years after startup, representing one-seventh of the total 2.3 million jobs created by all startups. Instead of excluding all nonemployer startups, we propose an alternative definition of entrepreneurship that might serve as a reasonable upper bound on job creation per entrepreneur and survival rates. We include all nonemployer startups that are incorporated, S corporations, partnerships, or sole proprietorships with EINs, but exclude sole proprietorships without EINs at startup. In each of these cases there is a much stronger business registration requirement than for sole proprietorships without EINs. Consultants and contract workers often show up as sole proprietorships without EINs. The use of this approach unfortunately results in the loss from our calculations of some growth-oriented sole proprietorships that eventually hire employees.

Based on this finding, we define a selective group of startups that excludes sole-proprietor-without-EIN startups. We find that the average entrepreneur creates 2.56 jobs in the first year after startup and 2.15 jobs five years later, after discounting jobs lost to exits. Although job creation is higher among this selective group of startups, survival rates remain low, with 64 percent surviving after two years and 45 percent surviving after five years. We view these levels of job creation per entrepreneur and survival rates as upper bounds.

Applying these lower and upper bound measures yields a picture of the US entrepreneur as one who creates relatively few jobs and experiences high exit rates on average. Survivors, however, contribute a significant number of jobs. This is in contrast to official statistics, which indicate that the average number of employees per new employer firm is roughly six, and that roughly 50 percent of all new employer establishments survive five years or longer.[14] Our statistics recognize that many business owners might choose to start a nonemployer business (often a sole proprietorship) because it offers low risk and yet provides the entrepreneur an opportunity to test her business idea before committing to a more formal business registration.[15] Our lower bound measure captures these startups, whereas our upper bound measure excludes them but captures most of the nonemployer startups that, as a group, create 319,000 jobs seven years after startup for the US economy. There is no right or wrong answer to the question of whether to include these startups; it depends on the goal of the analysis.[16]

The statistics we provide in this chapter summarize job creation by new businesses in the simplest way possible: the average number of jobs created by the average startup. However, it is well known and important to recognize that simple averages hide important heterogeneity and underlying job creation and destruction dynamics. Some businesses, most, do not grow at all, while many grow substantially and contribute a large share of all jobs. Exploring the heterogeneity of survivors with our Comprehensive Startup Panel in detail remains an area of further study.

Statistics that include the owner of the startup in job creation calculations provide yet another view, one that recognizes the importance of businesses as sources of jobs for the owners. The standard measure used for job creation is to count the number of employees per startup, which often ignores the owner's job. But at least in some cases the creation and potential loss of the business owner's job should also be considered in the economic welfare calculus for entrepreneurship policies that have a stated goal of creating self-employment jobs. Many nonemployer owners have no intention of hiring employees and seek only to create a job for themselves. Their goal is primarily to make a living or to supplement income through a self-employed business activity. Adding owners to the job creation numbers does not change the overall conclusion. Although in the first year after startup, total jobs per startup are as high as 1.33, the number drops to 0.97 in year 5. By year 7 the total jobs per startup, including the owner's job, of 0.86 has converged substantially toward the 0.57 number of employees per startup in that same follow-up year. Ownership jobs typically do not last very long because of high exit rates among startups.

7 Who Owns Startups?

Thus far we have painted a picture of how job creation and survival evolve in the first several years for startups, but we have not investigated who owns these startups. Are startups owned by a diverse group of people? Or are startups concentrated in the hands of a few? For example, do Blacks own a proportionate number of startups relative to their numbers in the labor force? Do women own more or fewer startups than men? Do only young entrepreneurs launch startups? Do entrepreneurs tend to be highly educated, or do they have education levels comparable to others'? These types of questions are important for addressing the larger issue of inequality. This chapter explores several related questions of who constitute the actual owners of these startups and how they differ by race, gender, and education.

Surprisingly, it is difficult to find nationally representative data providing information on the owners of startups. For this task, we use microdata from the Census Bureau's Survey of Business Owners (SBO), which is unusual in that it captures detailed information on the characteristics of owners, as well as the characteristics of the businesses. The SBO's sample is drawn from the underlying Business Register, which is the source for our new Comprehensive Startup Panel data set. The SBO data include nonemployer startups as well, but the SBO differs from our Comprehensive Startup Panel data set in three important ways. First, it includes detailed demographic information on each of the primary owners, such as age, gender, race, ethnicity, foreign-born status, veteran status, and education, whereas our Comprehensive Startup Panel data set does not contain this information. Second, it is a sample of businesses of all ages instead of only startups; similar to the Comprehensive Startup Panel, it excludes certain industries (e.g., parts of agriculture), but dissimilar to the Comprehensive Startup Panel, businesses must report receipts of $1,000 or more to be included.[1] Third, the SBO captures a cross section or point-in-time measure of existing businesses instead of a panel data set that follows businesses over time.

With the focus on startups, we select new businesses started in the year prior to when the SBO survey was conducted. Using these publicly available microdata, we can thus examine the demographic characteristics of the owners of the startups. We also explore other business information, such as the level of financial capital used to start the business and the number of employees hired in the startup year.

The goal of this exercise is threefold. First, we start by providing a detailed analysis of who starts businesses in the United States, exploring major demographic patterns and comparing them to the characteristics of both older, surviving businesses and the broader US labor force. The comparison to the US labor force, in particular, sheds light on the disproportionate ownership of startups by different groups of the population. Second, we examine levels and sources of financial capital used at startup because of the importance of capital in the early stages of business formation. Third, we examine how job creation differs by the race and ethnicity of entrepreneurs. Finally, we combine these three separate analyses to identify potential barriers to success faced by minority owners of startups. We focus on constraints imposed by limited access to financial capital and disparities in human capital among startups owned by underrepresented minority groups.

Exploring the intersection between race and barriers to startup success is especially pertinent to understanding economic inequities. An important link exists between racial inequality in business outcomes and broader racial inequality. Research on earnings inequality almost exclusively focuses on the wage and salary sector and ignores the other major form of making a living—owning a business. Roughly 10 percent of people in the workforce own a business and receive their income from this business rather than earn income from a wage or salary job. These owners hold a disproportionate amount of total wealth while potentially creating jobs for others. Another concern is the loss in economic efficiency resulting from unrealized opportunities for minorities to start and grow businesses. If minority entrepreneurs face liquidity constraints, discrimination, or other barriers to creating new business or expanding current businesses, these barriers will translate into efficiency losses in the economy. These barriers to entry and expansion are potentially costly to productivity and local job creation, especially as minorities represent a growing share of the population. Given these concerns, we explore some potential barriers to success among startups owned by different racial and ethnic groups.

Previous studies have identified disparities in wealth, access to financial capital, human capital, family business background, social capital, lending practices, and other factors as limiting minority business creation and success.[2] But information on levels of startup capital, and especially sources of startup capital, is difficult to find. Access to adequate levels of startup capital is clearly important for the successful launch of a business. Imagine, for example, a new restaurant that does not have enough startup capital to hire employees and rent space and equipment for at least a few months. That restaurant is unlikely to succeed. A retail store cannot sell goods until it has some in stock and rents a storefront.

In this chapter, we provide rare evidence on racial and ethnic differences in levels of financial capital used by startups and the sources of this capital. Much of the previous evidence focuses on constraints particular to Black entrepreneurs, with fewer studies focusing on constraints faced by Latinx entrepreneurs, and even fewer studies focusing on Asian entrepreneurs. We use the same data and analysis to examine constraints faced by Blacks and Latinxs and assess whether they mirror possible advantages experienced by Asians in business ownership and outcomes. Finally, information on Native American entrepreneurs is extremely difficult to find but is also examined here. Our analysis across all five major racial and ethnic groups in the United States—White, Black, Latinx, Asian, and Native American—sheds new light on our understanding of financial barriers to successful business ownership.

New Firms in the Survey of Business Owners

Chapter 2 first presented data from the published SBO 2007 showing the age distribution of businesses. We repeat this information in figure 7.1. Slightly more than 10 percent of businesses are less than a year old. Over time, the share of firms within each age category drops as firms exit. The share of firms that are one year old drops to 7 percent. By the fourth year, the share of firms drops to 4 percent, a decline of almost 60 percent. Averaging by the number of age years within each category, we find that each age-in-years in the age five to seven years group captures slightly less than

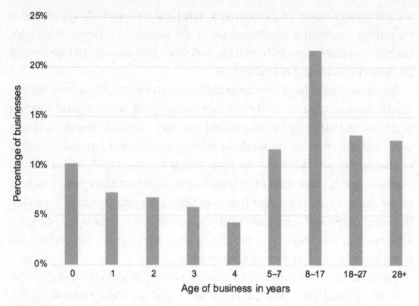

Figure 7.1
Age distribution of businesses. *Source*: Survey of Business Owners, 2007 (US Census Bureau 2013).

4 percent of the total, and each age-in-years in the age eight to seventeen years group captures 2 percent of the total. Declining percentages in each business category reflect the high exit rates for younger firms.

The SBO data capture only a snapshot in time of existing businesses. Many of the firms that existed in the years just prior to the survey no longer existed by the time the survey was conducted. The cross-sectional data do not allow for comparison of different startup cohorts over time since they capture only a percentage of the survivors to that point in time. Our Comprehensive Startup Panel data do not have this problem because they follow cohorts of businesses over time (i.e., panel data). In the SBO, only the businesses that survive to a given age make it into the survey. The older the business is the more selection it has undergone. Put differently, bad businesses exit early on while good businesses survive. As a result, comparisons made between new businesses and older businesses suffer from this form of inherent survivor bias.

Despite these concerns, we can still use SBO microdata to examine the characteristics of startups by identifying those firms that were established in the calendar year prior to the survey date, minimizing survivorship bias.

The survey was conducted after the end of calendar year 2007 and asks about businesses existing in 2007. A minimal level of survival bias might remain, however, because the survey was conducted after the end of the calendar year, and some owners of businesses that exited quickly might not be reachable for the survey.[3] Thus the group of respondent businesses are only an approximation to the startup cohort of 2007.

As already stated, the major advantage of the SBO microdata is that they capture detailed owner and business information, which allows us to examine patterns of ownership by race, gender, and education level of the owner, among other things. On the business side, we can examine levels and sources of startup capital. The information contained in the SBO allows an examination of the owners of the startups and what it takes to start a business. That information is not available in the Comprehensive Startup Panel data set that we create and analyzed in previous chapters.

The Survey of Business Owners Microdata

The 2007 SBO represents the first and only public use microdata version of the US Census Bureau's long-running Survey of Business Owners/Characteristics of Business Owners data series. The SBO questionnaire was mailed to a randomized sample of businesses selected from a list of all firms operating during 2007 with receipts of $1,000 or more (except those in crop and animal production, private households, public administration, and several other smaller industries), stratified across nine demographic groups.[4] Important for this chapter, the SBO's sampling is based on the underlying Business Register but separates firms along nine different demographic frames (seven frames classified by race/ethnicity, one frame for gender, and one frame for public ownership status). The underlying universe for the SBO sample was compiled from a combination of business tax returns and data collected on other economic census reports. For new businesses covered in the SBO, these came from the same universe of startups that we compiled and analyzed in previous chapters. The 2007 SBO for the startup cohort is essentially randomly selected and intended to be a nationally representative sample of the universe of startups in 2007. Information in the data set is collected from both administrative sources and survey questions.

The public use SBO microdata that we use differ from published estimates from the SBO in two major ways. First, the SBO microdata do not include publicly owned businesses. Many publicly owned firms are easily identifiable, and owner information on these businesses is difficult to obtain. These firms account for a significant share of employment in the economy, but there are relatively few of them. Second, the SBO microdata exclude businesses that are not classifiable by gender, ethnicity, race, or veteran status. One of the main goals of the SBO microdata is to make possible analyses of patterns among these demographic groups. Thus startups from the 2007 SBO microdata are intended to be a nationally representative sample of the universe of startups, excluding publicly owned startups and others that are not classifiable by gender, ethnicity, race, or veteran status.

Examining total business and employment counts for all businesses in the SBO microdata compared to the SBO published data, we find 26.4 million businesses hiring 59.3 million employees in the SBO microdata and 27.1 million businesses hiring 117.3 million employees in the published SBO. The data show roughly 800,000 unclassifiable businesses, hiring 60.7 million employees, that are not included in the public use SBO microdata that we use below. Identifying the gender and race of owners of publicly held businesses would be daunting and would also create problems with issues such as who has ownership control. More important, our focus is on describing startups and young firms, which are less affected by these issues.

The SBO contains information on business and owner characteristics for up to four owners of the business. The information on owner characteristics is very detailed and includes information on the race, ethnicity, gender, age, education level, and foreign-born status of the owner(s). The information on the business characteristics is also very detailed and includes information on the year of founding, employment, receipts, startup capital sources, and startup capital levels. For a large, nationally representative Census Bureau data set, the SBO microdata are unique in providing this level of detail on both business and owner characteristics in the same data set. Most business-level data sets (e.g., the Longitudinal Business Database [LBD]) have information only on the characteristics of the business, and most household-level data sets (e.g., the American Community Survey [ACS] and the Current Population Survey [CPS]) primarily have information on the characteristics of the business owners. The long-term goal of the Comprehensive Startup Panel data set is to match these longitudinal data to other data sets that have detailed information on various owner characteristics. We discuss a few possibilities in the next chapter.

Demographic Characteristics of New Firms

We explore some of the key demographic characteristics of the owners of startups. The SBO contains information on up to four owners of a business, including the percentage of their ownership. For businesses with multiple owners, we attribute demographic characteristics based on their percent ownership of the business. For example, if a business has two owners with equal ownership, one female and one male, we define this business as being 0.5 female owned and 0.5 male owned. If instead the business is 75 percent owned by the female partner and 25 percent owned by the male partner, we define this business as 0.75 female owned and 0.25 male owned in our tabulations. Similarly, a business with three female owners and one male owner, all four of whom equally own the business, is defined as 0.75 female owned and 0.25 male owned. In this way ownership shares implicitly "average" out different ownership characteristics of businesses, and the unit of analysis is a business.

The majority of startups are owned by men. Figure 7.2 displays the percentage ownership of startups by gender.[5] Thirty-nine percent of the ownership of startups is female and 61 percent is male.

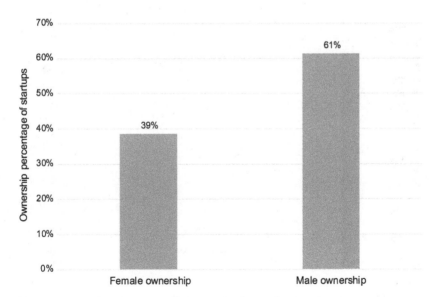

Figure 7.2
Ownership of startups by gender. *Source*: Authors' calculations from Survey of Business Owners Microdata, 2007 (US Census Bureau 2013).

There are also strong racial and ethnic patterns in ownership of start-ups. Figure 7.3 displays ownership by race and ethnicity. The categories do not add up to 100 percent because owners can report more than one race, and Latinx ethnicity is a separate question from race (although we separate White race from Latinx ethnicity). Blacks own 7 percent of all startups in the United States. Ten percent of startups are owned by Latinxs and 7 percent are owned by Asians. American Indian/Alaska Natives (Native Americans) own 1.0 percent of startups in the country. Non-Latinx White ownership accounts for 78 percent of startups. We discuss how these ownership patterns reflect patterns of ownership for older surviving businesses and the distribution of the US labor force to provide evidence on disparities by race and ethnicity in the next subsection.

We examine additional characteristics of owners of startups. Military veterans own 12 percent of startups. Foreign-born persons own 14 percent of startups. A graph of the age of owners of startups has an inverted U shape: ownership increases with age at first but then decreases with age. Figure 7.4 displays ownership of startups by age group. Ownership of startups is highest among those aged forty-five to fifty-four years, at 29 percent.[6]

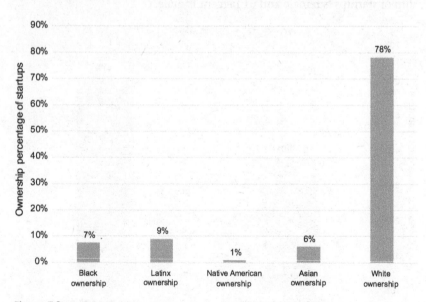

Figure 7.3
Ownership of startups by race/ethnicity. *Source*: Authors' calculations from Survey of Business Owners Microdata, 2007 (US Census Bureau 2013).

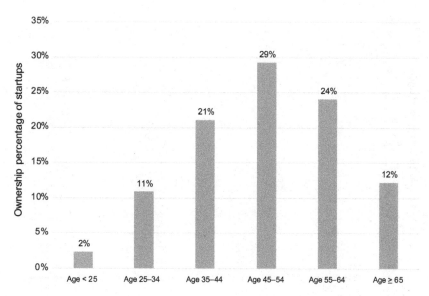

Figure 7.4

Ownership of startups by age class. *Source*: Authors' calculations from Survey of Business Owners Microdata, 2007 (US Census Bureau 2013).

Ownership of startups is skewed toward more educated individuals.[7] Figure 7.5 displays ownership of startups by major education level. Forty-four percent of startup ownership is among college-educated individuals. This contrasts with only a 6 percent ownership among high school dropouts and a 20 percent ownership among high school graduates with no additional education. Educational categories are defined as the individual's highest degree attained. Individuals classified as having "Some College" are recipients of associate's degrees, technical school degrees, and other college degrees that are less than a bachelor's degree, and they account for a substantial 30 percent ownership of all startups in the United States.

Comparisons to Surviving Older Firms

Using the SBO microdata, we can compare these characteristics of owners of startups to the owner characteristics of older, surviving businesses. The comparison captures two patterns. First, it captures how owner characteristics are related to the survival of startups. For example, if startups have a

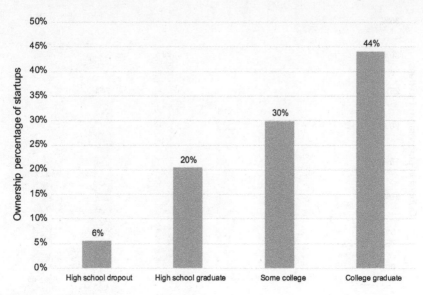

Figure 7.5
Ownership of startups by education. *Source*: Authors' calculations from Survey of Business Owners Microdata, 2007 (US Census Bureau 2013).

higher Latinx ownership percentage than older, surviving businesses, that might imply that Latinx-owned startups have lower survival rates. Second, it captures differences in the demographic composition of different cohorts of startups. If the number of Latinx-owned startups increases over time with each startup cohort, that will show up as a lower percentage of Latinx ownership among older, surviving businesses. Thus the changing composition of startups among surviving older firms might reflect either differential survival rates across demographic groups or the changing demographic composition of startup cohorts over time. Panel data are needed to separate these two explanations.[8]

The SBO microdata provide only one cross-sectional snapshot, and older firms may have changed ownership over time. As a consequence, owners in the latter years of a business are not necessarily the same as the founders of the business. Business ownership shares may get bought and sold over the life of the business. This requires us to exercise some caution in interpreting the results for these businesses. Business owners might differ in their propensity to sell their businesses over time, and this might affect the observed ownership numbers across racial categories. Even with all of these concerns about using cross-sectional data, the comparison of startups to older, surviving businesses is useful and interesting. With this caveat in mind, we present some comparisons.

Table 7.1 reports ownership shares by three types of businesses: (1) startups, (2) surviving businesses aged one to seven years, and (3) surviving businesses aged eight years and older. A couple of interesting patterns emerge from the findings. We start by looking at gender. Female ownership of businesses drops from 39 percent of startups to 34 percent of surviving businesses aged eight years and older. The finding may reflect either lower survival rates among female-owned businesses, fewer female startups in previous cohorts (i.e., cohorts started eight or more years earlier), or both.

Table 7.1

Ownership characteristics of startups versus older, surviving businesses

Ownership	Startups	Surviving businesses (%)	
		Aged 1–7 years	Aged 8+ years
Female ownership	39	40	34
Male ownership	61	60	66
Black ownership	7	5	3
Latinx ownership	9	8	4
Native American ownership	1.0	0.9	0.7
Asian ownership	6	7	4
White (non-Latinx) ownership	78	81	89
Veteran ownership	12	10	16
Immigrant ownership	14	17	10
High school dropout	6	5	5
High school graduate	20	19	21
Some college	30	30	29
College graduate	44	46	45
Age < 25	2	3	0
Age 25–34	11	17	3
Age 35–44	21	28	14
Age 45–54	29	28	32
Age 55–64	24	18	32
Age ≥ 65	12	6	19

Source: Authors' calculations from Survey of Business Owners Microdata, 2007 (US Census Bureau 2013).

As noted above, we cannot distinguish between the two explanations without panel data.[9]

Table 7.1 also reports ownership shares by race. Black ownership declines quickly from 7 percent of startups to 5 percent of businesses aged one to seven years, and then to 3 percent of businesses aged eight years and older, which represents a decline of more than 50 percent. Previous research finds low survival rates among Black-owned businesses, which is likely to explain some of these patterns (Fairlie and Robb 2007b, 2008).

Latinx ownership share of businesses also declines from startups to older, surviving businesses. Latinx ownership of startups is 9 percent but drops to only 4 percent among businesses surviving to age eight years or more. The decline in ownership share is consistent with lower survival rates and an increasing population share. Asian ownership drops less than that of the other minority groups: from 6 percent of startups to 4 percent of businesses aged eight years or more. Native American ownership also declines with age of the business. These findings for minority groups indicate that the opposite pattern must hold for non-Latinx White ownership of businesses by age. Indeed, we find that White ownership increases from 78 percent of startups to 81 percent of surviving businesses aged one to seven years, and then to 89 percent of surviving businesses aged eight years and older. Whether this reflects higher survival rates for White-owned businesses, an increasing share of minority-owned businesses in more recent cohorts, or a mix of both is an area for further study.

Examining other demographic patterns of startup ownership relative to patterns of ownership of older, surviving businesses, we find that veteran status drops and then rises with age of the business. Effects from changes in the size of the underlying veteran population that are likely to start a business as a result of military engagements might explain these patterns. Foreign-born ownership increases at first with surviving firm age but then drops. Ownership across education levels remains steady with business age groups (capturing both survival and cohort changes). For all three groups, ownership increases with higher levels of education. Finally, the age composition of the owner increases from startups to older surviving businesses. This is the result of natural aging—a business that is twenty years old, for example, is not very likely to have an owner who is twenty-five years old. However, it likely also reflects higher survival with owner age at time of founding.[10] Overall, startups exhibit a diverse set of ownership patterns across demographic characteristics, and these patterns differ somewhat from the ownership patterns of older, surviving businesses.

Comparison to the Labor Force

Are women and minorities underrepresented in the ownership of startups? The question cannot be answered using the SBO data alone because the data include only business owners. Instead, we need to compare ownership numbers to those in a relevant population. For this purpose, we rely on the Current Population Survey microdata to calculate shares of the labor force represented by women, racial/ethnic groups, and the same set of demographic groups that we examined using the SBO. We focus on the labor force to avoid issues around school enrollment, retirement, leaving the labor force to raise children, and other reasons for not working or not looking for a job. We can then compare, for example, the percentage of startups owned by Blacks to Blacks' share in the labor force to determine whether they are over- or underrepresented in the ownership of startups.

Table 7.2 reports the percentage ownership of startups and the percentages of the labor force by gender, race/ethnicity, veteran status, immigrant status, education level, and age group. Women are underrepresented in the ownership of startups when compared to their share of the US labor force: women own 39 percent of startups but constitute 46 percent of the labor force. Blacks are also underrepresented, owning 7 percent of startups but representing 12 percent of the total labor force. Latinxs are also underrepresented, with 9 percent of startup ownership but constituting 14 percent of the labor force. Native Americans are underrepresented and Asians are slightly overrepresented in startup ownership. As expected, given these patterns for minority groups, non-Latinx Whites are overrepresented in startup ownership relative to their share of the labor force.

Examining additional owner characteristics, we find that veterans are overrepresented in startup ownership and immigrants are slightly underrepresented in startup ownership.[11] The patterns by education level make it very clear that there is a strong positive relationship between startup ownership and education. Ownership of startups is clearly overrepresented by higher education groups and underrepresented by lower education groups

Table 7.2
Ownership characteristics of startups versus characteristics of the labor force

Ownership	Startups (%)	Labor force (%)
Female ownership	39	46
Male ownership	61	54
Black ownership	7	12
Latinx ownership	9	14
Native American ownership	1.0	1.5
Asian ownership	6	5
White (non-Latinx) ownership	78	69
Veteran ownership	12	8
Immigrant ownership	14	16
High school dropout	6	10
High school graduate	20	30
Some college	30	29
College graduate	44	31
Age < 25	2	13
Age 25–34	11	22
Age 35–44	21	24
Age 45–54	29	24
Age 55–64	24	14
Age ≥ 65	12	4

Sources: Authors' calculations of startup shares are from the 2007 SBO microdata and labor force shares from the 2007 Current Population Survey microdata.

when compared to the labor force. Finally, the relationship between startup ownership and age of the owner appears to reflect mostly an increasing representation among startups with age of the owner. Starting with the age forty-five to fifty-four years group, ownership of startups is higher than their share in the labor force. For the oldest age group, the overrepresentation of ownership of startups is even larger: ownership of startups by those aged sixty-five or older is 12 percent, compared with their 4 percent share in the labor force. This is consistent with the findings of Azoulay et al. (2020), who also show that startups are not created disproportionately by young people, which is often the impression we get when thinking about high-tech and other innovative startups. Instead, older, more experienced individuals are overrepresented in the ownership of startups across the vast range of different types of businesses that exist in the US economy.

Startup Capital

The SBO microdata provide additional information on startups that is not available in our panel data set covering the universe of startups. Importantly, the SBO includes information on the sources and levels of financial capital used to start businesses. Access to startup capital is an important determinant of business formation (e.g., Evans and Jovanovic 1989; Fairlie and Krashinsky 2012; Parker 2018). Figure 7.6 displays startup capital levels used by startups. Three quarters of startups use very little startup capital (less than $5,000). Another 7 percent of startups use between $5,000 and $10,000 in financial capital. Many businesses in the country are started with only a small level of investment, reflecting the wide range of types of business entities that exist (as noted in previous chapters using the Comprehensive Startup Panel data set). Turning to more substantial levels of capital investment, we find that 7 percent of startups use between $10,000 and $25,000 in startup capital, and 12 percent of startups use $25,000 or more in startup capital.

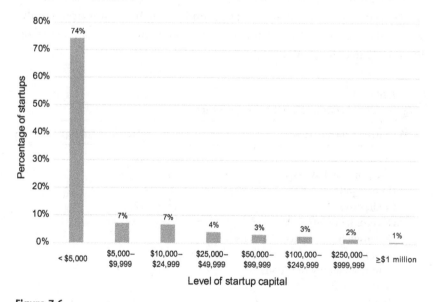

Figure 7.6
Composition of startups by startup capital. *Source*: Authors' calculations from Survey of Business Owners Microdata, 2007 (US Census Bureau 2013).

By far the most common source of this startup capital is the entrepreneur's own personal savings. Table 7.3 reports the composition of startups across sources of startup capital. Among startups, 84 percent report using personal savings for financial capital at business formation. The SBO does not provide information on amounts from each source, so it is possible that the use of personal savings is for relatively small amounts of total capital for some startups. The next most common source of startup capital is a credit card, with 17 percent of entrepreneurs using this source of startup capital. Although credit cards provide easy and fast access to startup capital, they also charge very high interest rates and are primarily valuable only as a short-term credit source. Owners of startups also obtain financial capital by tapping into other personal assets (9 percent) and home equity (7 percent). Overall, it is common for entrepreneurs to use their own resources to provide funding for startups.

Among startups, 7 percent obtain bank loans for startup capital. These loans are likely to be for larger amounts in many cases than the personal resources used by entrepreneurs. Venture capital plays a minor role in the overall funding of startups across the wide range of business entities in the US economy. The other sources of funding, such as loans from family or friends, grants, and government loans, represent very small shares of funding sources used by startups.

Table 7.3
Sources of startup capital among startups

Source of startup capital	Percent of startups
Personal savings	84
Other personal assets	9
Home equity	7
Credit cards	17
Government loan	0.4
Government guaranteed bank loan	0.4
Bank loan	7
Loan from family or friends	2
Venture capital	0.3
Grant	0.3
Other	2

Source: Authors' calculations from Survey of Business Owners Microdata, 2007 (US Census Bureau 2013).

Focusing on Minority-Owned Startups

We turn to a more in-depth exploration of racial disparities in the ownership of startups. Racial inequality is one of the most pressing societal issues.
A major component of economic inequality that has been documented and
studied extensively is earnings inequality by race and ethnicity (Altonji and
Blank 1999). But racial differences in business ownership and income also
contribute to income inequality and in many cases are larger (Fairlie and
Robb 2008). Although these disparities have received much less atten-
tion in the literature, they are alarming because of their magnitude and
the importance of business ownership as a way to make a living. Roughly
one out of ten workers in the United States is a self-employed business
owner. These business owners, however, hold roughly 40 percent of total
US wealth (Bucks, Kennickell, and Moore 2006).

Policymakers have been concerned for many years about improving
the success of minority-owned businesses and reducing disparities. In
the United States, for example, a variety of federal, state, and local government programs offer contracting goals, price discounts, and loans to
businesses owned by minorities, women, and other disadvantaged groups
(Boston 1999a; Chatterji, Chay and Fairlie 2014; Joint Center for Political and Economic Studies 1994). One of the goals of these programs is to
foster successful minority business development, which may have implications for reducing earnings and wealth inequality (Bradford 2003, 2014;
Kroeger and Wright 2021). Disadvantaged business owners have more
upward income mobility and experience faster earnings growth than disadvantaged wage and salary workers (Fairlie 2004; Holtz-Eakin, Rosen,
and Weathers 2000).[12]

Another concern is the loss in economic efficiency resulting from unrealized opportunities for minorities to start and grow businesses.[13] Business
formation is associated with the creation of new industries, innovation,
job creation, improvement in sector productivity, and economic growth
(Reynolds 2005). If minority entrepreneurs face liquidity constraints, discrimination, or other barriers to creating new business or expanding current businesses, there will be efficiency losses in the economy. Although it
would be difficult to determine the value of these losses, barriers to entry
and expansion that minority-owned businesses face are potentially costly
to productivity, especially as minorities represent a growing share of the

population in many industrialized countries. Barriers to business growth may be especially damaging for job creation in low-income neighborhoods (Boston 1999b, 2006; Stoll, Holzer, and Raphael 2001).

Thus it is concerning that our analysis indicates that Blacks, Latinxs, and Native Americans are underrepresented in startup ownership relative to their representation in the labor force. In this section, we explore racial and ethnic differences in startup characteristics. We first examine racial patterns in startup capital use. Access to financial capital among businesses at startup and for growth is important (see, e.g., Adelino, Schoar, and Severino 2015; Evans and Jovanovic 1989; Fairlie and Krashinsky 2012; Fairlie and Robb 2007b, 2008; Parker 2018).[14]

Figure 7.7 reports startup capital levels by the race/ethnicity of the owner. Only levels above $5,000 are displayed in the figure to highlight racial disparities in higher levels of startup capital. Black startups have lower levels of startup capital than non-Latinx White startups. Seven percent of Black startups have $25,000 or more, compared with 12 percent of

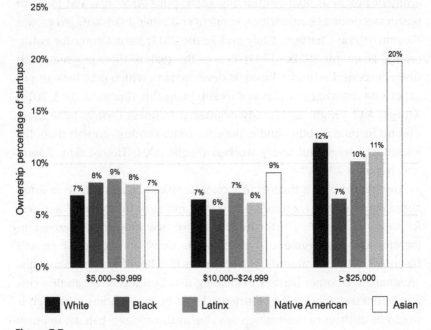

Figure 7.7
Ownership of startups by startup capital and race/ethnicity. *Source*: Authors' calculations from Survey of Business Owners Microdata, 2007 (US Census Bureau 2013).

White startups. Among Latinx startups 10 percent have more than $25,000 in startup capital. Native American startups have slightly more, with 11 percent at the $25,000 or more level. Asian American startups have the highest levels of startup capital: among Asian American startups 20 percent have $25,000 or more in startup capital.

Table 7.4 reports sources of startup capital by race and ethnicity of the owner. The distributions of sources of startup capital do not vary substantially across ownership by major racial and ethnic groups. A very large percentage from each ownership group rely on personal savings and assets to fund at least part of their startups. For all groups, the second most commonly used source of startup capital is credit cards. Home equity lines are also used by startup owners to fund their new businesses. Use of bank loans is relatively low but differs somewhat by race and ethnicity. Black- and Latinx-owned startups are less likely to use bank loans than White-owned startups.

Using the Kauffman Firm Survey (KFS), which captures a higher percentage of employer startups and growth-oriented startups, Fairlie, Robb, and Robinson (2022) find large disparities by race in average amount of capital used at startup. Their estimates indicate that the mean level of total financial capital among Black-owned startups is $35,200, compared with $106,700 among White-owned startups. The largest contribution to this total for Black-owned startups is from owner's equity, which is an average of $19,600. White-owned startups have an average of $34,400 of initial capital from owner's equity. One area of substantial disparity is outside debt, including bank loans. They find that Black-owned startups have an average of $10,800 compared with an average of $56,700 among White-owned startups.

Table 7.4
Sources of startup capital among startups by race/ethnicity of owner (%)

Source of startup capital	White	Black	Latinx	Native American	Asian
Personal savings and assets	94	92	90	94	92
Home equity	6	6	7	5	9
Credit cards	18	16	18	20	15
Bank loans	8	5	5	7	7
All other	6	7	6	6	8

Source: Authors' calculations from Survey of Business Owners Microdata, 2007 (US Census Bureau 2013).

The disparities in startup capital levels partly reflect broader racial inequality in wealth. The latest Census Bureau data indicate that the median level of wealth is $9,567 among Black families and $25,000 among Latinx families, compared with $171,700 among non-Latinx White families (US Census Bureau 2017). Personal wealth not only provides capital to directly invest in startups but also serves as collateral for obtaining bank loans and home equity lines of credit. Although we cannot link personal wealth to startup capital use in the data it is likely that they are correlated with each other. The reliance on the entrepreneur's personal savings and assets, credit cards, and home equity lines of credit provides evidence consistent with this link.

Education

The education level of the owner is also a strong predictor of business success, and low levels of education pose a limitation for minority business success (Fairlie and Robb 2007a; Moutray 2007; Parker 2018; van der Sluis, van Praag, and Vijverberg 2005) Racial and ethnic differences in the education levels of owners are large. Figure 7.8 displays education levels by race/ethnicity of the startup owner. Focusing on college graduates, 44 percent of White startup owners have this level of education. The education levels of minority-owned startups are much lower except for Asian startups. Among Black startups, 31 percent of owners have a college degree or higher. Among Latinx startups, 25 percent of owners have a college degree, and among Native American startups, 27 percent have a college degree. In contrast to these patterns, more than half of Asian startup owners have a college degree, a higher figure than for White startup owners.

If we turn now to the lowest level of education—less than a high school degree—the disparities in educational attainment are also very clear. Among Latinx startup owners, 21 percent have less than a high school degree, which is a substantially higher percentage than for Whites (5 percent). Ten percent of Black startup owners and 10 percent of Asian startup owners have less than a high school degree. The Native American startup ownership percent with less than a high school degree is 12 percent.

Initial Employer Status and Job Creation at startup

We can examine whether there are racial differences in employer versus nonemployer status at startup. The SBO microdata contain a measure of

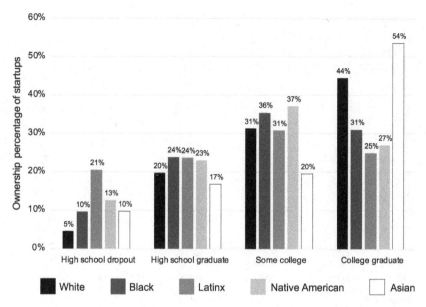

Figure 7.8
Ownership of startups by education level and race/ethnicity. *Source*: Authors' calculations from Survey of Business Owners Microdata, 2007 (US Census Bureau 2013).

whether the business employed someone anytime during the calendar year. The measure is clearly not perfect for startups because some might have started at the beginning of the year while others might have started halfway through the year. If a startup started halfway through the year, then it will have a lower probability, all else equal, of having any employees than a startup that started at the beginning of the year. Nevertheless, the information is useful for identifying racial disparities in this proxy for growth potential and commitment by startups. As shown in chapter 5, employer startups have a much stronger upward trajectory in terms of hiring employees than nonemployer startups.

Figure 7.9 displays the percentage of employer (versus nonemployer) startups by racial/ethnic ownership. The disparities are large. Among White owners, 7 percent of startups are employer startups. In contrast, only 3 percent of Black startups are employer startups. Latinxs also have relatively low percentages of employer versus nonemployer startups at 5 percent. Among Native American startups, 5 percent are employer startups, and Asian startups have the highest percentage of employer startups at 12 percent.

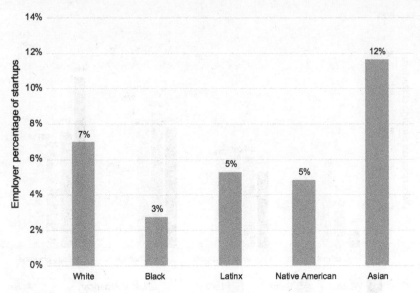

Figure 7.9
Percentage employer versus nonemployer startup by racial/ethnic ownership. *Source*:
Authors' calculations from Survey of Business Owners Microdata, 2007 (US Census
Bureau 2013).

We can also examine the number of employees per startup in the first
year. One issue, however, is that the number of employees is measured as
of March 12. The measure will undercount the total number of employees
by missing jobs created after March 12 by existing startups and all jobs created by new businesses that started after March 12.[15] But the measure does
offer a comparison of very early-stage job creation across racial and ethnic groups that might shed light on longer-term disparities in growth and
employment. Inequality by race in early-stage job creation is even larger
when we switch to comparing the number of employees per startup. Figure 7.10 displays the number of employees per startup in the initial year
by race and ethnicity. Black startups hire 0.06 employees on average compared with 0.19 employees per non-Latinx White startup. Latinx startups
also have relatively low employment levels at 0.12 employees per startup,
and Native American startups have even lower employment levels at 0.08
employees per startup. On the other hand, Asian startups have the highest
employee per startup levels at 0.28 employees per startup.

In earlier chapters, we estimate multivariate regression models to control for confounding factors to isolate the independent effects of follow-up

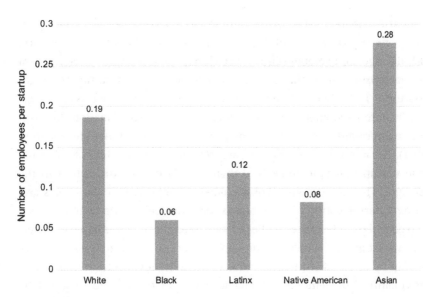

Figure 7.10
Early measure of number of employees per startup by racial/ethnic ownership.
Source: Authors' calculations from Survey of Business Owners Microdata, 2007 (US Census Bureau 2013).

year and industry on job creation levels per startup. In the regressions, we control for geographic areas, which removes the effects of regional variation in business policies or local economies, and for differences in job creation across startup cohorts, which removes macroeconomic trends. We use multivariate regression analysis here to also control for potentially confounding factors, but we can push the analysis even further to examine what might explain racial disparities in job creation among startups. We can explore, for example, whether Black startups are less likely to create jobs in the first year because of differences in industry concentrations, locations across states in the country, owner's education, or startup capital. Or we might find that all these factors contribute to racial disparities in startup employment levels.

We first estimate a series of multivariate regressions in which we use an employer indicator as the dependent variable. We estimate the following equation:

$$Y_i = \alpha + \sum_{d=1}^{D} \delta^d D_i^d + \sum_{c=1}^{C} \delta^c D_i^c + \sum_{k=1}^{19} \beta^k I_i^k + \lambda_g + u_i \qquad (7.1)$$

where Y_i equals 1 if startup I has employees in the startup year (and equals 0 otherwise), D_i^d is a set of demographic characteristics that includes race, gender, age, and veteran status for startup I, D_i^c is a set of owner and firm characteristics that includes owner's education level and startup capital for startup I, I_i^k is a set of dummy variables for major industry classifications, λ_g is state fixed effects, and u_i is the error term. The equation differs in three important ways from the earlier regressions represented by equation (3.1). Because only one year of data is available in the SBO (2007), only the startup year is included and there is only one startup cohort in the sample. The earlier regressions included subsequent follow-up years and several startup cohorts. The public use data also necessitate switching from zip code fixed effects used earlier to state fixed effects. The main parameters of interest are δ^d, which capture job creation in the startup year for ownership by race and ethnicity relative to the left-out classification of White, non-Latinx. All demographic characteristics of owners are weighted by their ownership percentage of the business when there are multiple owners.

Table 7.5 reports a series of multivariate regressions with different sets of controls. Specification 1 is the base model, which includes only the race/ethnicity variables. The left-out race/ethnicity is non-Latinx White. The coefficients capture disparities between groups (as seen in figure 7.9). Black startups are 4.2 percentage points less likely than White startups to be employers in the first year. Latinx startups are also less likely to hire employees in the first year (–1.5 percentage points). Native American startups also have a lower probability of hiring employees in the initial year (–1.9 percentage points). All these disparities are large—the base rate of hiring employees in the startup year is 6.9 percentage points. Asian-owned startups have much higher rates of hiring employees in the first year than White-owned startups: Asian-owned startups are 4.9 percentage points more likely to hire employees.

One method of exploring how these disparities in startup employment rates across race are related to other characteristics of owners is to sequentially add controls to the regressions. The remaining columns reported in table 7.5 do just this. Specification 2 adds controls for gender, age, veteran status, states, and major industry classifications.[16] The addition of these controls exacerbates somewhat the disparities for Latinx and Native American startups. The interpretation is that once we control for composition effects (e.g., Latinx businesses might disproportionately operate

Table 7.5
Regressions for the probability of employer startup (versus nonemployer startup)

Explanatory variables	(1)	(2)	(3)	(4)
Black ownership	−0.04180 (0.00307)	−0.03894 (0.00303)	−0.03577 (0.00303)	−0.02707 (0.00290)
Latinx ownership	−0.01533 (0.00262)	−0.01875 (0.00266)	−0.01194 (0.00269)	−0.00947 (0.00257)
Native American ownership	−0.01919 (0.00778)	−0.02103 (0.00753)	−0.01787 (0.00752)	−0.01733 (0.00719)
Asian ownership	0.04860 (0.00298)	0.03231 (0.00301)	0.03222 (0.00301)	0.01539 (0.00288)
High school drop out			−0.02695 (0.00392)	−0.01882 (0.00375)
Some college			0.00323 (0.00255)	0.00145 (0.00244)
College graduate			0.03233 (0.00252)	0.02169 (0.00241)
Startup capital: $5,000–$9,999				0.04984 (0.00281)
Startup capital: $10,000–$24,999				0.09024 (0.00292)
Startup capital: $25,000–$49,999				0.13337 (0.00371)
Startup capital: $50,000 and over				0.27127 (0.00279)
Gender, age, and veteran status of owner	No	Yes	Yes	Yes
State controls	No	Yes	Yes	Yes
Industry controls	No	Yes	Yes	Yes
Mean of dependent variable	0.069	0.069	0.069	0.069
Sample size	112,357	112,357	112,357	112,357

Notes: The sample consists of new businesses in the SBO 2007 microdata. The dependent variable equals 1 if the startup has employees in 2007 and equals 0 if no employees. *Source*: Authors' calculations from Survey of Business Owners Microdata, 2007 (US Census Bureau 2013).

in industries or states with high shares of nonemployer businesses), the disparities are even larger. The effect moves substantially in the opposite direction for Asian businesses which tend to enter industries with a disproportionate number of employer businesses. Specification 3 also controls for education. As shown above, Black, Latinx, and Native American startup owners tend to have lower levels of education than White startup owners, and Asian startup owners tend to have higher levels of education. Owner's education is a strong predictor of having employees in the startup year. The addition of education variables to this specification changes the disparities across groups, with the Latinx and Native American variables becoming smaller in absolute value. After controlling for education and other characteristics, Latinx-owned startups are roughly one percentage point less likely to be employer startups than are White-owned startups. The finding of a smaller coefficient in absolute value after controlling for education implies that lower levels of education among Latinx startup owners partly explains why Latinx startups are less likely to hire employees in the initial year.

Specification 4 adds startup capital. Some caution is warranted when exploring the relationship between this measure of startup capital and employment (Fairlie and Robb 2008). The problem is that potentially successful business ventures or ones that need to hire employees at startup are likely to generate more startup capital than business ventures that are viewed as being potentially less successful or that have less need for startup capital. Thus we cannot determine with certainty that lower levels of startup capital are primarily driven by constraints in obtaining financing, which would suggest that the main direction of causation is from these measured startup capital levels to employment in the startup year.[17] We view the coefficients in the regression as providing evidence on the association between startup capital levels and early-stage employment by startups without necessarily implying a direction of causation. We find, as expected, that each higher level of startup capital is strongly associated with a higher probability of hiring employees at startup. For example, increasing from $0–$4,999 of startup capital to $5,000–$9,999 of startup capital is associated with an increase of 5.0 percentage points in the likelihood of being an employer startup versus a nonemployer startup.

The addition of startup capital controls has a notable effect on the Black startup coefficient, suggesting that lower levels of startup capital among Black startup owners contribute to lower levels of employment at startup.

Black-owned startups may be undercapitalized, leading to longer-term growth problems. Controlling for startup capital also results in a smaller (in absolute value) Asian startup coefficient, implying that Asian startup capital levels are initially higher. As shown in figure 7.7, Asian startups indeed tend to have higher levels of startup capital than White startups. Controlling for these higher levels of startup capital thus reduces the employment probability among Asian startups relative to White startups. Interestingly, Latinx startups and Native American startups are not affected strongly by controlling for startup capital.

We next explore our second measure of employment in the startup year: the number of employees per startup. Table 7.6 reports the same set of multivariate regressions as table 7.5, but now the dependent variable is the number of employees hired by the startup. Specification 1 is the base model, which includes only the race/ethnicity variables. The disparities between groups reflect those displayed in figure 7.10. As before, adding the main controls in specification 2, such as geographic differences (i.e., states) and industry differences, increases the estimated disparities for Latinx- and Native American–owned businesses and reduces them significantly for Asian-owned startups. Asian-owned startups hire 0.10 more employees at startup than White-owned startups, but after controlling for the main controls, the difference disappears.

Specification 3 adds education to the regression for the number of employees per startup. The owner's education level is a strong predictor of the number of employees at startup. College graduate owners hire 0.17 more employees per startup than high school graduate owners, for example. Controlling for differences in education levels explains part of differences in the number of employees per startup across racial and ethnic groups. The number of employees at startup decreases in absolute value for Latinx-, Black-, and Native American–owned startups, partly owing to lower levels of owner's education.

Turning to specification 4, we find that startup capital is strongly associated with the number of employees per startup. Moving from less than $5,000 in startup capital to $5,000–$9,999 in startup capital is associated with an increase of 0.05 employees per startup. Controlling for differences in startup capital also alters the coefficients on race and ethnicity. Number of employees per startup level at Black startups increases after controlling for startup capital, which is consistent with Black-owned startups being

Table 7.6
Regressions for the number of employees at startup

Explanatory variables	(1)	(2)	(3)	(4)
Black ownership	–0.12234	–0.11979	–0.10566	–0.08068
	(0.08195)	(0.08398)	(0.08410)	(0.08411)
Latinx ownership	–0.06208	–0.08657	–0.05818	–0.04606
	(0.07001)	(0.07365)	(0.07463)	(0.07460)
Native American ownership	–0.09523	–0.10803	–0.09431	–0.08956
	(0.20762)	(0.20868)	(0.20872)	(0.20860)
Asian ownership	0.09616	0.00070	–0.00031	–0.05156
	(0.07967)	(0.08329)	(0.08345)	(0.08355)
High school dropout			–0.07384	–0.05117
			(0.10891)	(0.10887)
Some college			0.04268	0.04481
			(0.00255)	(0.07080)
College graduate			0.16828	0.13791
			(0.06985)	(0.06994)
Startup capital: $5,000–$9,999				0.05281
				(0.08156)
Startup capital: $10,000–$24,999				0.12837
				(0.08467)
Startup capital: $25,000–$49,999				0.20008
				(0.10775)
Startup capital: $50,000 and over				0.92232
				(0.08101)
Gender, age, and veteran status of owner	No	Yes	Yes	Yes
State controls	No	Yes	Yes	Yes
Industry controls	No	Yes	Yes	Yes
Mean of dependent variable	0.180	0.180	0.180	0.180
Sample size	112,357	112,357	112,357	112,357

Notes: (1) The sample consists of new businesses in the SBO 2007 microdata. (2) The dependent variable is the number of employees hired at startup.
Source: Authors' calculations from Survey of Business Owners Microdata, 2007 (US Census Bureau 2013).

undercapitalized. To a lesser extent, Latinx levels of employment increase, as do Native American levels of employment, after controlling for relatively low levels of startup capital (figure 7.7). The coefficient for Asian startups becomes much more negative, suggesting that relatively high startup capital among Asian-owned startups partly explains why their employment levels are also relatively large.

Overall, the results for having any employees (table 7.5) and for the number of employees (table 7.6) do not differ substantially. Controlling for the education level of the owner and the startup capital used to launch the business explains some of the racial and ethnic differences in employment by startups. The two main findings are that Black startups tend to be undercapitalized, limiting their startup employment levels, and that Latinx owners have both relatively low levels of education and lower levels of startup capital, which limits their startup employment levels. On the other hand, Asian owners have relatively high levels of startup capital, contributing to higher levels of employment for this group of startups.

New Data

The Census Bureau recently replaced the SBO data with two data sets, the Annual Business Survey (ABS) and the Nonemployer Statistics by Demographics series (NES-D). The ABS provides information on the demographic characteristics and business characteristics of a sample of employer businesses. The NES-D provides information on the demographic characteristics of all nonemployer businesses.

The advantages of the Census Bureau's switch to the NES-D data is that it leverages administrative records and preexisting census data to assign demographic information to business owners instead of relying on survey results.[18] The NES-D will include the full nonemployer universe instead of a sample of businesses such as in the SBO. Another major advantage is that the NES-D will be reported annually with a shorter dissemination lag instead of the five-year rotation and three-year dissemination lag of the SBO.

The combined ABS and NES-D data set will provide a detailed and comprehensive statistics on US businesses by the demographic characteristics of the business owners (US Census Bureau 2020b). In the future, it will be possible to link these data to the Comprehensive Startup Panel data set providing valuable information on the race, gender, and other demographic characteristics of the owners of startups and how these dimensions are related to job creation and survival.

Conclusions

Ownership of startups is not limited to one or two groups of the population. We find a diverse set of startup owners by race, ethnicity, gender, age, education level, immigrant status, and veteran status. Our Comprehensive Startup Panel data set does not include information on the demographic characteristics of owners. Instead, we use a sample from the universe of startups—new businesses covered in the 2007 SBO (US Census Bureau 2013). The SBO provides detailed information on both owner characteristics and business characteristics of startups. We find that 39 percent of startups are owned by women. Black ownership of startups is 7 percent of the total, Latinx ownership is 9 percent, and Asian ownership is 6 percent. The immigrant ownership share of startups is 14 percent and the veteran share of ownership is 12 percent. Ownership shares of startups increase with owner's age at first but then decline with owner's age. The largest ownership share of startups is for the middle age group (ages forty-five to fifty-four), accounting for 29 percent of startups. Ownership shares of startups increase with owner's education. Forty-four percent of startups are owned by college graduates.

Although startups have a diverse set of owners, we find some inequality in ownership of startups when we compare the composition of startup ownership to the composition of the US labor force. The comparison provides evidence on whether groups are under- or overrepresented in startup ownership. We find several interesting patterns. First, women are underrepresented, constituting 52 percent of the labor force but only 39 percent of startup owners. Minorities are also underrepresented in startup ownership when compared to their share of the labor force. Blacks constitute 12 percent of the labor force but account for only 7 percent of startups. Latinx constitute 14 percent of the labor force but account for only 9 percent of startups. The comparisons for owner's age and education level indicate increasing levels of overrepresentation in both owner characteristics. The age group twenty-five to thirty-four years accounts for 11 percent of startups but 22 percent of the labor force, and the age group fifty-five to sixty-four years accounts for 24 percent of startups but only 14 percent of the labor force. College graduates are overrepresented in ownership of startups, constituting 44 percent of ownership but 31 percent of the labor force.

We turn to exploring levels and sources of startup capital. Most new businesses start with small amounts of capital. Three quarters of startups use less than $5,000. Twelve percent of startups use $25,000 or more in initial financial capital. The differences in startup capital reflect the diversity of startups in the United States, as also shown in earlier chapters. To fund these startups, owners often rely on their own personal savings, assets, and credit sources. Personal savings were used by 84 percent of startups, credit cards were used by 17 percent of startups, other personal assets were used by 9 percent of startups, and home equity lines of credit were used by 7 percent. Certainly, large levels of startup capital are obtained through bank loans, but fewer than 10 percent of startups used these loans as a source of initial financial capital.

We combine the two analyses to explore potential barriers to employment size faced by minority-owned startups, especially startup capital. Startups owned by Blacks are less likely to hire employees at startup and have fewer employees per startup than startups owned by non-Latinx Whites. The disparities are large, with Black startups being 4.2 percentage points less likely to hire any employees than White startups and hiring 0.12 (or 65 percent) fewer employees per startup on average. Latinx startups are also less likely to hire employees at startup, with 0.06 (or 33 percent) fewer employees on average. Native Americans startups have 0.10 (51 percent) fewer employees on average. In contrast, startups owned by Asians have 0.10 (51 percent) more employees on average than White startups.

What contributes to these racial and ethnic differences in startup employment? We focus on the role played by differences in human capital (as measured by owner's education level) and financial capital (as measured by startup capital) in contributing to these disparities in early-stage employment levels among startups. Black-owned startups tend to be undercapitalized, which limits their startup employment levels, but relatively low levels of human capital (as measured by education) also contribute. For Latinx startup owners relatively low levels of human capital partly explain lower levels of employment by these startups. There is also some evidence of capital constraints for these startups, too. Asian-owned startups have the highest level of startup capital, which is associated with the highest level of early-stage employment among startups owned by any major racial/ethnic group. Native American–owned startups also have relatively low levels of human and financial capital, both findings associated with lower employment levels, but the contributions are not as large as for other groups.

The findings discussed in this chapter make several contributions to the previous literature on the potential barriers limiting business ownership and performance among minorities. Previous studies have identified wealth disparities, access to financial capital, discrimination in lending, other types of discrimination, and relatively less human capital, family business background, social capital, and other factors as limiting minority business creation and success.[19] We focus here on startups instead of on all existing businesses or business owners, which is the focus of most previous work. In the most closely related previous work, Fairlie and Robb (2008) draw on confidential, restricted-access microdata from the 1992 Characteristics of Business Owners (CBO) to explore why Asian American–owned firms perform well in comparison to White-owned businesses, while Black-owned firms typically do not. The study finds that access to financial capital is the largest factor limiting success among Black-owned businesses and is also the largest factor explaining why Asian-owned businesses outperform White-owned businesses on average. Family business experience also plays a role in explaining differences in outcomes. The findings presented here focusing on startups and using more recent data reinforce and build on those earlier findings.

Previous research on race and business success mostly drew on data from public use household data sets such as the ACS and CPS, where race and ethnicity information are readily available. In a recent study, for example, Fairlie (2018) examines potential barriers created by human capital, wealth, demographic, geographic, and industry constraints for each group. Low levels of wealth contribute to lower business ownership rates of Blacks and Latinx, and high levels of wealth increase Asian business ownership rates. Low levels of education contribute to why Blacks and Latinx have lower business income, and high levels of education increase Asian business income. Black, Latinx, and Asian business owners are relatively young compared to White business owners, which also reduces business ownership rates. Focusing on Mexican American entrepreneurship, Fairlie and Woodruff (2010) find that low levels of education and wealth explain the entire gap between Mexican immigrants and non-Latino Whites in business formation rates; together with language ability, these factors explain nearly the entire gap in business income. Legal status represents an additional barrier for Mexican immigrants. These findings from the ACS and CPS are generally consistent with previous research using other household data sets. For example, Fairlie (1999) uses the Panel Study of Income Dynamics (PSID) and finds that wealth and education disparities are important for Black men, and Lofstrom and Wang (2009) use the Survey of Income and Program Participation (SIPP) and find that low levels of wealth for Mexican Americans and other Latinx work to lower self-employment entry rates.

Switching the focus to racial disparities in the early-stage use of financial capital, Fairlie, Robb, and Robinson (2022) use confidential and restricted-access panel data from the KFS and matched administrative data on credit scores to explore disparities in capital use between Black- and White-owned startups. Black-owned startups start smaller in terms of capital and stay smaller over the entire first eight years of their existence. Black startups face more difficulty in raising external capital, especially external debt. Disparities in creditworthiness constrain Black entrepreneurs, but perceptions of treatment by banks also hold them back. Black entrepreneurs apply for loans less often than White entrepreneurs largely because they expect to be denied credit, even when they have a good credit history and in settings where strong local banks favor new business development. The causes of racial disparities in early-stage financial capital and their consequences on job creation among startups are complex and require further study in light of their importance for racial inequality in business success.

8 ⸱Policy Implications and Future Research

Each year, several million new business entities take the plunge and enter the market, creating a massive number of jobs in the US economy. Counting the number of jobs created, not only in the startup year but also through the first several years of existence, depends heavily on the nature of these new startups and their survival rates, and is essential for identifying the economic contributions of entrepreneurs and for evaluating the government's business development policies. For policymaking purposes, we are particularly interested in calculating the number of jobs created by each startup, as well as how long these jobs and startups survive. Understanding the nature of business startups—their types, how many jobs they create for others and for the business owner—sheds light on the fundamental nature of entrepreneurship (i.e., Schumpeterian entrepreneurship versus job independence and flexibility).

In this book, we take a new approach to measuring entrepreneurship by recharacterizing the start date of a business from when it hires its first employee to when it hires its first employee *or* when it first has revenues. This more nuanced definition of a startup adds all businesses that generate revenues but start without employees and moves the start date back in time for those that hire employees after their entry year. We create and analyze a new compilation of administrative data covering the universe of startups in the United States. The new Comprehensive Startup Panel tracks job creation and survival of every business startup in the US economy from the initial startup year up to seven follow-up years. Government policies promoting entrepreneurship are not limited to high-growth-potential startups. Often, these same programs target individuals interested in starting smaller-scale businesses whose primary goal is simply to make a living for the owner. Thus we create the data set to first allow the broadest definition possible of a startup but later to allow narrower definitions.

Using the new Comprehensive Startup Panel, we provide the first answers, based on all US startups, to three fundamental questions about entrepreneurial job creation and survival: (1) How many jobs are created by the average entrepreneur? (2) Do these jobs last over time? And (3) How many entrepreneurial firms survive each year after startup? In addition to providing answers to these fundamental questions about entrepreneurship, we test several proposed explanations for the underlying causes of patterns in entrepreneurial job creation and survival. How many nonemployer firms transition to become employers? How does the employment size distribution evolve over time for these startups? Do nonemployer startups make notable contributions to employment several years after startup? We also examine which sectors of the economy are job creators and which have relatively low turnover rates.

Our analysis of this new US startup panel data set produces several novel findings on entrepreneurship and job creation that have important implications for policy, economic welfare, and an understanding of entrepreneurship. First, entrepreneurs make major contributions to total job creation in the United States. We find that, on average, each annual cohort of startups creates a total of 3.0 million jobs in the first year after startup and employs a total of 2.6 million workers five years later. Businesses that start without employees contribute a nontrivial share of the total. Nonemployer startups create an average of 319,000 jobs seven years after startup, representing one-seventh of total employment by all startups seven years after startup, and one-fifth of firms hiring their first employee have a previous nonemployer history. The Comprehensive Startup Panel we create formally incorporates their contribution to the job creation statistics, a contribution not fully recognized until now. Without the job creation contributions of startups through their first several years of existence, job creation by all businesses would be negative in most years in the United States.

Although startups make enormous contributions to total job creation in the US economy, the contributions are mostly driven by the sheer number of new businesses created each year (approximately 4.1 million). Job creation is not high on average per entrepreneur—we find that, using our most inclusive definition of entrepreneurship, the average startup employs roughly 0.74 workers in the first year after startup. Five years later this number drops to 0.63 (a 15 percent decline). This suggests that we should revise the fundamental question about job creation to: How many entrepreneurs does it take to create a job? To be sure, when we exclude sole-proprietor-without-EIN startups to create a more selective definition of entrepreneurship, job creation rates per startup are higher. Using this definition, we find that the average startup employs 2.56 workers in the first year after startup and 2.15 workers five years later. Although the most reasonable definition of entrepreneurship is likely to lie somewhere between the two, these numbers do not imply high levels of job creation per entrepreneur and are substantially less than the often cited statistic of six jobs created per new employer firm (US SBA 2017), which focuses on more successful new employer businesses, does not include nonemployer businesses, and does not account for firms' previous history as nonemployers.

Third, in a broader sense, job creation is higher once we account for the jobs entrepreneurs create for themselves, since those jobs are usually not counted as employee jobs in the data. Although the "entrepreneurs create jobs for themselves" argument is often made in the policy arena, the results presented here indicate that business ownership jobs do not last very long. In fact, when we generate a new measure of total jobs per startup, we find that total jobs per startup is 1.33 in the first year after startup (compared to 0.74). Five years after startup the total number of jobs, including the owner's, is 0.97 per startup (a 27 percent decline), and seven years later it is 0.86 total jobs per startup.

Why does the total number of jobs per startup when the owner's job is included decline so quickly? We find high exit rates among the universe of startups and even among our selective group of startups. We find that only 47–64 percent of startups survive two years after startup, and 33–45 percent survive five years after startup. Except for the upper bound on this range, these survival rates are considerably lower than the popular statistic of 50 percent survival after five years among new employer establishments (US SBA 2017). Furthermore, we find that all major industry groups have high exit rates, and highly visible businesses such as those in Accommodation and Food Services, a category that includes hotels and restaurants, have survival rates of only 21–29 percent five years after startup. The potential loss of business owner jobs as well as the potential benefits from gaining entrepreneurial experience should also be included in the economic welfare calculus for entrepreneurship policies.

Fourth, average patterns conceal a substantial amount of heterogeneity in the underlying dynamics of job creation and survival by startups and heterogeneity across startup types. We test several hypotheses for why the average number of jobs per entrepreneur remains relatively constant over years since startup and find that although startups have extremely high exit rates, the resulting job losses from these exits are almost fully offset by the opposite pattern of strong employment growth among surviving startups and the large number of nonemployer startups that eventually hire employees. This is consistent with often reported results that consider only the population of businesses with employees.

Turning to heterogeneity across startup types, we find that nonemployer startups make sizable contributions to employment several years after startup (one-seventh of jobs seven years later). We argue that instead of excluding all nonemployer startups, a preferred alternative upper bound measure of job creation and survival among entrepreneurs could perhaps exclude only sole-proprietor-without-EIN startups. Job creation levels per entrepreneur are higher, but remain much lower than levels found when the analysis focuses on number of jobs per new employer business. Examining heterogeneity across industry groups, we find that some sectors are job creators—for example, Manufacturing and Accommodation and Food Services have average employment levels that are much higher than those in other sectors (although Accommodation and Food Services survival rate is relatively low).

Fifth, we build on the analysis of startup job creation and survival rates to explore the characteristics of the owners of these startups. We find a diverse set of startup owners by race, ethnicity, gender, age, education level, immigrant status, and veteran status. Of particular note, we find that 39 percent of startups are owned by women. Seven percent are owned by Blacks, 9 percent are owned by Latinxs, and 6 percent are owned by Asians. When we compare these figures to the composition of the US labor force, however, we find both gender and racial inequality in the ownership of startups. Women constitute 52 percent of the labor force, Blacks constitute 12 percent, and Latinxs constitute 14 percent. Focusing on racial patterns, we also find inequality in startup outcomes. Startups owned by Blacks hire fewer employees per startup than startups owned by non-Latinx Whites. The disparities are quite large, with Black startups hiring 0.13 (or 67 percent) fewer employees per startup on average compared to White startups. Latinx startups are also less likely to hire employees at startup, with 0.07 (or 36 percent) fewer employees, and Native American startups have 0.10 (or 56 percent) fewer employees on average. In contrast, startups owned by

Asians have 0.09 (or 49 percent) more employees on average than White-owned startups.

What explains these racial and ethnic differences in startup employment? Although we cannot investigate all potential causes, we focus on the role that differences in human capital and financial capital play in contributing to these disparities in early-stage employment among startups. Black startups tend to be undercapitalized, limiting their employment levels at startup. But relatively low levels of human capital also seem to contribute. For Latinx startup owners, relatively low levels of human capital partly explain lower levels of employment among these startups. There is also some evidence of capital constraints for these startups, too. Native American startups also have relatively low levels of human and financial capital. Asian-owned startups, by contrast, have the highest level of startup capital, which is associated with the highest level of early-stage employment among startups owned by any major racial or ethnic group.

The Timeline of Business Creation

Throughout the book we identify the start of a business based on the underlying US Census Bureau Business Register. The definition of a startup used in this book is based on the first time a business entity has revenues or employment because this is when business activity can first be observed by tax filings. The measure is not based on surveys but instead is based on administrative records in the system, which is an important difference, because the measure is derived from the universe of startups, thus avoiding sample attrition problems, and does not rely on survey questions, which are subject to interpretation and response bias.

It is useful to take a step back and examine where our definition of a startup fits into a typical timeline for the different stages of starting a business. To be sure, any of these stages could potentially be used to identify the start of a business. The decision of where on the timeline to measure the start of a business is often based on the research question posed and on available data.

A general timeline for starting a business might be the following:

1. Entrepreneur first comes up with an idea for the business.
2. Entrepreneur makes first tangible effort to start the business (e.g., takes a business plan writing class, researches online how to start a business, investigates sources of capital, or files a patent application).

3. Entrepreneur files for a business license, registration, employer identification number (EIN), tax ID, partnership, business loan, and/or incorporation.

4. Entrepreneur secures financial capital for business.

5. Entrepreneur first commits work effort in business.

6. Business receives first revenues.

7. Business hires first employees.

Although entrepreneurs might not follow these stages in this exact order or may skip some of them, these stages are illustrative of the various options for and challenges faced in creating strict definitions of entrepreneurship and precisely identifying the timing of startups. As noted in earlier chapters, previous research and government statistics often focus on new employer businesses for measuring startups. We expand this definition to include when a business first has revenues *or* first hires employees. But what about all the other stages along this timeline for business creation?

Previous attempts at defining entrepreneurship or startups along this timeline have been made in the literature. A well-known attempt at identifying a very early stage of business creation focuses on what is termed "nascent entrepreneurship," which has been measured in the Panel Study of Entrepreneurial Dynamics (PSED) and the Global Entrepreneurship Monitor (GEM).[1] Nascent entrepreneurship tries to capture stage 1, with the added restriction of also requiring one of the subsequent steps. Nascent entrepreneurs are individuals currently trying to start a new business or venture in which they are active in the startup effort and anticipate some ownership of the business. Additional criteria are used to rule out whether the startup activity was already an infant business based on cash flows.

Some studies have used writing a business plan or applying for a business loan as demonstrating a first-stage or intermediate step in starting a business. For example, Fairlie, Karlan, and Zinman (2015) examine the effectiveness of the Growing America Through Entrepreneurship (GATE) training program. Before turning to estimating the effects of randomly allocated training on business starts, ownership, sales, and employment, they examine whether there are treatment effects on writing business plans or applying for business loans. They find that treated individuals were much more likely to write a business plan by the time of the follow-up survey than the control group but were not more likely to apply for a business loan. Many individuals receiving training did not write a business plan, and only a small share applied for a business loan. One problem with using one of these stages to define when a business starts is that they are not all undertaken by all entrepreneurs and thus might mean something different for various would-be entrepreneurs and types of businesses.

An alternative approach that has not yet been fully studied in the context of entrepreneurship is how the filing for protection of intellectual property, such as a patent, is related to the starting of a business. Recent research has highlighted the importance of patents in protecting household innovations (Miranda and Zolas 2018), but little is known regarding how acquiring intellectual property such as patents can be used to secure future funding for startups, attract new employees, or incentivize the owners to expand or commercialize their idea. Patents might fit into the timeline at stage 2, but it is definitely not clear. Perhaps the patent is applied for and granted with no thought on the owner's part of developing a business around the invention, and the business plan takes shape several years after the invention (prior to stage 1). Or perhaps the patent is a consequence of the business plan and filing for protection takes place sometime around the various other filing processes? We do know that while the vast majority of patents are assigned to corporate and government entities, a significant share of US patents assigned to US or foreign individuals never get linked to a business. What is also known is that most patented household innovations tend to be concentrated in consumer products and in technological areas that differ from those of the average patent. A household business with patents tends to have a significantly higher revenue level and is 70 percent more likely to transition into an employer business than a nonpatenting home-based business, indicating that patent ownership may be a powerful tool for startups early in their life cycle.

Household surveys that include repeated observations over time for the same person can be used to identify the first time an individual reports working in their business. Panel data sets such as matched Current Population Survey (CPS) files, the Panel Study of Income Dynamics (PSID), and National Longitudinal Surveys (NLS) typically have questions on work effort and business ownership. Fairlie (2006, 2013), for example, uses matched monthly or yearly CPS data to measure new business owner work activity.[2] The measure captures movement into main work activity in business ownership of all types, including incorporated or unincorporated businesses and employer and nonemployer businesses. Measures based on household panel data typically identify all individuals who report not owning a self-employment business as their main job in the initial survey month or year, and then examine whether they report owning a self-employment business in the subsequent month or year.[3] In some cases an hours restriction is imposed, such as working fifteen or more usual weekly hours in the self-employment business. The start of the business is thus defined as the first reported work effort in the business.

Yet another effort at documenting entrepreneurship that starts from a different point along the general timeline for starting a business is the Business Formation Statistics of the US Census Bureau.[4] This effort identifies business formations based on the universe of administrative applications for an EIN (Form SS-4). In essence, this new database identifies the population of potential new businesses with an EIN. Many of these businesses never actually generate any revenue or hire any employees and remain unrealized in the mind of their potential entrepreneurs. It pushes us closer to stage 1 and the formation of a business idea. The database has been linked to the population of businesses with employees, so transitions to becoming an actual employer business can now be observed. These data could also potentially be linked to the population of nonemployer business. The high-frequency nature of applications for an EIN are such that these data are currently being used to track in almost real time potential business activity across industries and detailed geographies.[5]

There is not necessarily a right or wrong answer to the question of how to define entrepreneurship or how to identify the start of a new business. Our approach in this book is to identify a business entity as starting the moment the owner files a tax record, which has a few advantages for our purposes. First, it covers the universe of businesses with real measurable activity—many of the other stages in the timeline of starting a business are difficult to measure or pinpoint in time. Second, some of the stages of the timeline may be skipped, and the timing itself may be subject to interpretation by different entrepreneurs. Third, measurement of some stages requires surveys and questionnaires, which potentially creates problems with item nonresponse, response bias, variable interpretation, and sample attrition, among other problems.

Promise for Future Research

The emerging field of entrepreneurship has struggled with finding adequate data and agreement on definitions of entrepreneurship. The new

Comprehensive Startup Panel data set that we generate affords substantial flexibility in how one defines entrepreneurship and allows the exploration of many questions around entrepreneurial job creation, survival, and growth. The massive number of observations—an average of more than four million startups each year—furnishes unprecedented detail useful in analyzing different types of entrepreneurs. The Comprehensive Startup Panel data set also eliminates concerns over survivorship, recall, and attrition bias. The new data set and the findings presented here provide a jumping-off point for future research on entrepreneurship.

Job creation is one of the most important aspects of entrepreneurship, but we know relatively little about the early-stage hiring patterns and decisions of startup owners. The advantages of the Comprehensive Startup Panel data set for studying these questions include having access to an exhaustive universe of startups, the ability to follow annual startup cohorts over time with panel data, and having access to information on the number of jobs, total payroll, and other related outcomes, such as survival. Information on legal form of organization, EINs, and employment in the initial year permits tailoring the definition of entrepreneurship to the needs of the study based on different classifications and combinations of classifications of businesses, such as nonemployer, employer, EIN, incorporated, S corporation, partnership, and sole proprietorship. Most of the examples presented here use the full universe of startups, which includes all classifications, but there is much flexibility in creating various restrictive samples by using the microdata.

Many future questions about entrepreneurship can be addressed using these data. For example, what drives the up-or-out dynamics of nonemployer businesses? What is the contribution of continuers and high-growth nonemployer startups to overall growth? What is the nature and what are the growth patterns of high-tech startups compared to other startups? How do firms that start off without employees differ from firms that start with employees? How do their growth patterns differ over time? What are the employment dynamics of different startup cohorts? Is survival among startups related to whether they were started in a recession or in a growth period? How did the COVID-19 pandemic shape the new cohort of startups, and how does it compare in that respect to the Great Recession?

These are just a few examples of the plethora of questions on entrepreneurship that can be addressed with the new Comprehensive Startup Panel data set introduced here.

Linking the Startup Panel Data Set to Other Data Sets

Another area of promise for future research derives from the ability to link the startup panel data set to other Census Bureau data sets. Matching the startup panel data forward or backward can satisfy three major goals for future research. First, it can extend the timeline for measuring startups, as noted above. This could be especially useful for improving our understanding of the dynamics of entrepreneurship over various stages of the startup process. Second, it can provide more information on the characteristics of startups. Learning more about different types of startups can be useful for identifying the determinants of startup success and for studying equity issues in business formation (e.g., formation by race and gender). Third, it can be forward-looking and shed more light on business outcomes in the first several years of existence among startups.

We first discuss extending the timeline backward. The Comprehensive Startup Panel data set permits defining a startup by time of first revenue or first employee. Matching to data before this is possible for various components of intellectual property, such as patents and trademarks, that have been linked to new businesses prior to their inception. However, linking to the Census Bureau's Business Formation Statistics database might allow us to dig even further back, to the time before a business has its first receipts.[6] This would allow researchers to answer a number of interesting questions introduced in this book: What is the length of time between the business application and first revenues? How often do sole proprietorships submit business applications for EINs, and how long does it usually take the owner after startup to file the application?

Another promising property useful for future research is the ability to merge the Comprehensive Startup Panel data set with other Census Bureau data sets that provide more detailed information on owner characteristics. For example, data from the American Community Survey (ACS), which provides detailed demographic, home ownership, and educational information, can be merged to a segment of startup owners. Data from the Longitudinal Employer-Household Dynamics (LEHD) can be merged to provide information on owners of startups, including detailed information on their work histories, such as their prior earnings and their employer. These would primarily be limited to the sole proprietor startups in our sample.

What is clear, however, is that linking administrative records to our panel data can open up new avenues for describing the demographics of entrepreneurs and startups. A recent Census Bureau project, the Nonemployer Statistics by Demographics (NES-D), utilizes administrative records from the Business Register, tax data, the Decennial Census, the ACS, and the Department of Veteran Affairs to provide detailed demographic data on nonemployer businesses in the United States (see Luque et al. 2019 for more details). These combined data replace data that were formerly captured exclusively by surveys, such as the Survey of Business Owners (SBO), and demonstrates how administrative records can provide information on a large and comprehensive set of businesses. Applying a similar method to describe the demographics for the subset of startups could yield a significant return. Use of administrative K-1 data can extend the demographics to owners of pass-through entities.

Another example of information on owner characteristics that can be matched to the startup panel data set is the recently introduced UMETRICS data at the Census Bureau. The data feature information on university students (undergraduate and graduate) who were paid by federally funded grants at more than twenty-five large research universities in the United States, allowing the tracking of entrepreneurial activity by a dynamic and highly educated set of entrepreneurs. Goldschlag et al. (2019) provide an example along these lines but focus on employer firms and highlight the importance of human capital in startup survival, growth, and innovative activity.

There is also the potential to match the Comprehensive Startup Panel data set with other data sets to look forward. Linking data sets in this way is promising for providing insights into the early-stage outcomes of startups, beyond job creation and survival. For example, merging the Comprehensive Startup Panel data set with the LEHD yields more information on worker pay and worker longevity at new firms (i.e., in the startup year and subsequent years). Is turnover among employees at startups high in the startups' first few years of existence? How do additional new employees and increasing firm tenure on the part of employees contribute to pay dynamics at startups? Additionally, the Comprehensive Startup Panel data set could be linked to the SBO and Annual Business Survey (ABS) to provide some information on financing and other outcomes collected with survey questions.

Of special interest is linking the startup panel data set to information on government programs promoting entrepreneurship. Although confidentiality requirements and the logistics of merging data sets would this more difficult, it might be possible in the future to link the startup panel data set to the receipt of government loans, entrepreneurship training, emergency assistance, or tax incentives. The Ryan-Murray bill, passed by Congress in 2018 as the Foundations for Evidence-Based Policymaking Act, was signed into law in January 2019. The law incorporates many of the recommendations of the US Commission on Evidence-Based Policymaking to improve the use of evidence and data to generate policies and inform programs underwritten by the federal government. As the law is implemented, taking on these types of studies may become the norm rather than the exception.

We hope that this book provides a stepping stone for future research in the area because one goal is to make the data and its ability to match to other sources available in Federal Statistical Research Data Centers (FSRDCs) across the country. As noted in chapter 1, the Comprehensive Startup Panel data set can be accessed through a "data package." The data package consists of the ILBD, the LBD, and SAS code that links the ILBD and LBD; identifies startups; and includes all startups starting in 1994 or later. The provided SAS code can be run to create the Comprehensive Startup Panel data set, which will be ready for analysis.

Studying Racial Inequality

One area ripe for additional research concerns racial disparities in job creation, firm survival, and success among startups. Future work could build on the findings presented here on the demographics of startup owners. A key finding of chapter 7 is that Blacks, Latinxs, and Native Americans are underrepresented in the ownership of startups compared to their representation in the US labor force. Additionally, initial job creation per startup levels are relatively low for each of these minority groups. Financial and human capital constraints appear to be partly responsible for the disparities in early-stage employment outcomes, but data limitations (i.e., our reliance on the SBO data) preclude us from also examining disparities in longer-term employment levels and survival rates.

New findings on racial inequality in financing, human capital growth, and business outcomes will likely be important for addressing broader racial inequality. Most previous research on earnings inequality focuses on the wage and salary sector and ignores the other major form of making a living—owning a business. Ten percent of the workforce, or 12 million people, own a business instead of having a wage or salary job, and these owners hold a disproportionate amount of total wealth and create jobs for others. Another concern is the loss of economic efficiency resulting from blocked opportunities for minorities to start and grow businesses. If minority entrepreneurs face liquidity constraints, discrimination, or other barriers to creating new businesses or expanding current ones, there will be efficiency losses in the economy. These barriers to entry and expansion are potentially costly to US productivity and local job creation, especially as minorities represent a growing share of the population. Minority-owned businesses are important for local job creation (as minority owners disproportionately hire minority workers), economic advancement, and longer-term wealth inequality (Boston 1999b, 2006; Bradford 2003, 2014; Fairlie and Robb 2008; Stoll et al. 2001).

Although our findings on racial inequality in startup ownership and initial employment are interesting and important, much more can be learned by matching our startup panel to information on the race of owners. It is difficult to find comprehensive information on race and ethnicity to match to the Comprehensive Startup Panel data set, but some recent developments might help in making progress toward this goal. This work has started with the new NES-D program, which has begun to capitalize on using the existing surveys and administrative records maintained by the Census Bureau on demographics to replace the loss of survey information that was previously collected for nonemployer businesses.[7] This program relies on a variety of different data sources, including the ACS, the Census Bureau's Numident file (used to link persons with their protected identification key), the SBO, the ASE, and the Department of Veteran Affairs. Surveys such as the ABS, which includes employer businesses, can provide even more details on startup owners' demographic and financial status, as well as on innovation outcomes of startups at the time of their founding.

Using these data sets and others matched to the startup panel data set, it is possible to conduct critically needed research on three aspects of racial inequality in business. First, because of the importance of startup capital to wealth accumulation and wealth gaps, more research is needed on racial barriers to accessing capital for startups.[8] Efforts to bring into the Census Bureau individual and business credit score data and banking history data are under way. Home mortgage data are already available but need to be matched. The ACS has information on home ownership and values, and the Survey of Income and Program Participation (SIPP) has additional information on ownership and values of detailed assets. Second, a careful examination of the stages of the startup timeline during which minority startups are especially likely to fail would be useful. Survival rates among minority firms are relatively low, and an important unanswered question is whether there is a critical make-or-break point early in the life cycle of the firm. Third, certain policy interventions might be found to be effective in reducing racial disparities in startup success, employment, and survival.[9] Do these policies help minority startups survive and create jobs, and are those jobs created for co-ethnics and in their local communities? All of these questions and underresearched areas are important for reducing racial disparities in business outcomes and thus in reducing broader societal racial inequality. Future research matching the Comprehensive Startup Panel data set to information on race should be able to address these and related questions centered on inequality.

Studying the Economic Effects of the COVID-19 Pandemic

Although the data and analysis discussed in this book predate the unprecedented economic turmoil created by the COVID-19 pandemic, we note a few possibilities for future research. A young but rapidly growing literature is exploring the impacts of the COVID-19 on small businesses. The research examines the early negative impacts of the pandemic on business activity, closures, sales, consumer demand, and other outcomes (e.g., Bartik, Bertrand, et al. 2020; Bloom, Fletcher, and Yeh 2021; Bohn, Mejia, and Lafortune 2020; Desai and Looze 2020; Fairlie 2020; Fairlie and Fossen 2021b; Farrell, Wheat, and Mac 2020; Kim, Parker, and Schoar 2020; US Census Bureau 2020a). For example, estimates of active business ownership from the CPS indicate that the number of working business owners plummeted from 15.0 million in February 2020 to 11.7 million in April 2020 (Fairlie 2020). In contrast to this two-month drop of 22 percent at the beginning of the pandemic, the entire Great Recession resulted in a drop of only 5 percent in business owner activity.[10] Even more growth-oriented and stable incorporated business owners experienced a drop in work activity of 20 percent from February to April 2020.

Losses by female, minority, and immigrant business owners were especially severe in April 2020. Blacks experienced the largest losses—41 percent of active business owners. Latinxs also experienced major losses—32 percent. Immigrant business owners suffered a 36 percent drop, and female business owners suffered a 25 percent drop. In comparison, losses were 17 percent for non-Latinx White business owners, 18 percent for US-born owners, and 20 percent for male owners. The concentrations of female, Black, Latinx, and Asian businesses in industries hit hard by the pandemic were partly responsible for why losses were higher for these groups than for all business owners. When the analysis is extended into the second and third months following widespread shelter-in-place restrictions—May and June 2020—business owner activity partially rebounded, but the disproportionate impacts of COVID-19 by gender, race, and immigrant status lingered. Black owners continued to experience the largest losses, with 26 percent of active business owners still not active in May and 19 percent not active in June relative to pre-pandemic levels. Fall-offs in non-Latinx White business owner activity rates were 11 percent in May and 5 percent in June.

One limitation to these findings on business owner activity in the CPS is that there is no way to determine at present whether pandemic-induced business closures are temporary or permanent. Furthermore, the data do not provide insights into the impacts on the revenues, profits, and employees of these businesses—and the likelihood of the businesses ever reopening.[11] The startup panel data set can be analyzed to explore all these important questions in the future.

Several emerging studies focus on the government's provision of financial help to small businesses in the pandemic, especially through the Paycheck Protection Program (PPP) (e.g., Atkins, Cook, and Seamans 2022a, 2022b; Bartik, Cullen, et al. 2020; Cole 2020; Erel and Liebersohn 2020; Fairlie and Fossen 2021a, 2022; Granja et al. 2020; Howell et al. 2021; Hubbard and Strain 2020; Humphries, Neilson, and Ulyssea 2020; Lederer et al. 2020). The findings from these early studies of the pandemic have provided some insight into what happened during these tumultuous times, but there is much more to uncover. The new Comprehensive Startup Panel data set will be extremely useful for studying job creation, survival, and other outcomes during the pandemic. Linking startups in the new panel data set to PPP loans, local social distancing restrictions, and COVID-19 cases would be expected to shed considerable light on what happened during this extremely disruptive time.

Bounding Job Creation and Survival and Implications for Policy

The two most important sets of numbers that we calculate using the new startup panel are the number of jobs per startup and the survival rate. Both are calculated in the startup year and up to seven years after the startup year. The inclusion or exclusion of sole-proprietor-without-EIN startups is an important decision in measuring entrepreneurial job creation and survival. We consider the two measures as lower and upper bounds, respectively.

Table 8.1 reports the lower and upper bounds on job creation per startup and survival rates (as previously reported in tables 6.7 and 6.8). These bounds result in a wide range of values for job creation levels per startup. Job creation levels per startup range from 0.74–0.57 at the lower bound to 2.56–1.94 at the upper bound. Calculating lower and upper bounds on survival rates, however, does not result in such a wide range of values. For most follow-up years, the survival rates differ by ten to fifteen percentage points. For both job creation per startup and survival rates, the trends over years since startup are roughly similar.

Table 8.1
Range of measures for employment per entrepreneur and survival rates

Years since startup	Employees per entrepreneur (N)		Survival rates (%)	
	Lower bound	Upper bound	Lower bound	Upper bound
1	0.74	2.56	59	76
2	0.73	2.50	47	64
3	0.70	2.38	40	56
4	0.66	2.26	36	50
5	0.63	2.15	33	45
6	0.60	2.04	31	41
7	0.57	1.94	29	38

Note: The lower bound includes the universe of startups, and the upper bound excludes sole-proprietor-without-EIN startups.
Source: Authors' calculations from the newly compiled Comprehensive Startup Panel data set (1995–2018). The startup year (year 0) is the first calendar year in which the business has revenues or payroll. The following year (year 1) captures the first complete calendar year of information on number of employees and survival in the data. Startup cohorts include the years 1995 to 2011, and follow-up years include 1996 to 2018.

For bounding measures of job creation and survival, our removal of some types of entrepreneurs follows the approach taken in a few recent studies (including the incorporated self-employed, partnerships, and patent holders). Using this approach, we lose a small portion of the total jobs created, but job creation per entrepreneur is now higher and perhaps more in line with that of entrepreneurs who have some potential interest in growing. But it is important to keep in mind that many new businesses start out as sole proprietorships and grow to become successful businesses. Starting out as a sole proprietorship is easy, fast, and allows the owner to test the waters. We do not necessarily want to throw these entrepreneurs out of the calculations. Or, put differently, we want to understand the challenges and constraints these types of entrepreneurs face as well.

We also expand the definition of job creation to include the owner's job, which might be important for thinking about the large number of sole proprietor businesses whose owners have no intention of ever hiring employees and are solely focused on providing themselves with income. Given these concerns, we add the owner's job to job creation counts to create an alternative measure of the total number of jobs (including owner's job) per startup. Table 8.2 reports the new measure of total jobs created per startup in addition to the lower bound measure of job creation per startup (as previously reported in table 6.9). We use the lower bound definition as a starting point because it includes the universe of startups to capture all types of business activities, which is consistent with the idea of many sole proprietors of startups having a primary goal of creating a job for themselves. We also assume for these calculations that each startup has one owner as an approximation for simplification and because of the very large percentage of startups that are sole proprietorships, which have only one owner by definition. Using this alternative measure, we find that total jobs per startup is 1.33 in the first year after startups but drops to 0.97 five years after startup and 0.57 seven years after startup.

At startup and in the first couple of follow-up years, adding the owner's job to total employee counts per startup makes a difference. In the startup year, for example, the number of jobs per startup increases by threefold. The concern, however, appears several years after startup. Startups generally have low survival rates, and this translates into wiping out the owner's job. Five years out we start to see many fewer owners of surviving startups. Low survival rates over time limit the contribution that counting the owner's

Table 8.2
Employees per entrepreneur and total jobs per startup, including the owner's job

Years since startup	Employees per entrepreneur (lower bound)	Surviving owners	Total jobs per startup (including owner's job)
1	0.74	0.59	1.33
2	0.73	0.47	1.19
3	0.70	0.40	1.10
4	0.66	0.36	1.03
5	0.63	0.33	0.97
6	0.60	0.31	0.91
7	0.57	0.29	0.86

Note: The lower bound includes the universe of startups.
Source: Authors' calculations from the newly compiled Comprehensive Startup Panel data set (1995–2018). The startup year (year 0) is the first calendar year in which the business has revenues or payroll. The following year (year 1) captures the first complete calendar year of information on number of employees and survival in the data. Startup cohorts include the years 1995 to 2011, and follow-up years include 1996 to 2018.

job can make to measuring total jobs per startup. Another issue that might be important to study and consider is that the owner's job is not equivalent to an employee's job. Often early in the startup phase of a business the owner is not taking home much in pay and is instead focused on the survival and growth of the business, whereas employees get paid regardless and obtain competitive wages.

How should we view these numbers for policy? If the goal is to create business tax incentives and job creation incentives to attract more growth-oriented startups, then the upper bound measure might be the preferred benchmark. If instead the goal is to create self-employment training, counseling, or education programs to help disadvantaged workers start their own business or become self-employed, then the lower bound measure might be more applicable. In this case, however, we might want to include the job created for the owner of the startup even if this job is not comparable to an employee's job. The recent PPP program, for example, included funding to sole proprietors, independent contractors, and the self-employed, in addition to employer small businesses. These are difficult and important questions, and there are no right or wrong answers to them.

Although choosing a baseline measure of job creation levels and survival probabilities is difficult, the range of measures we present is important for setting expectations about policy interventions. Federal, state, and local governments spend billions of dollars each year on incubators, training programs, loan programs, tax breaks, and investor incentives to encourage business creation with one of the primary goals being to create jobs. The US Small Business Administration (SBA), for example, administers several programs to support small businesses, including loan guaranty, training, federal contracting, and other programs, partly through more than a thousand subsidized Small Business Development Centers (SBDCs). There are also at least eight hundred other nonprofit programs providing self-employment training and other assistance (Edgcomb and Girardo 2012). The popularity of public policies to foster entrepreneurs is not limited to the United States but is widespread around the world (OECD 2017b). Why do governments invest such vast amounts of financial resources and effort into helping startups succeed? One reason is that starting and growing a business and then surviving are not easy, but the overall payoffs in terms of innovation, job creation, and productivity growth might be large.

Although there might be a justification for interest in policies to foster entrepreneurship, government and philanthropic expenditures are often made without measurement of the benefits in terms of the number of businesses, number of jobs, or total payroll created relative to the costs of these programs. To address this concern, the federal government recently emphasized the importance of measuring job creation for policy evaluation. The US Government Accountability Office (GAO), for example, recommended that the SBA use job creation and other outcome-based measures to evaluate the effectiveness of its programs (Congressional Research Service 2020). In 2018, Congress passed the Ryan-Murray bill to improve government performance. The Foundations for Evidence-Based Policymaking Act established a fifteen-member commission to study how best to strengthen and expand the use of data to evaluate the effectiveness of federal programs and tax expenditures. As the law is implemented, conducting these types of studies should become the norm rather than the exception.

Several recent evaluations of entrepreneurship policy programs provide some insights into the effectiveness of a wide range of policies. Starting with programs that target more growth-oriented businesses, for example, Brown and Earle (2016) evaluate the effects of SBA lending programs on job creation. For each $1 million in loans, they estimate an increase of 3 to 3.5 jobs. They also estimate that taxpayer costs per job created are in the range of $21,000–$25,000. Lerner (1999) examines the Small Business Innovation

Research (SBIR) program and finds that awardees grew considerably faster than similar companies that did not receive awards. Howell (2017) shows these effects are stronger for more financially constrained firms. In the ten years after receipt of SBIR funding, the workforce of the average award recipient in a high-tech region grew to double the number of employees. The superior performance, as measured by growth in employment and other measures, however, was confined to awardees in areas that already had private venture activity. Chrisman (2016) uses a survey of recipients of SBDC services to compare their performance after receiving assistance to the performance of all US businesses, and extrapolates job creation levels to the full client base. He estimates that 96,095 new jobs are generated from the assistance received, and the average cost of generating each job is $2,476.

Moving to policies that emphasize creating stable income for the owner in addition to potential job creation, Fairlie, Karlan, and Zinman (2015) find that entrepreneurship training increases business ownership only in the short run and has no effects on business sales, earnings and employment. However, more recent evidence on entrepreneurship training shows stronger positive effects on creating a job for the owner (Fairlie, Hock, et al. 2022). Weigensberg et al. (2017) examine outcomes among Self-Employment Assistance program recipients, which is targeted to unemployed workers, and find mixed results. Elert, Andersson, and Wennberg (2015) examine entrepreneurship education through the Swedish version of the international Junior Achievement Company Program and find that participation in high school in the program is associated with a future higher probability of starting a business and deriving income from this business, but not with firm survival.

Overall, the evidence on the effectiveness of programs to spur entrepreneurship and create jobs for owners and others is mixed. Despite the lack of solid, consistent evidence of effectiveness, the popularity of public policies to attract and foster entrepreneurs continues to grow around the world (OECD 2017b).

Policymakers and governments need to carefully assess the cost and benefits of programs to promote entrepreneurship. We find that with our most inclusive definition of entrepreneurship, the average startup employs roughly one-half of a worker. When we exclude sole-proprietor-without-EIN startups to create a more restrictive definition of entrepreneurship, job creation rates increase to two workers per startup five years later. If instead we add the owner's job to the total job count, then startups create an average of three quarters of a job five years later. All of these numbers are substantially lower than the often cited six jobs per new employer business (US SBA 2017). Therefore, public policies attempting to spur business creation need to be realistic about how many jobs can be created by new entrepreneurs. These policies generally do not target solely employer startups. Additionally, racial disparities in first-year job creation suggests that other confounding barriers, such as access to startup capital, need to be addressed or the potential of entrepreneurship policies to create jobs might be more pessimistic.

In light of these levels of job creation per entrepreneur, programs to spur entrepreneurship might target high-growth entrepreneurs to end up with a positive benefit-cost ratio (at least in terms of generating jobs). A few sectors, such as Manufacturing and Accommodation and Food Services, appear to be relative job creators, although businesses in Accommodation and Food Services are also more likely to fail. Although the "entrepreneurs create jobs for themselves" argument is often made in the policy arena, business owner jobs often do not last very long. The potential loss of business owner jobs after several years should also be factored into the economic welfare calculus for entrepreneurship policies, as should the potential benefits to be derived from acquiring entrepreneurial experience.

More generally, new policies to attract and create entrepreneurs might not have long-term success because of the relatively low survival rates that we find. These policies likely will need to also address entrepreneurial survival, possibly through additional or continued support, particularly for disadvantaged populations with limited outside opportunities. Simply attracting or creating startups will not guarantee new jobs and businesses five to seven years later. Efforts to remove barriers to entrepreneurship and financing, to foster an innovative environment, and to create opportunities for all groups might prove fruitful.

Measuring job creation and survival rates using a broad definition versus a narrow definition of entrepreneurs is relevant for policy discussions, especially to generate realistic benefit projections from these programs. The higher job creation and survival rates associated with new employer businesses might be useful for programs that provide tax incentives and credits for startups. But the lower rates derived from using the universe of startups might be more useful for a broader set of programs such as self-employment training programs, counseling services, and assistance. Such programs, which are widespread around the world, do not restrict beneficiaries to entrepreneurs with high growth or employee intentions. And, as we show in chapter 6, nonemployer startups eventually contribute a large share of the total jobs in the US economy.

Findings from analyzing the newly compiled Comprehensive Startup Panel data set comprising the universe of US startups, alone or linked with other government data sources, could have important implications for policy and research in many areas, including macroeconomics, labor, public policy, and entrepreneurship. For example, local governments often compete with each other to lure startups with tax breaks and other incentives, with the goal of creating jobs for residents, economic growth, and longer-term tax revenues. If a city wants to create a tax incentive to spur entrepreneurship, then the startup panel data set could be used to analyze how many startups moved to comparable cities that previously implemented similar policies and where those startups moved from after the policy was implemented. How many jobs did those startups have prior to leaving the previous location, and how many jobs did they create in the new location? On the other hand, cities could evaluate how many startups and resulting jobs left their area to go to other locations, and investigate possible reasons for why they left. There is often the assumption, for example, that just by attracting startups, locales will experience long-term job growth. This assumption might be optimistic in light of the low startup survival rates we find even using a more restrictive definition of startups.

What if a state wants to create a new lending program? Our new Comprehensive Startup Panel data set could not only be used to analyze how many new startups were created in that state, it could also be used to observe how long those startups survived and how many jobs were created. The costs of creating this type of program could then be weighed against the benefits measured as jobs created for others and possibly the owners. If exit rates are high, then it will be important to measure these benefits not only in the first year but also for several years after the business receives loans, grants, or other types of assistance. The Comprehensive Startup Panel is ideal for this purpose and could provide much-needed information to help in evaluating the impacts of a wide range of policies on startup numbers, job creation, and survival.

The analysis of the startup panel data set sheds new light on the fundamental nature of entrepreneurship in addition to providing implications for evaluating policies. Low levels of job creation per startup and high exit rates suggest that much of entrepreneurship as measured as the universe of startups is likely to be motivated by experimentation or a desire for job independence, contract or consulting work, schedule flexibility, or to be part of the gig economy. A small percentage of these businesses end up creating innovative products, services, and jobs (i.e., Schumpeterian entrepreneurship). The administrative data do not include information on individual motives for creating a business, but it appears that entrepreneurship is more about creating *a job* than about creating *jobs*, and many of the business owners' jobs created are short term, perhaps to help smooth out spells of underemployment or unemployment. Entrepreneurship is also about experimentation. Regardless of the type of legal form, the pace of churning of businesses and ideas is breathtaking.

The new Comprehensive Startup Panel, which captures the universe of US startups, has much potential for aiding future research on these questions and others. Further research using these data to evaluate the cost-effectiveness of the multitude of proposed and existing policies designed to encourage entrepreneurship and to study the underlying causes of racial inequality in startup activity is especially needed.

Notes

Chapter 1: Introduction

1. The evidence on the effectiveness of programs to spur entrepreneurship is mixed. For a few recent examples, see Brown and Earle (2016) on US Small Business Administration (SBA) lending programs, Chrisman (2016) on Small Business Development Centers (SBDCs), Lerner (1999, 2009) on the Small Business Innovation Research and other public venturing programs, Fairlie, Karlan, and Zinman (2015) on entrepreneurship training, Elert, Andersson, and Wennberg (2015) on entrepreneurship education, Chatterji, Chay, and Fairlie (2014) on contracting programs, and Weigensberg et al. (2017) on Self-Employment Assistance programs.

2. Small Business Development Centers, which are partly funded by the SBA, measure job creation resulting from their training and assistance centers around the country from surveys of participants (Chrisman 2016).

3. SBDCs list counseling, training, financial, marketing, production, organization, engineering, and technical assistance as services provided.

4. In general, however, there is no universally agreed-upon or official definition of "entrepreneur" in government data or research (Decker et al. 2014; Parker 2018).

5. The previous research on job creation among businesses focuses almost exclusively on employer firms (e.g., Brown, Hamilton, and Medoff 1990; Davis, Haltiwanger, and Schuh 1998; Decker et al. 2014; Garcia-Macia, Hsieh, et al. 2016; Glaeser, Kerr, and Kerr 2015; Glaeser, Kerr, and Ponzetto 2010; Haltiwanger, Jarmin, and Miranda 2013; Kulick et al. 2016; Tracy 2011). Data on nonemployer startups are more difficult to find and are not reported by age of business over time. Among OECD countries, the United States is one of the few countries that do not report nonemployer business creation rates (see OECD 2017a, figure 3.1, for example).

6. A simple example illustrates this point. If a business with no employees starts in 2001 and hires its first employee three years later, data focusing on employer firms will capture this business as a startup in 2004. The jobs created by this business will also be attributed to startup cohort 2004 instead of startup cohort 2001.

7. Entrepreneurs need to navigate filing for an employer identification number, federal wage and tax statements, employee eligibility verification, state new hire reporting program, workers' compensation insurance program, unemployment insurance tax registration program, and disability insurance in some states.

8. We contribute to a large literature focusing on these patterns. For broader discussions and reviews of these literatures, see, for example, Bates (1997), Fairlie and Robb (2008), Dávila and Mora (2013), Jennings and Brush (2013), Kerr and Kerr (2020), Fairlie and Lofstrom (2015), and van der Sluis, van Praag, and Vijverberg (2005).

9. Black startups refer to Black and African American startups.

10. As discussed in more detail in chapter 6, to simplify this calculation we assume that each business has one owner.

Chapter 2: Business and Startups in the United States

1. There is a small revenue threshold placed to qualify for inclusion in the US Census Bureau's Business Register.

2. Administrative data are the by-product of some administrative processes. For example, employer businesses are required to operate with a tax identifier called the employer identification number (EIN). The EIN is used by businesses to fulfill their tax liabilities with the IRS. The process of first requesting an EIN and then filing income and payroll taxes generates large amounts of administrative data.

3. Specifically, it captures all nonfarm business establishments. In 1974 the Office of Management and Budget directed the Census Bureau to create and maintain a register of all US businesses for statistical purposes.

4. Published nonemployer statistics by the US Census Bureau restrict reporting to nonemployer businesses with annual business receipts of $1,000 or more. In construction industries, revenues of $1 or more are needed to be included in the published statistics.

5. The Business Register allows us to measure both employment and payroll for employer businesses. However, employment is a point-in-time measure. Employers are required to report the number of employees on payroll during the week of March 12.

6. Although the Business Dynamics Statistics (BDS) database is based on the same source data as the Census Bureau's County Business Patterns (CBP) and Statistics of US Business (SUSB) programs, differences in how the source data are processed lead to differences in the published statistics. The LBD program involves many edits and updates that are done for longitudinal consistency but that are not done for the CBP and SUSB. Since the BDS is sourced from the LBD, these differences are carried

through to the BDS tabulations. For more information, see https://www.census.gov /programs-surveys/bds/documentation/comparability.html. Information about the LBD and the BDS can be found in Jarmin and Miranda (2002a, 2002b) and Haltiwanger, Jarmin, and Miranda (2009).

7. See https://www.bls.gov/webapps/legacy/cpsatab9.htm. Recent research uses the CPS data to study the determinants of business ownership. See Levine and Rubinstein (2016), Wang (2019), and Fairlie and Fossen (2020) for a few recent examples. See also Hipple and Hammond (2016) for more information on measuring self-employment in the CPS.

8. Similarly, the American Community Survey (ACS) can be used to measure self-employment/business ownership. See Fairlie (2018) for a recent analysis.

9. For example, if an individual works ten hours per week on her business but thirty hours per week in a wage or salary job then that individual will not be classified as a business owner.

10. The 2007 Survey of Business Owners (SBO) questionnaire, Form SBO-1, was mailed to a random sample of all firms operating during 2007 with annual receipts of $1,000 or more. A few industries are excluded (e.g., Agriculture, Public Administration). See US Census Bureau (2013).

11. The Business Dynamics Statistics data capture only employer businesses and defines a startup (a firm of age 0) based on the year it first reports employees during the payroll week covered by March 12.

12. These are two alternative ways of defining firm age. The choice of definition is a practical consideration based on data constraints. We do not argue there is a true birth year that can readily be identified in any administrative data. A simple example illustrates how using revenue versus employment can lead to different birth years. If a business with no employees first generates revenue in 2001 and hires its first employee three years later, data focusing on the employer definition will capture this business as a startup in 2004. The jobs created by this business will also be attributed to the 2004 startup cohort. If we were to use a revenue-based definition of birth, the jobs created will be attributed instead to the 2001 startup cohort.

13. The Kauffman Firm Survey (KFS), which provides data on a sample of roughly 4,000 nonemployer and employer startups, has also been used to study nonemployer-to-employer transitions (Fairlie and Miranda 2017). Because of the underlying sampling frame of the KFS, however, the sample is skewed toward including employer firms.

14. Nonemployer businesses do not file payroll taxes.

15. The PIK is an individual identifier that replaces the Social Security number (SSN) in all files maintained by the US Census Bureau. The PIK ensures no Census Bureau

employee or researcher has access to SSNs. The linkage between the nonemployer and the employer universes makes use of the name of the business and the tax identifiers: the EIN and the PIK. If any of these changes then it might not be possible to form a link. This is more likely when there is a change in legal form of organization at the time of the transition. For additional discussion of these issues, see Davis et al. (2007).

16. Improved algorithms lead to more precise estimates although not qualitatively different findings.

17. For details about the LBD, see Jarmin and Miranda (2002a, 2002b) and Chow et al. (2021).

18. This seven-year reactivation window is also used in the redesigned LBD as the threshold for deciding when to assign new establishment or firm identifiers (see Chow et al. 2021). Note that for a firm identified by a PIK (i.e., nonemployer sole proprietorships) rather than an EIN, one may argue that a shorter window would be more appropriate. Since PIKs are attached to a person rather than a location, there may be less confidence that the reactivation of a PIK after several years is truly the reactivation of the same business. For consistency, however, we impose the same reactivation window for all firms regardless of identifier.

19. To be specific, we track the original nonemployer and/or employer firm identifier for a startup and classify a change to its first employer identifier as an exit in our analysis (a change from a nonemployer identifier to an employer identifier is considered a continuation, not an exit). In the Census data sets, employer businesses can change firm identifiers for a variety of reasons, including expanding their business from a single establishment to multiple establishments (or vice versa), ownership changes, reorganization, acquisitions (either as an acquirer or acquiree) and more. Unfortunately, it is difficult to identify the precise reasons for why a firm changes its identifier, which in many cases will require evaluating firms on a case-by-case basis to determine whether a reorganization or ownership change should be considered more of an exit or continuation of the business. This definition of firm exits will primarily impact employer startups and slightly underestimate survival rates (mostly in later follow-up years) and underestimate job creation (to a larger degree, but also presumably slightly and mostly in the later years) of startups.

20. The Business Dynamic Statistics (BDS) produced by the Census takes a more methodical approach for those interested in the exit dynamics of employer firms. This difference in methodology can also explain some key differences in the job creation and survival rates of employer firms between the BDS and our results.

21. We do not impose the $1,000 annual revenue restriction used in published nonemployer statistics.

22. In our analysis, we define a startup's "survival" as the startup being present in either the employer or nonemployer universe in a follow-up year. Thus a startup

may "exit" in a given year and return in a later year as a "surviving" firm, which is similar to how the business's activity is recorded in the BDS.

23. Information about the application process and more generally about FSRDCs is available at http://www.census.gov/fsrdc. See also Fairlie et al. (2019) for more information.

24. To avoid the disclosure of confidential information, in our analysis throughout this book we report the Utilities sector and Construction sector together as one group rather than separately. While we do not report the separate shares of non-employer firms in these two firms, it is worth noting that over the period of our analysis (1995–2018), the Utilities sector represents on average 0.1 percent of total employer firms, and the Construction sector represents on average 11.7 percent of total employer firms in the economy (see the Census Bureau's 2019 Business Dynamics Statistics).

Chapter 3: Job Creation by Startups

1. We do not report the number of jobs in the startup year because employment is measured in March and thus does not capture the number of employees at new businesses started after March in that calendar year. Our payroll-based definition focuses on whether a startup has any employees over the calendar year and not on the number of employees.

2. Total employment by all US businesses is from US Census Bureau (2020b).

3. This is not a general equilibrium statement, but it highlights the importance startups play in the economy.

4. The Census Bureau's Longitudinal Employer Household Dynamics (LEHD) data set is compiled from Unemployment Insurance Earnings Records and provides a link between workers and their employers. The LEHD data have been used to study a wide range of topics on workers (see, e.g., Andersson et al. 2013; Goldin et al. 2017; McKinney and Abowd 2020).

5. The cumulative total also includes the partial year of payroll in the year of startup for most startups (unless they were started in January).

6. The average number of employees per new business is high in Management of Companies and Enterprises, but this industry group is very small and difficult to categorize.

7. Although the Utilities sector is grouped with the Construction sector, it represents only a small fraction of the total for this major industry group.

8. Future research will be able to follow job creation and survival over the business cycle, for example.

9. Although not reported in the table, we also control for the differences in job creation across startup cohorts. We do not find major differences across startup cohorts, and do not focus on that here.

10. Using income tax return data, Carroll et al. (2000) find that among their sample of individuals who were sole proprietors in both 1985 and 1988, roughly one-third hired workers. They also found that 9 percent took on workers and 22 percent stopped hiring workers between the two years.

Chapter 4: Startup Survival

1. This definition is similar to the BDS's in that we allow a startup to "exit" in a given year and return in a later year as a "surviving" firm. As noted in chapter 2, we do not distinguish exits from a firm reorganization, ownership change, or acquisition. This primarily impacts employer firms and places a strict definition of firm exit on our data which has the effect of slightly underestimating survival for employer firms mostly in later follow-up years. For more precise survival rates on employer businesses, see the Business Dynamic Statistics (BDS) produced by the Census, which incorporates a more detailed methodology for identifying exits.

2. Note that after year 1, the true probabilities of survival are actually lower than the approximations reported here. Because of our definition of survival, a subset of "surviving" firms in a given year may have been absent the previous year and are reentering. For a true conditional probability of survival, these reentering firms should be excluded from the numerator.

3. See Headd (2003) and Parker (2018) for discussions on the limitations of focusing solely on business exits.

Chapter 5: The Dynamics of Job Creation and Survival among Startups

1. We exclude age zero firms from the chart to avoid assigning zero employment to startups that hire their first employee after March 12.

2. We considered estimating a selection model that simultaneously estimates the exit probability and employment level, but we could not identify a credible instrument that affects exits but is uncorrelated with unobservables in the employment equation. Thus we estimate a conditional model that focuses on the employment decision for only surviving startups to complement the unconditional model that captures both exit and employment.

3. The administrative data also show many transitions from employer to nonemployer status as businesses adjust to changing circumstances and as employees transition in and out of jobs. We do not explore the nature of these transitions and how small businesses adjust to shocks further in the book. This is an area of research that is understudied.

4. See https://www.sba.gov/business-guide/manage-your-business/hire-manage-employees.

5. Information about the Kauffman Firm Survey can be found at https://www.kauffman.org/wp-content/uploads/2019/12/kauffmanfirmsurvey2013.pdf.

6. Only categorical information on revenues is available in the KFS.

7. Note from figure 5.2 that roughly 40 percent of startups exit by year 1.

8. Note from table 5.4 that smaller startups are more likely to exit by year 5. For this reason, including all year 1 startups in our comparison would bias the year 1 distribution downward.

Chapter 6: Refining Our Definition of an Entrepreneur

1. See https://www.sba.gov/sites/default/files/advocacy/SB-FAQ-2017-WEB.pdf. These statistics are derived from underlying Census Bureau or BLS data.

2. Interested readers can reproduce these numbers from the Census Bureau's Business Dynamics Statistics(BDS) series found at https://www.census.gov/data/developers/data-sets/business-dynamics.html. This and the Statistics of US Business data set are generated from the same underlying data.

3. See https://www.bls.gov/bdm/entrepreneurship/entrepreneurship.htm. The BED is generated from the Quarterly Census of Employment and Wages (QCEW) database. The underlying QCEW data come from employment and total wage information covered by state and federal unemployment insurance programs.

4. Note that the BLS series does not identify de novo businesses but rather new establishments. They need not be one and the same; for example, there are many new establishments that are opened by existing firms (e.g., a chain restaurant).

5. As noted in Haltiwanger, Jarmin, and Miranda (2013), prior to the release of the published BDS series there was no age information in publicly available data, leading to the perception of an inverse relationship between firm size and growth in the data.

6. For employer business data by firm age, see https://www.census.gov/ces/dataproducts/bds/data_firm.html.

7. A version of the KFS is available that corrects sampling weights based on Census Bureau administrative data. These data are available through the Federal Statistical Research Data Centers.

8. Data are from the BDS and the Census Bureau's Nonemployer Statistics.

9. Comparing the jobs created by surviving nonemployer and surviving employer startups over time, we find that the jobs created by the two types of startups in terms

of payroll per employee do not differ. Average pay per employee is very similar between nonemployer and employer startups.

10. In the data all incorporated, S corporation, and partnership startups have EINs even if they do not have employees. The IRS requires EINs for all corporations and partnerships. On the other hand, LLCs are not required to file for an EIN, with many sole-proprietorships registered as an LLC in order to limit their liability. We do not make this distinction in our analysis (e.g., we do not keep the sole proprietorships that filed as LLCs but do not file for an EIN).

11. See https://www.sba.gov/business-guide/launch-your-business/choose-business -structure.

12. Their sample covers fifteen states, capturing roughly 50 percent of the economy.

13. As in figure 4.3, note that after year 1, the true probabilities of survival are actually lower than the approximations reported here. Because of our definition of survival, a subset of "surviving" firms in a given year may have been absent the previous year and is reentering. For a true conditional probability of survival, these reentering firms should be excluded from the numerator.

14. See https://www.sba.gov/sites/default/files/advocacy/SB-FAQ-2017-WEB.pdf.

15. See https://www.sba.gov/business-guide/launch-your-business/choose-business -structure.

16. While the average entrepreneur contributes relatively few jobs to the economy, because of their large number, in aggregate they contribute significantly to net job creation in any given year. Startups are the only net job contributor to jobs, as shown in previous chapters.

Chapter 7: Who Owns Startups?

1. In the Comprehensive Startup Panel, we do not impose the $1,000 annual revenues restriction used in published nonemployer statistics and the SBO.

2. For broader discussions and reviews of this literature, see, for example, Fairlie and Robb (2008), Bates (2011), and Dávila and Mora (2013). Also, for discussions and reviews of the literature on barriers faced by women and immigrants, see Jennings and Brush (2013), Kerr and Kerr (2020), Fairlie and Lofstrom (2014), and Parker (2018).

3. An advantage of the SBO relative to many other surveys is that completing it is mandatory (required by federal law), resulting in high response rates.

4. See https://www.census.gov/programs-surveys/sbo/technical-documentation/method ology.2007.html for more details. The excluded industries are Crop and Animal

Production (NAICS 111 and 112), Rail Transportation (NAICS 482), Postal Service (NAICS 491), Central Banks (NAICS 521), Religious Organizations (NAICS 813), Private Households (NAICS 814), and Public Administration (NAICS 92).

5. All startups are included. We cannot create a second sample similar to our "upper bound" discussed in chapter 6 (i.e., one that excludes sole proprietors with EINs) because the public use version of the data does not include information on legal form of organization.

6. This is consistent with findings from administrative data in Azoulay et al. (2020).

7. See van der Sluis, van Praag, and Vijverberg (2005), Moutray (2007), and Parker (2018) for more on the relationship between education and business ownership and success.

8. Comparisons across time and racial characteristics can only be considered indicative owing to the selection issues discussed earlier.

9. An alternative method of exploring this question is to create "synthetic cohorts" that examine startups in each previous year and survivors in each year. The approach is not as useful as having panel data for exploring the question but can shed some light on the competing questions. Also, we cannot access previous or later cohorts of SBO microdata to perform this exercise, and the data were released only every five years.

10. Evidence in Azoulay et al. (2020) shows startups founded by older individuals are more likely to succeed.

11. Azoulay et al. (2022) show, in contrast, that for the population of startups with employees, immigrants are disproportionally likely to start a business relative to their size in the population.

12. It has also been argued that some disadvantaged groups historically facing discrimination or lack of opportunities in the wage/salary sector, such as Chinese, Greek, Italian, Japanese, and Jewish immigrants, have used business ownership as a source of economic advancement. See Glazer and Moynihan (1970), Loewen (1971), Light (1972, 1979), Baron and Kahan (1975), Bonacich and Modell (1980), and Sowell (1981).

13. Hsieh et al. (2016) find that falling occupational barriers for minority workers may explain one-fourth of aggregate growth in per capita GDP from 1960 to 2010.

14. We cannot examine survival with the SBO microdata, but there is evidence of a positive relationship between startup capital and survival using precursors to the SBO. Robb (2000), using the 1992 CBO linked to the 1992–1996 Business Information Tracking Series, finds that higher levels of startup capital are positively correlated with business survival among employer firms. Headd (2003), using the 1992

CBO for a sample of firms started between 1989 and 1992, also finds that startup capital is negatively associated with closure of the firm between 1992 and 1996.

15. A similar problem arises with the Comprehensive Startup Panel as noted in chapter 3, which is why we focus there on job creation in the first year after startup. Unfortunately, the SBO is not a panel data set and does not track the nonsurviving startups in the first year after startup, setting their employment to zero.

16. Foreign-born status is not controlled for in the regressions because of the overlap with race and ethnicity. We focus on race and ethnicity and allow these classifications to absorb differences in immigrant status. Separately estimating foreign-born status would remove some of these overall disparities.

17. In support of the use of this measure, however, there is evidence suggesting that the size of inheritances received by individuals increases the amount of capital invested in the business (Holtz-Eakin, Joulfaian, and Rosen 1994). This finding suggests that the receipt of inheritances might relieve liquidity constraints and thus lower levels of startup capital, at least partly reflecting barriers to access to financial capital.

18. See https://www.census.gov/programs-surveys/abs/data/nesd.html for a more complete discussion. The primary source of data for race and Hispanic origin information is Decennial Census and ACS data, with the Census Numident serving as a secondary source. The Census Numident is the primary source for the age, sex, place of birth, and US citizenship status of the business owner, with Decennial and ACS data used as a secondary source. Finally, the Department of Veteran Affairs USVETS data provide administrative records on veteran status.

19. For broader discussions and reviews of this literature, see, for example, Fairlie and Robb (2008), Bates (2011), and Dávila and Mora (2013).

Chapter 8: Policy Implications and Future Research

1. See, for example, Reynolds et al. (2004) and GEM (2019).

2. See Fairlie (1999) and Dunn and Holtz-Eakin (2000) for examples using the PSID and NLS, respectively.

3. A refinement is possible by using whether the individual was previously unemployed prior to starting the business. In this case, the new entrepreneur is defined as a "necessity" entrepreneur instead of an "opportunity" entrepreneur (Fairlie and Fossen 2020).

4. See the website at https://www.census.gov/econ/bfs/index.html.

5. See Bayard et al. (2018), Asturias et al. (2021), and Haltiwanger (2021).

6. See https://www.census.gov/econ/bfs/index.html.

7. The SBO collected information on nonemployers but was replaced by the Annual Survey of Entrepreneurs (ASE) and, more recently, by the Annual Business Survey (ABS). In moving to the ASE and ABS, however, the SBO excluded nonemployers.

8. See, for example, Fairlie, Robb, and Robinson (2022) for an examination of racial differences in startup financing using the Kauffman Firm Survey.

9. For example, see Bates and Williams (1996), Boston (1999a), Blanchflower (2009), and Chatterji, Chay. and Fairlie (2014) for evidence on the effects of minority contracting programs.

10. On March 19, 2020, the State of California imposed shelter-in-place restrictions, with New York State following the next day. By early April, most states had imposed social distancing restrictions that closed "non-essential" businesses and added to consumer health concerns in the emerging pandemic.

11. An interesting area for future research would be to investigate the contractions and spikes in applications for EINs during the pandemic as measured in the BFS. Will these applications turn into actual businesses in the future?

References

Abowd, John M., Francis Kramarz, and David N. Margolis. 1999. "High Wage Workers and High Wage Firms." *Econometrica* 67, no. 2: 251–333.

Acemoglu, Daron, Ufuk Akcigit, Harun Alp, Nicholas Bloom, and William Kerr. 2018. "Innovation, Reallocation, and Growth." *American Economic Review* 108, no. 11: 3450–3491.

Acs, Zoltan J., Brian Headd, and Hezekiah Agwara. 2009. "The Nonemployer Start-Up Puzzle." Working Paper no. SBAHQ-08-M-0195. US Small Business Administration, Office of Advocacy.

Adelino, Manuel, Antoinette Schoar, and Felipe Severino. 2015. "House Prices, Collateral, and Self-Employment." *Journal of Financial Economics* 117, no. 2: 288–306.

Altonji, Joseph G., and Rebecca M. Blank. 1999. "Race and Gender in the Labor Market." *Handbook of Labor Economics* 3, part C: 3143–3259.

Andersson, Fredrik, Harry J. Holzer, Julia I. Lane, David Rosenblum, and Jeffrey Smith. 2013. "Does Federally-Funded Job Training Work? Nonexperimental Estimates of WIA Training Impacts Using Longitudinal Data on Workers and Firms." NBER Working Paper no. w19446. Cambridge, MA: National Bureau of Economic Research.

Asturias, Jose, Emin Dinlersoz, John Haltiwanger, and Rebecca Hutchinson. 2021. "Business Applications as Economic Indicators." US Census Bureau, Center for Economic Studies.

Atkins, Rachel, Lisa Cook, and Robert Seamans. 2022a. "Discrimination in Lending? Evidence from the Paycheck Protection Program." *Small Business Economics* 58, no. 2: 843–865.

Atkins, Rachel, Lisa Cook, and Robert Seamans. 2022b. "Using Technology to Tackle Discrimination in Lending: The Role of Fintechs in the Paycheck Protection Program." *AEA Papers and Proceedings* 112: 296–298.

Audretsch, David B. 1991. "New-Firm Survival and the Technological Regime." *Review of Economics and Statistics* 73, no. 3: 441–450.

Audretsch, David B., and Talat Mahmood. 1995. "New Firm Survival: New Results Using a Hazard Function." *Review of Economics and Statistics* 77, no. 1: 97–103.

Audretsch, David B., Max C. Keilbach, and Erik E. Lehmann. 2006. *Entrepreneurship and Economic Growth*. Oxford: Oxford University Press.

Azoulay, Pierre, Ben Jones, J. Daniel Kim, and Javier Miranda. 2020. "Age and High-Growth Entrepreneurship." *American Economic Review: Insights* 2, no. 1: 65–82.

Azoulay, Pierre, Ben Jones, J. Daniel Kim, and Javier Miranda. 2022. "Immigration and Entrepreneurship in the United States." *American Economic Review: Insights* 4, no. 1 (2022): 71–88.

Ballou, Janice, Tom Barton, David DesRoches, Frank Potter, E. J. Reedy, Alicia Robb, Scott Shane, and Zhanyun Zhao. 2008. "Kauffman Firm Survey: Results from the Baseline and First Follow-Up Surveys." Kansas City: Kauffman Foundation.

Baron, Salo W., and Arcadius Kahan. 1975. *Economic History of the Jews*. Jerusalem: Keter Publishing House.

Bartik, Alexander W., Marianne Bertrand, Zoe Cullen, Edward L. Glaeser, Michael Luca, and Christopher Stanton. 2020. "The impact of COVID-19 on Small Business Outcomes and Expectations." *Proceedings of the National Academy of Sciences* 117, no. 30: 17656–17666.

Bartik, Alexander W., Zoe B. Cullen, Edward L. Glaeser, Michael Luca, Christopher T. Stanton, and Adi Sunderam. 2020. "The Targeting and Impact of Paycheck Protection Program Loans to Small Businesses." NBER Working Paper no. w27623. Cambridge, MA: National Bureau of Economic Research.

Bates, Timothy. 1997. *Race, Self-Employment & Upward Mobility: An Illusive American Dream*. Washington, DC: Woodrow Wilson Center Press; Baltimore: Johns Hopkins University Press.

Bates, Timothy. 2011. "Minority Entrepreneurship." *Foundations and Trends® in Entrepreneurship* 7, no. 3–4: 151–311.

Bates, Timothy, and Darrell Williams. 1996. "Do Preferential Procurement Programs Benefit Minority Business?" *American Economic Review* 86, no. 2: 294–297.

Bayard, Kimberly, Emin Dinlersoz, Timothy Dunne, John Haltiwanger, Javier Miranda, and John Stevens. 2018. "Early-Stage Business Formation: An Analysis of Applications for Employer Identification Numbers." NBER Working Paper no. w24364. Cambridge, MA: National Bureau of Economic Research.

Birch, David L. 1979. *The Job Generation Process*. Report prepared for the US Department of Commerce, Economic Development Administration, Washington, DC.

Bjelland, Melissa, John Haltiwanger, Kristin Sandusky, and James Spletzer. 2006. "Reconciling Household and Administrative Measures of Self-employment and

Entrepreneurship." CES Working Paper. Washington, DC: Center for Economic Studies.

Blanchflower, David G. 2009. "Minority Self-Employment in the United States and the Impact of Affirmative Action Programs." *Annals of Finance* 5, no. 3: 361–396.

Blanchflower, David G., and Andrew J. Oswald. 1998. "What Makes an Entrepreneur?" *Journal of Labor Economics* 16, no. 1: 26–60.

Bloom, Nicholas, Robert S. Fletcher, and Ethan Yeh. 2021. "The Impact of COVID-19 on US Firms." NBER Working Paper no. w28314. Cambridge, MA: National Bureau of Economic Research.

Bohn, Sarah, Marisol Cuellar Mejia, and Julien Lafortune. 2020. "The Economic Toll of COVID-19 on Small Business." Public Policy Institute of California, PPIC blog post, May 19.

Bonacich, Edna, and John Modell. 1980. *The Economic Basis of Ethnic Solidarity in the Japanese American Community.* Berkeley: University of California Press.

Boston, Thomas D. 1999a. *Affirmative Action and Black Entrepreneurship.* New York: Routledge.

Boston, Thomas D. 1999b. "Generating Jobs through African American Business Development." In *Readings in Black Political Economy*, ed. J. Whitehead and C. Harris. Dubuque, IA: Kendall-Hunt.

Boston, Thomas D. 2006. "The Role of Black-Owned Businesses in Black Community Development." In *Jobs and Economic Development in Minority Communities: Realities, Challenges, and Innovation,* ed. Paul Ong. Philadelphia: Temple University Press.

Bradford, William D. 2003. "The Wealth Dynamics of Entrepreneurship for Black and White Families in the U.S." *Review of Income and Wealth* 49, no. 1: 89–116.

Bradford, William D. 2014. "The 'Myth' That Black Entrepreneurship Can Reduce the Gap in Wealth between Black and White Families." *Economic Development Quarterly* 28, no. 3: 254–269.

Brown, J. David, and John S. Earle. 2016. "Finance and Growth at the Firm Level: Evidence from SBA Loans." *Journal of Finance* 72, no. 3: 1039–1080.

Brown, Charles, James Hamilton, and James L. Medoff. 1990. Employers Large and Small. Cambridge, MA: Harvard University Press.

Brown, Charles, and James L. Medoff. 2003. "Firm Age and Wages." *Journal of Labor Economics* 21, no. 3: 677–697.

Bucks, Brian K., Arthur B. Kennickell, and Kevin B. Moore. 2006. "Recent Changes in U.S. Family Finances: Evidence from the 2001 and 2004 Survey of Consumer Finances."

Federal Reserve Bulletin. Washington, DC: Board of Governors of the Federal Reserve System.

Burton, M. Diane, Michael S. Dahl, and Olav Sorenson. 2018. "Do Start-Ups Pay Less?" *Industrial and Labor Relations Review* 71, no 5: 1179–1200.

Carroll, Robert, Douglas Holtz-Eakin, Mark Rider, and Harvey S. Rosen. 2000. "Income Taxes and Entrepreneurs' Use of Labor." *Journal of Labor Economics* 18, no. 2: 324–351.

Chatterji, Aaron, Kenneth Y. Chay, and Robert W. Fairlie. 2014. "The Impact of City Contracting Set-Asides on Black Self-Employment and Employment." *Journal of Labor Economics* 32, no. 3: 507–561.

Chow, Melissa C., Teresa C. Fort, Christopher Goetz, Nathan Goldschlag, James Lawrence, Elisabeth Ruth Perlman, Martha Stinson, and T. Kirk White. 2021. "Redesigning the Longitudinal Business Database." Working Paper no. w28839. Washington, DC: National Bureau of Economic Research.

Chrisman, James J. 2016. "Economic Impact of Small Business Development Center Counseling Activities in the United States: 2014–2015." Faculty paper, Mississippi State University, Department of Management and IS.

Cole, Allison. 2020. "The Impact of the Paycheck Protection Program on Small Businesses: Evidence from Administrative Payroll Data." Faculty paper, MIT Sloan School of Business, November 13.

Congressional Research Service. 2020. "Small Business Administration and Job Creation." Washington, DC: Congressional Research Service.

Cullen, Julie Berry, and Roger H. Gordon. 2007. "Taxes and Entrepreneurial Risk-Taking: Theory and Evidence for the U.S." *Journal of Public Economics* 91, no. 7–8: 1479–1505.

Dávila, Alberto, and Marie Mora. 2013. *Hispanic Entrepreneurs in the 2000s: An Economic Profile and Policy Implications*. Stanford: Stanford University Press.

Davis, Steven J., John C. Haltiwanger, and Scott Schuh. 1998. *Job Creation and Destruction*. Cambridge, MA: MIT Press.

Davis, Steven J., John Haltiwanger, Ron Jarmin, C.J. Krizan, Javier Miranda, Al Nucci and Kristen Sandusky. 2007. "Measuring the Dynamics of Young and Small Businesses: Integrating the Employer and Nonemployer Universes." NBER Working Paper no. w13226. Cambridge, MA: National Bureau of Economic Research.

Decker, Ryan, John Haltiwanger, Ron Jarmin, and Javier Miranda. 2014. "The Role of Entrepreneurship in US Job Creation and Economic Dynamism." *Journal of Economic Perspectives* 28, no. 3: 3–24.

Desai, Sameeksha, and Jessica Looze. 2020. "Business Owner Perceptions of COVID-19 Effects on the Business: Preliminary Findings." *Trends in Entrepreneurship* 10. Kansas City: Kauffman Foundation.

Dunn, Thomas A., and Douglas J. Holtz-Eakin. 2000. "Financial Capital, Human Capital, and the Transition to Self-Employment: Evidence from Intergenerational Links." *Journal of Labor Economics* 18, no. 2: 282–305.

Edgcomb, Elaine, and William Girardo. 2012. "The State of Business Development Services." Washington, DC: Aspen Institute, May.

Elert, Niklas, Fredrik W. Andersson, and Karl Wennberg. 2015. "The Impact of Entrepreneurship Education in High School on Long-Term Entrepreneurial Performance." *Journal of Economic Behavior & Organization* 111, no. 1: 209–223.

Erel, Isil, and Jack Liebersohn. 2020. "Does FinTech Substitute for Banks? Evidence from the Paycheck Protection Program." NBER Working Paper no. 27659. Cambridge, MA: National Bureau of Economic Research.

Evans, David, and Boyan Jovanovic. 1989. "An Estimated Model of Entrepreneurial Choice under Liquidity Constraints." *Journal of Political Economy* 97, no. 4: 808–27.

Evans, David, and Linda Leighton. 1989. "Some Empirical Aspects of Entrepreneurship." *American Economic Review* 79, no. 3: 519–535.

Fairlie, Robert W. 1999. "The Absence of the African-American-Owned Business: An Analysis of the Dynamics of Self-Employment." *Journal of Labor Economics* 17, no. 1: 80–108.

Fairlie, Robert W. 2004. "Does Business Ownership Provide a Source of Upward Mobility for Blacks and Hispanics?" In *Public Policy and the Economics of Entrepreneurship*, ed. Doug Holtz-Eakin and Harvey S. Rosen. Cambridge, MA: MIT Press.

Fairlie, Robert W. 2013. "Entrepreneurship, Economic Conditions, and the Great Recession." *Journal of Economics and Management Strategy* 22, no. 2: 207–231.

Fairlie, Robert. 2018. "Racial Inequality in Business Ownership and Income." *Oxford Review of Economic Policy* 34, no. 4: 597–614.

Fairlie, Robert. 2020. "The Impact of COVID-19 on Small Business Owners: Evidence from the First Three Months after Widespread Social-Distancing Restrictions." *Journal of Economics & Management Strategy* 29, no. 4: 727–740.

Fairlie, Robert W., and Frank M. Fossen. 2020. "Defining Opportunity versus Necessity Entrepreneurship: Two Components of Business Creation." *Research in Labor Economics* 48: 253–289.

Fairlie, Robert W., and Frank M. Fossen. 2021a. "Did the $660 Billion Paycheck Protection Program and $220 Billion Economic Injury Disaster Loan Program Get Disbursed to Minority Communities in the Early Stages of COVID-19?" NBER Working Paper no. w28321. Cambridge, MA: National Bureau of Economic Research.

Fairlie, Robert W., and Frank M. Fossen. 2021b. "Sales Losses in the First Quarter of the COVID-19 Pandemic: Evidence from California Administrative Data."

NBER Working Paper no. w28414. Cambridge, MA: National Bureau of Economic Research.

Fairlie, Robert, and Frank M. Fossen. 2022. "The 2021 Paycheck Protection Program Reboot: Loan Disbursement to Employer and Nonemployer Businesses in Minority Communities" *AEA Papers and Proceedings*, 112: 287–289.

Fairlie, Robert, Heinrich Hock, Irma Perez-Johnson, and Robert Santillano. 2022. "Is Training a Sufficient Condition for Starting a Business? Experimental Evidence on Entrepreneurship Training with Screening, Personalized Services and Microgrants." UC Santa Cruz Working Paper. Santa Cruz: University of California.

Fairlie, Robert W., Dean Karlan, and Jonathan Zinman. 2015. "Behind the GATE Experiment: Evidence on Effects of and Rationales for Subsidized Entrepreneurship Training." *American Economic Journal: Economic Policy* 7, no. 2: 125–161.

Fairlie, Robert W., and Harry A. Krashinsky. 2012. "Liquidity Constraints, Household Wealth, and Entrepreneurship Revisited." *Review of Income and Wealth* 58, no. 2: 279–306.

Fairlie, Robert W., and Magnus Lofstrom. 2015. "Immigration and Entrepreneurship." In *Handbook of the Economics of International Migration*, vol. 1. Amsterdam: North-Holland, 877–911.

Fairlie, Robert W., and Javier Miranda. 2017. "Taking the Leap: The Determinants of Entrepreneurs Hiring Their First Employee." *Journal of Economics & Management Strategy* 26, no. 1: 3–34.

Fairlie, Robert W., Javier Miranda, and Nikolas Zolas. 2019. "Measuring Job Creation, Growth, and Survival among the Universe of Start-ups in the United States using a Combined Start-up Panel Data Set." *ILR Review* 72, no. 5: 1262–1277.

Fairlie, Robert W., and Alicia M. Robb. 2007a. "Families, Human Capital, and Small Business: Evidence from the Characteristics of Business Owners Survey." *ILR Review* 60, no. 2: 225–245.

Fairlie, Robert W., and Alicia M. Robb. 2007b. "Why Are Black-Owned Businesses Less Successful Than White-Owned Businesses: The Role of Families, Inheritances, and Business Human Capital." *Journal of Labor Economics* 25, no. 2: 289–323.

Fairlie, Robert W., and Alicia M. Robb. 2008. *Race and Entrepreneurial Success: Black-, Asian-, and White-Owned Businesses in the United States*. Cambridge, MA: MIT Press.

Fairlie, Robert, Alicia Robb, and David Robinson. 2022. "Black and White: Access to Capital among Minority-Owned Startups." NBER Working Paper no. 28154. Cambridge, MA: National Bureau of Economic Research.

Fairlie, Robert, and Christopher M. Woodruff. 2010. "Mexican-American Entrepreneurship." *BE Journal of Economic Analysis & Policy* 10, no. 1: 1–42.

Farrell, Diana, Chris Wheat, and Chi Mac. 2020. *Small Business Financial Outcomes during the Onset of COVID-19*. New York: JPMorgan Chase & Co. Institute Report.

Foster, Lucia, Cheryl Grim, John C. Haltiwanger, and Zoltan Wolf. 2018. "Innovation, Productivity Dispersion, and Productivity Growth." NBER Working Paper no. 24420. Cambridge, MA: National Bureau of Economic Research.

Foster, Lucia, John Haltiwanger, and Chad Syverson. 2016. "The Slow Growth of New Plants: Learning about Demand?" *Economica* 83, no. 329: 91–129.

Garcia-Macia, Daniel, Chang-Tai Hsieh, and Peter J. Klenow. 2016. "How Destructive Is Innovation?" NBER Working Paper no. w22953. Cambridge, MA: National Bureau of Economic Research.

Glaeser, Edward L., Sari Pekkala Kerr, and William R. Kerr. 2015. "Entrepreneurship and Urban Growth: An Empirical Assessment with Historical Mines." *Review of Economics and Statistics* 97, no. 2: 498–520.

Glaeser, Edward L., William R. Kerr, and Giacomo A. M. Ponzetto. 2010. "Clusters of Entrepreneurship." *Journal of Urban Economics* 67, no. 1: 150–168.

Glazer, Nathan, and Daniel P. Moynihan. 1970. *Beyond the Melting Pot: The Negroes, Puerto Ricans, Jews, Italians, and Irish of New York City*, 2nd ed. Cambridge, MA: MIT Press.

Global Entrepreneurship Monitor. 2019. "Global Entrepreneurship Monitor: Overview." London: London Business School.

Goldin, Claudia, Sari Pekkala Kerr, Claudia Olivetti, and Erling Barth. 2017. "The Expanding Gender Earnings Gap: Evidence from the LEHD-2000 Census." *American Economic Review* 107, no. 5: 110–114.

Goldschlag, N., R. Jarmin, J. Lane, and N. Zolas. 2019. "Research Experience as Human Capital in New Business Outcomes." In *Measuring and Accounting for Innovation in the 21st Century*. Chicago: University of Chicago Press.

Granja, João, Christos Makridis, Constantine Yannelis, and Eric Zwick. 2020. "Did the Paycheck Protection Program Hit the Target?" NBER Working Paper no. w27095. Cambridge, MA: National Bureau of Economic Research.

Guzman, Jorge, and Scott Stern. 2016. "The State of American Entrepreneurship: New Estimates of the Quantity and Quality of Entrepreneurship for 15 US States, 1988–2014." NBER Working Paper No. 222095. Cambridge, MA: National Bureau of Economic Research.

Haltiwanger, John C. 2021. "Entrepreneurship during the COVID-19 Pandemic: Evidence from the Business Formation Statistics." NBER Working Paper no. w28912. Cambridge, MA: National Bureau of Economic Research.

Haltiwanger, John, Steven Davis, C. J. Krizan, Ron Jarmin, Javier Miranda, Al Nucci, and Kristin Sandusky. 2009. "Measuring the Dynamics of Young and Small

Businesses: Integrating the Employer and Nonemployer Businesses." In *Producer Dynamics: New Evidence from Micro Data*, ed. Timothy Dunne, J. Bradford Jensen, and Mark J. Roberts. Chicago: University of Chicago Press.

Haltiwanger, John, Henry Hyatt, Erika McEntarfer, and Liliana Sousa. 2012. "Job Creation, Worker Churning, and Wages at Young Businesses." Kauffman Business Dynamics Statistics Briefing. Kansas City: Kauffman Foundation.

Haltiwanger, John, Ron S. Jarmin, Robert Kulick, and Javier Miranda. 2017. "High Growth Young Firms: Contribution to Job, Output, and Productivity Growth." In *Measuring Entrepreneurial Businesses: Current Knowledge and Challenges*, ed. John Haltiwanger, Erik Hurst, Javier Miranda, and Antoinette Schoar, 11–62. Cambridge, MA: National Bureau of Economic Research.

Haltiwanger, John, Ron Jarmin, and Javier Miranda, 2009. *The Business Dynamic Statistics: An Overview*. Kauffman Foundation Statistical Brief. Kansas City: Kauffman Foundation.

Haltiwanger, John C., Ron S. Jarmin, and Javier Miranda. 2013. "Who Creates Jobs? Small vs. Large vs. Young." *Review of Economics and Statistics* 95, no. 2: 347–361.

Hamilton, Barton H. 2000. "Does Entrepreneurship Pay? An Empirical Analysis of the Returns to Self-Employment." *Journal of Political Economy* 108, no. 3: 604–631.

Headd, Brian. 2003. "Redefining Business Success: Distinguishing between Closure and Failure." *Small Business Economics* 21, no. 1: 51–61.

Headd, Brian, and Radwan Saade. 2008. "Do Business Definition Decisions Distort Small Business Research Results?" Working Paper. Washington, DC: SBA Office of Advocacy.

Hipple, Steven F., and Laurel A. Hammond. 2016. *Self-Employment in the United States*, Washington, DC: US Bureau of Labor Statistics.

Holtz-Eakin, Douglas, David Joulfaian, and Harvey Rosen. 1994. "Entrepreneurial Decisions and Liquidity Constraints." *RAND Journal of Economics* 25, no. 2: 334–347.

Holtz-Eakin, Douglas, Harvey S. Rosen, and Robert Weathers. 2000. "Horatio Alger Meets the Mobility Tables." *Small Business Economics* 14, no. 4: 243–274.

Howell, Sabrina T. 2017. "Financing Innovation: Evidence from R&D Grants." *American Economic Review* 107, no. 4: 1136–1164.

Howell, Sabrina T., Theresa Kuchler, David Snitkof, Johannes Stroebel, and Jun Wong. 2021. "Racial Disparities in Access to Small Business Credit: Evidence from the Paycheck Protection Program." National Bureau of Economic Research Working Paper no. w29364. Washington, DC: National Bureau of Economic Research.

Hsieh, Chang-Tai, Erik Hurst, Charles I. Jones, and Peter J. Klenow. 2016. "The Allocation of Talent and U.S. Economic Growth." Stanford University Working Paper.

Hubbard, R. Glenn, and Michael R. Strain. 2020. "Has the Paycheck Protection Program Succeeded?" NBER Working Paper no. w28032. Cambridge, MA: National Bureau of Economic Research.

Humphries, John Eric, Christopher A. Neilson, and Gabriel Ulyssea. 2020. "Information Frictions and Access to the Paycheck Protection Program." *Journal of Public Economics* 190, no. 1: 104–144.

Hurst, Erik, and Benjamin Wild Pugsley. 2011. "What Do Small Businesses Do?" *Brookings Papers on Economic Activity*, Fall, 73–142.

Hvide, Hans K., and Paul Oyer. 2018. "Dinner Table Human Capital and Entrepreneurship." NBER Working Paper no. w24198. Cambridge, MA: National Bureau of Economic Research.

Jarmin, Ron, and Javier Miranda. 2002a. "The Longitudinal Business Database." CES Working Paper 02–17. Washington, DC: US Census Bureau, Center for Economic Studies.

Jarmin, Ron, and Javier Miranda, 2002b. "The Longitudinal Business Database: A Primer," *2002 Proceedings of the American Statistical Association*. New York: American Statistical Association.

Jarmin, Ron, and Javier Miranda. 2002b. "The Longitudinal Business Database." CES Working Paper no. 02–17. Washington, DC: US Census Bureau, Center for Economic Studies.

Jennings, Jennifer E., and Candida G. Brush. 2013. "Research on Women Entrepreneurs: Challenges to (and from) the Broader Entrepreneurship Literature?" *Academy of Management Annals* 7, no. 1: 663–715.

Joint Center for Political and Economic Studies. 1994. *Assessment of Minority Business Development Programs*. Report to the US Department of Commerce Minority Business Development Agency. Washington, DC: JCPES.

Jovanovic, Boyan. 1982. "Selection and the Evolution of Industry." *Econometrica* 50, no. 3: 649–670.

Katz, Lawrence F., and Alan B. Krueger. 2016. "The Rise and Nature of Alternative Work Arrangements in the United States, 1995–2015." NBER Working Paper w22667. Cambridge, MA: National Bureau of Economic Research.

Kerr, Sari Pekkala, and William Kerr. 2020. "Immigrant Entrepreneurship in America: Evidence from the Survey of Business Owners 2007 & 2012." *Research Policy* 49, no. 3: 103–118.

Kihlstrom, Richard, and Jean-Jacques Laffont. 1979. "A General Equilibrium Entrepreneurial Theory of Firm Formation Based on Risk Aversion." *Journal of Political Economy* 87, no. 4: 719–748.

Kim, Olivia S., Jonathan A. Parker, and Antoinette Schoar. 2020. "Revenue Collapses and the Consumption of Small Business Owners in the Early Stages of the COVID-19 Pandemic." NBER Working Paper no. w28151. Cambridge, MA: National Bureau of Economic Research.

Knight, Frank. 1921. *Risk, Uncertainty, and Profit.* New York: Houghton Mifflin.

Kroeger, Teresa, and Graham Wright. 2021. "Entrepreneurship and the Racial Wealth Gap: The Impact of Entrepreneurial Success or Failure on the Wealth Mobility of Black and White Families." *Journal of Economics, Race, and Policy* 4: 183–195.

Kulick, Robert, John C. Haltiwanger, Ron S. Jarmin and Javier Miranda. 2016. "High Growth Young Firms: Contribution to Job, Output and Productivity Growth." In *Measuring Entrepreneurial Businesses: Current Knowledge and Challenges,* ed. John Haltiwanger, Erik Hurst, Javier Miranda, and Antoinette Schoar. Cambridge, MA: National Bureau of Economic Research.

Lafontaine, Francine, and Kathryn Shaw. 2016. "Serial Entrepreneurship: Learning by Doing?" *Journal of Labor Economics* 34, Suppl. 2: S217–S254.

Lederer, Anneliese, Sara Oros, Sterling Bone, Glenn Christensen, and Jerome Williams. 2020. *Lending Discrimination within the Paycheck Protection Program.* Washington, DC: National Community Reinvestment Coalition.

Lerner, Josh. 1999. "The Government as Venture Capitalist: The Long-Run Impact of the SBIR Program." *Journal of Private Equity* 3, no. 2: 55–78.

Lerner, Josh. 2009. "Boulevard of Broken Dreams." In *Boulevard of Broken Dreams.* Princeton University Press.

Levine, Ross, and Yona Rubinstein. 2016. "Smart and Illicit: Who Becomes an Entrepreneur and Do They Earn More?" *Quarterly Journal of Economics* 132, no. 2: 963–1018.

Levine, Ross, and Yona Rubinstein. 2018. "Selection into Entrepreneurship and Self-Employment." NBER Working Paper no. 25350. Cambridge, MA: National Bureau of Economic Research.

Light, Ivan. 1972. *Ethnic Enterprise in America.* Berkeley: University of California Press.

Light, Ivan. 1979. "Disadvantaged Minorities in Self Employment." *International Journal of Comparative Sociology* 20, no. 1–2: 31–45.

Loewen, James W. 1971. *The Mississippi Chinese: Between Black and White.* Cambridge, MA: Harvard University Press.

Lofstrom, Magnus, and Chunbei Wang. 2009. "Mexican-American Self-Employment: A Dynamic Analysis of Business Ownership." *Research in Labor Economics* 29:197–227.

Luque, Adela., Rhenuka Bhaskar, James Noon, Kevin Rinz, and Victoria Udalova. 2019. "Nonemployer Statistics by Demographics (NES-D): Using Administrative and Census Records Data in Business Statistics." US Census Bureau Working Paper no. 19-01.

McKinney, Kevin L., and John M. Abowd. 2020. *Male Earnings Volatility in LEHD before, during, and after the Great Recession*. US Census Bureau Working Paper no. 20-31. 2020.

Miranda, Javier, and Nicholas Zolas. 2018. "Measuring the Impact of Household Innovation Using Administrative Data." NBER Working Paper no. w25259. Cambridge, MA: National Bureau of Economic Research.

Moutray, C. 2007. *Educational Attainment and Other Characteristics of the Self-Employed: An Examination Using the Panel Study of Income Dynamics Data*. Washington, DC: US Small Business Administration.

OECD (Organization for Economic Cooperation and Development). 2017a. *Entrepreneurship at a Glance 2017*. Paris: OECD Press.

OECD. 2017b. *SME and Entrepreneurship Policy Series*. Paris: OECD Press.

Oi, Walter Y., and Todd L. Idson. 1999. "Firm Size and Wages." In *Handbook of Labor Economics*, ed. Orley C. Ashenfelter and David Card, vol. 3, part B, Amsterdam: Elsevier/North Holland, 2165–2214.

Ouimet, Paige, and Rebecca Zarutskie. 2014. "Who Works for Startups? The Relation between Firm Age, Employee Age, and Growth." *Journal of Financial Economics* 112, no. 3: 386–407.

Parker, Simon C. 2018. *The Economics of Entrepreneurship*. Cambridge: Cambridge University Press.

Phillips, Bruce D., and Bruce A. Kirchhoff. 1989. "Formation, Growth and Survival: Small Firm Dynamics in the U.S. Economy." *Small Business Economics* 1, no. 1: 65–74.

Pugsley, Benjamin W., and Ayşegül Şahin. 2019. "Grown-Up Business Cycles." *Review of Financial Studies* 32, no. 3: 1102–1147.

Reynolds, Paul. 2005. *Entrepreneurship in the US: The Future Is Now*. New York: Springer.

Robb, Alicia. 2000. *The Role of Race, Gender, and Discrimination in Business Survival*. Ann Arbor: University of Michigan Press.

Robb, Alicia, and Joseph Farhat. 2013. *An Overview of the Kauffman Firm Survey: Results from 2011 Business Activities*. Kansas City: Kauffman Foundation.

Robb, Alicia M., E. J. Reedy, Janice Ballou, David DesRoches, Frank Potter, and Zhanyun Zhao. 2010. *An Overview of the Kauffman Firm Survey: Results from the 2004–2008 Data*. Kansas City: Kauffman Foundation.

Schumpeter, J. A. 1934. *The Theory of Economic Development*. Cambridge, MA: Harvard University Press.

Sowell, Thomas. 1981. *Markets and Minorities*. New York: Basic Books.

Stoll, Michael A., Steven Raphael, and Harry J. Holzer. 2001. "Why Are Black Employers More Likely Than White Employers to Hire Blacks?" Institute for Research on Poverty Working Paper. Madison: University of Wisconsin.

Tracy, Spencer L. 2011. *Accelerating Job Creation in America: The Promise of High-Impact Companies*. Washington, DC: US Small Business Administration.

US BLS (Bureau of Labor Statistics). 2017. *Survival Rates of Establishments, by Year Started and Number of Years since Starting, 1994–2015, Business Employment Dynamics, Entrepreneurship in the U.S. Economy*. Washington, DC: US Bureau of Labor Statistics.

US BLS (US Bureau of Labor Statistics). 2020. *Entrepreneurship and the U.S. Economy*. Washington, DC: US Bureau of Labor Statistics.

US Census Bureau. 2013. *Survey of Business Owners 2007*. Washington, DC: US Census Bureau.

US Census Bureau. 2017. *Definitions—Business Dynamics Statistics*. Washington, DC: US Census Bureau.

US Census Bureau. 2020a. *Small Business Pulse Survey*. Washington, DC: US Census Bureau.

US Census Bureau. 2020b. *Technical Documentation 2017 Nonemployer Statistics by Demographics*. Washington, DC: US Census Bureau.

US SBA (Small Business Administration). 2017. "Frequently Asked Questions about Small Business." Washington, DC: US Small Business Administration.

US SBA. 2020. Office of Small Business Development Centers (website). Washington, DC: US Small Business Administration.

van der Sluis, J., M. van Praag, and W. Vijverberg. 2005. "Education and Entrepreneurship in Industrialized Countries: A Meta-Analysis." *World Bank Economic Review*, 19, no. 2: 225–261.

Wang, Chunbei. 2019. "Tightened Immigration Policies and the Self-Employment Dynamics of Mexican Immigrants." *Journal of Policy Analysis and Management* 38, no. 4: 944–977.

Weigensberg, Elizabeth, Karen Needels, Alix Gould-Werth, Ankita Patnaik, and Joanne Lee. 2017. *A Study of the Self-Employment Assistance Program: Helping Unemployed Workers Pursue Self-Employment. Final Evaluation Report*. Washington, DC: US Department of Labor.

Index